The
Musical Dialogue

NIKOLAUS HARNONCOURT

The Musical Dialogue

Thoughts on Monteverdi, Bach and Mozart

Translated by
Mary O'Neill

Reinhard G. Pauly
General Editor

AMADEUS PRESS
Portland, Oregon

© 1984 as *Der musikalische Dialog* by Residenz Verlag,
Salzburg and Wien

Translation © 1989 by Amadeus Press
All rights reserved
ISBN 0-931340-08-X
Printed in Singapore

Amadeus Press
9999 S.W. Wilshire
Portland, Oregon 97225

Library of Congress Cataloging-in-Publication Data

Harnoncourt, Nikolaus.
   [Musikalische Dialog. English]
   The musical dialogue : thoughts on Monteverdi, Bach, and Mozart /
Nikolaus Harnoncourt ; translated by Mary O'Neill ; Reinhard G.
Pauly, general editor.
     p.   cm.
   Translation of: Der musikalische Dialog.
   Discography: p.
   ISBN 0-931340-08-X
   1. Music--History and criticism. 2. Monteverdi, Claudio,
1567-1643. 3. Bach, Johann Sebastian, 1685-1750. 4. Mozart,
Wolfgang Amadeus, 1756-1791. 5. Music--Interpretation (Phrasing,
dynamics, etc.) I. Pauly, Reinhard G. II. Title.
ML60.H33713 1988
780'.903'2--dc19   88-38033
                                                                 CIP
                                                                 MN

Contents

Preface

This book contains a collection of lectures, talks and essays devoted primarily to a discussion of the works of Monteverdi, Bach and Mozart. It is not a scholarly treatise; I do not cite all the sources known to me in order to substantiate my views. I am not interested in proving anything, but simply wish to convey some personal insights, acquired in the course of intensive theoretical and practical experience, in a form that can be understood by the general public. Even though I use the sources in a very critical and conscientious way (cf. the article on evaluating the sources which appeared in my first book, *Baroque Music Today*), I give the quotations in translated form and dispense with footnotes, references and bibliographic information.

I do not believe that quotations from the sources can serve as proof, because their very selection betrays the intention and tendency of the person quoting them. They are used here only for purposes of illustration. I strongly recommend that readers who are interested in more detailed technical understanding read the source material in its entirety. In doing so, they will encounter many contradictions, or at least what are commonly regarded as contradictions. It should be remembered, however, that it is above all in the contradictions, which can only be apparent contradictions, that the varied approaches to a topic can be revealed. Only the simplest concepts and thoughts are amenable to either an "a" or "b" answer; most things upon closer inspection include both, and much more besides. Almost every opinion has its opposite as well, and at times only a very slight shift is needed in order to turn a statement into its own contradiction. An honest colleague must be trusted even when he contradicts himself, much more than an intellectual bureaucrat who is capable of arranging everything in irrevocably correct little boxes.

50.5% "yea" and 49.5% "nay" means yes in a democracy. Should a tiny shift of 1% be able to swing the vote? Similarly, each statement, each decision is composed of many conflicting elements, each of which will at some point emerge.

The Tonal Image of Medieval Music

We know almost nothing with certainty of the sound of music prior to 1500. Anyone interested in this music must always keep this fact in mind and use extreme caution in assessing statements made by those alleging that they are in possession of incontrovertible evidence. Everything achieved up to the present in this area is hypothetical in nature, and will remain so forever because this music in its true form has died away once and for all. The only option open to us is to try to imagine, as precisely as possible, the way in which music was made at that time, using eye-witness accounts and contemporary documentation. Nor should we forget that the musical practice of that time, above all in secular works, almost always utilized improvisation that was more or less bound by a specific set of rules. In the actual performance of this music particularly, we must rely largely on our feelings for musical style. The greater our comprehension of the entire spiritual and intellectual milieu of those times, the more performance of this music will communicate to us. But, since complete understanding is unattainable, the "Music of the Gothic Age" will never again be heard in a completely authentic way—we would have to become the people who lived during that period to realize a full understanding. We are only able to approach its true form through intuition and knowledge; the closer we come, the more convincing the results will be.

It is almost impossible to discuss sonority in a structured and comprehensible way. Musical sound is a phenomenon that eludes any attempt to describe it. Just a short time after a tone has faded away, the fine points of its particular qualities can hardly be recalled to memory. Each of us knows how difficult it is to recall the sound of an instrument that we have heard, to imagine it with all its nuances. Furthermore, it is well-nigh impossible to convey tonal qualities in words in a generally accessible way. There simply are no linguistic means to describe such qualities. We must make do with visual or other comparisons, such as bright and dark, open and muffled. However, these expressions themselves are by no means unambiguous; the same words suggest quite different sounds to different people. Physical criteria offer us the only possibility of describing sounds unambiguously. However, even when presented graphically, this type of analysis is so abstract that very few people can imagine the corresponding tones when they see the numbers or wave forms, and thus this method is not suitable for a discussion of this topic. However, such an analysis is extremely valuable for assisting the ear in systematic studies of tones.

Why are we interested in questions of musical sound? What is the nature of the interrelationships between a composition and its tonal reproduction? Are there binding rules which mandate the selection of certain sound combinations in performance, especially the performance of early music? For music which is generally familiar, let us say from Viennese classicism on, it goes without saying for us that the specific instrumentation is given. This means that the composer determines not only the purely musical content of his work, but he also defines, unequivocally and precisely, the "Klangbild" or tonal image of the rendition. There are works for harpsichord, for organ, for all the usual instruments, and the individual instruments, even in the case of large orchestras, are precisely prescribed. During the act of composition, composers have in mind the sound and the special way in which these instruments are played and articulated; they write with these instruments in mind.

But the further back we go in time, the sparser and more generalized are the composer's directions. "For singing and playing on all manner of instruments" is a common instruction for music of the 16th century. Medieval music very seldom prescribes particular instruments, such as is found in the "in Saeculum viellatoris" of the Bamberg Codex. Yet these spare directives by no means imply that selection of instruments was a matter of complete indifference. Earlier music was not composed in its polished, final shape as was the music of later ages. For many of these works, we cannot speak of a specific vocal or instrumental style for particular instruments; instead, the music was adapted to the characteristics of the instruments which were used. The music provided the compositional substance which could be performed with the most varied types of groups, in accordance with available resources. The idiosyncratic musical figures that were typical of specific instruments were improvised only during performance.

The primary reason underlying these practices—thoroughly departing from those prevailing today—is to be found in the fundamental difference in the profession of musician then and now. When Western music had only entered its development, when nothing had yet been written down, the composer and the performing musician were identical. Music was simply improvised in public, as we would say today. The separation between these two functions, i.e. that of the composer and that of the performer, developed gradually as a result of the devising of more elaborate means of notation to describe a composition in a concrete way, and the desire of the composers to give their works a definitive form. Only recently has the absolute separation been reached. Musicians today ordinarily have no knowledge of the art of composition; they have a downright slavish relationship to the written music they receive from the composer. Their task is simply to perform the compositions of others as perfectly as possible in terms of technique and expression. The precise designation of all the ornaments which were to be played, a compositional practice which began in the late Baroque period, was initially regarded by musicians as a degrading insult. During the Middle Ages, composers were performing musicians, and almost every musician was also a composer. In any case, every good musician had to master the rules of composition and of improvisation, and so it was taken for granted that the latest form of a work would emerge only on the occasion of its current performance.

I wish to avoid here a discussion of the question of which instruments are to be used for which music and what effects the many prohibitions on instrumental music in the church have had. This topic is too complex to be included in a discussion devoted principally to questions of musical sound. However, I must at least point out the incredible disparity that exists between the instrumental music which was undoubtedly and extensively played and the ridiculously few instrumental compositions which have been preserved—as compared with the host of extant vocal works. This disparity cannot be explained by accidental losses which occurred over the course of the centuries. There are two possible reasons for this difference. First: much instrumental music was improvised. Second: instrumentalists used composed vocal music, which they modified and adapted to given conditions and available resources. This practice can be seen from the later tablatures for lute, harpsichord and organ, as well as treatises such as the *Tratado de Glosas* of Diego Ortiz of 1553, and from many other sources as well.

The value of many of the written sources for studying the musical practice of the Middle Ages is seriously compromised by the disparity that existed for centuries between theory and practice, which, particularly in the Middle Ages, was insurmountably large. Theory was regarded as a field in itself. Studies were constantly based on Boethius (around 520 A.D.), or later on Guido d'Arezzo (c. 1000–c. 1050), even at a time when musical practice had greatly advanced. The theorist was described as *musicus*, the performing musicians as *cantores*. Learned theorists scornfully disregarded all secular musical practice, and even surrounded sacred music with a purely theoretical framework of doctrine, which was theory for its own sake, unrelated to actual practice. Since most music was not written down, the predominance of theory over practice arose out of the written tradition, a fact which has been greatly misunderstood.

In his definitive study on musical improvisation, Ernest Ferand repeatedly pointed out this fact in a convincing and emphatic manner. In any case, according to testimony from Ekkehard of St. Gall, instrumental music was included in the basic education of young noblemen in the 9th and 10th centuries. An educated man living around 1200 was expected to have mastered the fiddle, flute, harp, rebec and psaltery.

Of course there were a whole series of unwritten rules stipulating which instruments could and could not be used together. Certain combinations always appear in the pictures we have from that period, and sources such as Sebastian Virdung's *Musica getutscht,* and the writings of Michael Praetorius convey a clear idea of the various ways in which the instrumentarium could be properly assembled. Although Praetorius lived in a different period, his works provide us with important information concerning the structure and properties of musical sound and the performance practice of earlier times. This ability to utilize available resources may well be the first skill we should attempt to acquire.

From c. 1200 to c. 1500, the instrumentarium remained largely unchanged. The most commonly used string instruments were the fiddle, rebec and tromba marina or "nun's fiddle." The winds included trumpet, bass shawm, shawm, bagpipe, portative organ, recorder, and transverse flute. Plucked instruments included the harp, psaltery, lute, mandola, and guitar. Percussion instruments included the tambourine, cymbals, triangle and timbrel ring. Very typical combinations of two instruments include the portative organ and fiddle, fiddle and lute, portative organ and harp, portative organ and lute, all often also used to accompany singers. For three instruments, fiddle, harp and portative organ; portative organ, lute and harp; portative organ, fiddle and lute, were often combined. In some pictures we see a recorder replacing the portative organ or another instrument.

The instruments in those days were described either as loud/strong or as soft/quiet. The loud instruments included trumpets, shawms, bagpipes, and kettle drums; the quiet ones included fiddles, recorders, lutes, and harps. It is likely that loud instruments were used primarily out-of-doors, while the quiet instruments were reserved for chamber music played in smaller rooms. Heinrich Besseler believes that open-air music played on shawms, bass shawms and trumpets had a homogeneous sound as early as the 15th century, a characteristic found in the other categories of instrumental music only after the great transition that occurred around the year 1500.

The wide variety of this instrumentarium is counterpointed by the human voice, the only "instrument" that has been preserved unchanged up to our own day, at least in terms of physiology. Nonetheless, we must not assume that the sound of singing has gone unchanged since those early days. After all, the roots of Western music reach back to the Orient. Both the earliest instrumental practices as well as choral music, the monophonic choral and solo singing in church, were taken from the East and only gradually transformed into what we describe today as Western music.

Oriental singers use a singing technique that is fundamentally different from our own. Professor Hans Hickmann, who lived for many years in Egypt in order to study the sources of Western music on the basis of surviving Oriental musical practices, points out the similarity of facial positions of singers depicted in old paintings with the facial positions of Oriental singers. Thus, until 1500 or shortly thereafter, we can imagine the sound of the human singing voice as being somewhat similar to Turkish, Egyptian and sometimes even Spanish folk singers today. The sound is throaty and nasal, and has a large dynamic range.

If we now consider the instruments, the question is much more difficult, because, practically speaking, no instruments of the 13th or 14th centuries have been preserved. We are forced to rely exclusively on pictorial representations. The earliest extant instruments are from the 15th century, and they are individual specimens (rebec of the Figdor Collection, rebec in Modena) which can hardly be regarded as representative of the actual instrumentarium used during the period. Moreover, the present condition of these instruments precludes serious study of their original sound.

Quite a number of instruments of the 16th century have been preserved. Nonetheless, in studying these instruments we must constantly ask whether we are examining instruments which were actually used or perhaps only collectors' items which derived their value, even at that time, primarily from their rarity or highly artistic workmanship. After all, whatever has been preserved consists primarily of richly ornamented showpieces from the private collections or "Kunstkammer," as they were called at that time, of noble families. Only after about the second half of the 16th century is it possible for us to derive a somewhat adequate sense of the instrumentarium, of the sound of the instruments and of their playing technique.

The study of the oldest extant instruments requires an uncompromising and critical examination of all of the pertinent data, particularly with regard to the age of the instrument, since most early instruments are not dated and since private collectors and (at times) museums alike have a completely understandable tendency to pre-date their oldest instruments in order to make them appear older. From the very beginning, the difference between the gentle/quiet and the loud instruments, described centuries later by Michael Praetorius, is very evident. An admixture of these two types is very unattractive in terms of sound and is rarely expressed in pictures.

At this point, I would like to discuss the most important instruments individually. The fiddle was evidently the most widely-used instrument. It existed in very diverse forms: oval, shaped like a "figure-8," but most frequently in the familiar guitar-like shape. The written sources extol the superior qualities of the fiddle. Around 1300, for example, Johannes de Groccheo writes: "It seems to me that the fiddle deserves preeminence among all the stringed instruments." Ulrich von Eschenbach speaks of its sweet sound. Unfortunately, since no medieval fiddles have been preserved, we have no idea how they sounded. We can only draw conclusions based on the earliest preserved instruments about the sound of their predecessors, an approach which appears to me the most reliable.

12

The Kunsthistorisches Museum in Vienna owns a number of the very earliest extant string instruments, from shortly after 1500. Without exception, these instruments have an extraordinarily beautiful and sweet sound. They speak very readily, and lightness is one of their special tonal characteristics—there is no trace of coarseness or harshness. The fact that such sonority characterizes all the instruments that have been preserved may well indicate that this is no coincidence. I own a bass instrument from the year 1558. It is somewhat larger than a cello and has the guitar-shape of the old fiddles. This instrument also has a wonderfully mellow and smooth tone that is immediately noticeable to any musical person, a tone that can be clearly distinguished from the sound of the gamba or cello. An expert can see immediately from the masterful execution, the choice of wood and varnish, that this cannot be simply a primitive lower rung on the ladder to the further development and perfection of string instrument making. On the contrary, it is a mature and skillfully executed work of art, the equal of any later master instrument. If we study all of these instruments in depth, we are bound to come to the conclusion that the string instruments of that time are not the result of fumbling attempts in the direction of a sound ideal which would be achieved only at a later date. They are genuine masterpieces which correspond perfectly to the tonal ideal of their age. After all, even at that time instrument makers looked back on a centuries-old tradition which reached to the Orient. It is not likely that the fiddles of the 13th– 16th centuries sounded much worse than the earliest preserved instruments, and such an assumption would be difficult to prove in any case, on the basis of pictorial and sculptural representations.

In some remote areas, such as in the Caucasus or Balkan regions, we occasionally find instruments similar to the fiddle or the rebec, which are used today for folk music. However, using such instruments to investigate the tonal aspects of medieval instruments appears to me a rather dubious undertaking, for a number of reasons. In terms of their tonal qualities, such stringed folk instruments (e.g. the fiddles played by American hillbillies) are usually a far cry from the art-music prototypes after which they were modeled. Any similarity is based purely on external appearance. It is also clear that the peasants who made, and still make, such primitive instruments for their own use cannot compete with the professional string instrument makers who practiced their craft as a highly complex art form handed down from generation to generation. No one would think of using peasant violins of the 18th and 19th centuries as a basis for studying the tonal qualities of stringed instruments of those times. Such a notion would be absurd.

The recorders of the Middle Ages probably sounded similar to those built at a somewhat later time, e.g. the 16th century, many of which are preserved. The technical features of their construction, the work from *one* piece, the very wide boring, the large finger-holes and the relatively high cutout of the mouth-hole result in a full, velvety tone which differs greatly from the sound of the Baroque recorder as it is generally found today. Baroque recorders sound much brighter than Renaissance recorders, or, to put it somewhat differently, their sound is richer in harmonics. The Baroque recorder is primarily a solo instrument, while Renaissance recorders, and probably the earlier recorders as well, were used for ensemble playing. The latter also have a much smaller tone range, in keeping with the purpose for which they were used.

It is not easy to imagine the sound of the lute, which had metal strings during the Middle Ages and was plucked with a quill plectrum. If we were to use similar metal strings on a Renaissance lute, we would have an approximate idea of how the Gothic lute might have sounded. I do not think that the construction of earlier instruments was essentially different from that of Renaissance lutes, and this experiment thus seems meaningful to me. The sound of a Renaissance lute with metal strings, plucked with a quill, resembles that of an old Flemish spinet: very clear, but not very loud, full in the fundamental tone, but nonetheless with brilliant overtones. Only one melodic line is usually played on it. The transition to the Renaissance lute with gut strings and plucked with the fingers probably occurred around 1500. From that point on, the lute appears as a preferred solo instrument for polyphonic playing, similar to the keyboard instruments. The main difference between the two types does not exist in the instrument itself, but rather in the type of strings used and in the fundamentally different ways of playing.

In the case of the portative organ, however, it is possible to give more detailed information. For several centuries, this was one of the most frequently used instruments. Although no portative organ has come down to us, it is relatively easy to reconstruct its sound. Much visual material is available, some of it (the paintings of Memling or Van Eyck, for example) of almost photographic clarity. Moreover, we know the scaling of the pipes and the way in which wind was supplied. In the earliest portative organs, all pipes had the same diameter, which is described as being about the size of a pigeon's egg, meaning that the sound changed from the lower to the upper tones. The low pipes have a very narrow scaling and for that reason have a sound somewhat like a bowed string instrument, while the high pipes have an extremely wide scaling, sound more flute-like and have fewer harmonics. From the purely musical point of view, the portative organ should probably be included among the quiet instruments. It is used exclusively with such instruments, and a balance between, say, a fiddle, harp and a loud-sounding portative organ is unthinkable. In his study of the portative organ, Hickmann mentions this instrument's capacity for varying both the volume and pitch, which is praised in old sources. From the wealth of visual material on this instrument, it appears that most portative organs, especially the Flemish ones, had a single bellows, which was lifted and depressed by hand. This means, on the one hand, that one has to breathe and cannot play without a pause, like playing a wind instrument, and on the other hand that the wind pressure can be controlled by hand, which is of critical importance in actual practice. In terms of the technical aspects of organ-building, relatively narrow limits are set here with regard to volume and timbre as well. The intensity of sound is dependent on wind pressure and on the scaling or mensuration of the pipes, i.e. on their diameter, mouth-width, cut-up, etc. Tne wind pressure cannot be selected at will; it is approximately 50 mm H_2O. It would hardly be possible to demand greater wind pressure from the player, because this would make it too difficult to press the bellows. Only in the case of portative organs with small bellows could one select a somewhat higher wind pressure without overtaxing the strength of the player. To be sure, this instrument would then be very short-winded. But there is a second important reason for low wind pressure: the very narrow, lowest pipes can produce a correct tone only with very low wind pressure, without the use of artificial means of voicing. One could strengthen the higher pipes, but that would result in an impossible proportion between lower and higher tones, since the higher tones are by nature more prominent than the lower tones. Furthermore, this would be practically unbearable for the ears of the player, which are directly beside the pipes. If a sharper sound were desired, higher cut-ups and more wind pressure must be selected, something which is unlikely because of the excessive wind consumption. Illustrations of instruments in old paintings also show quite clearly that this was not the case. Close attention must therefore be paid to seeing to it that the extremely narrow low pipes speak at all, and that the extremely wide high pipes sound without too much secondary noise. The ability to adjust the intonation to the other instruments by regulating wind pressure with the left hand is of great importance, as the performer can greatly influence the tone in this way as well. In summary, it can be said that the portative organ is probably the only medieval instrument whose sound we can reproduce with a fair degree of accuracy, through conscientious reconstruction.

The quiet cornet was used relatively commonly after the second half of the 15th century. This problematic instrument was always described as very difficult to master. Based on examples from the 16th century which are preserved in museums, most of which speak relatively lightly, I can imagine that the timbre of this instrument was very supple and variable, most closely resembling that of the a clarinet.

The harp, usually with gut strings, was probably rather soft and mellow in tone.

The shawms, which were used primarily outdoors and for dance music, were probably the loudest of all the wind instruments, yet their sound was certainly neither rough nor vulgar. I had an opportunity to hear a very good recording of Catalan shawm players. Even though these instruments have undergone some modifications as compared with the old instruments, nonetheless in essential points they largely resemble the old shawms, e.g. in the use of a pirouette at the reed, in the boring, and probably even in the reeds. The tone of the shawm is very full and rather incisive, but never rough and by no means rigid, as claimed by many musicologists, but fully capable of shadings. Thus, despite the pirouette, a little roll that is placed around the reed so that it only partly emerges, the players can influence the tone with their lips to a very great extent; it is quite likely that this was also true of old shawms.

At the beginning of the 15th century, the slide trumpet and the trombone were developed from trumpets which had been in use for quite some time. The trombone has remained relatively unchanged and has been an important wind instrument up to the present. The earliest preserved trombones are from the 16th century, but in terms of mensuration they appear to bear a strong resemblance to instruments of the 15th century which we know only from pictures, and thus we can also draw conclusions about their sound. The sound of this trombone (I am thinking particularly of an instrument made in 1551 which I once heard played by a superb trombonist) is extraordinarily velvety and lyrical. The attack of the tone is very mellow and full, like that of a very old gamba. The dynamic possibilities are greater than in any other instrument of the period. I own a trombone from about 1700, which is very similar in tone and almost identical in the bore to the older instrument. It appears that the design and sound of the trombone underwent no fundamental changes until late in the 18th century.

What has been said of the trombone is also largely true of the trumpet, except that a very clear change in tone can be observed, from the low register, where the tone is penetrating and blaring, to the upper register, where the sound is very lyrical, much softer and almost string-like. However, this is true only when played with original mouthpieces.

Thus, it is possible to get a general idea of the sound of the music of the Middle Ages and the Renaissance, even though this can certainly not be identical to the actual sounds of that period, which are irrevocably lost and forgotten. Not much remains of the sharp and penetrating sound which many musicians and music lovers think of in connection with Medieval music. In any case, a large proportion of the most frequently used combinations of instruments, such as fiddle, harp, and recorder; fiddle, portative, psaltery; and others, rule out this incisive tone. The use of relatively incisive instruments, such as shawms, is probably restricted to very particular kinds of music and should not be thought of as standard practice.

Furthermore, even those instruments themselves were by no means as hard and rough in tone as is widely assumed today. And what about the much-debated cornett or Zink? The quiet cornetts, which were most likely primarily used for this early music, have a tone that is just as mellow as and no louder than that of the recorders. The fact they usually sound much louder today is due to imperfect copies and to players who have yet to master the instrument. When beginners play wind instruments, their attack is harsher and their sound louder and rougher than that of experienced players. Moreover, the present-day renaissance of cornett playing is so oriented to the curved cornett that the quiet cornett is either completely disregarded or is played like a curved one, with a mouthpiece, in the manner of a trumpet. And the curved and loud cornetts belong in the same category with the shawms.

A few quotes to substantiate my conviction that the sound of medieval music was sweet and of the highest quality: in the 9th century, Walafried Strabo writes of the organ in the Cathedral at Aachen: "The melos was sweet, and so affected the senses that one woman, overwhelmed by the magical tones, lost consciousness and even her very life." In the 14th century, Adam von Salimbene writes: "In Pisa I encountered girls and boys who had vielles, zithers and other musical instruments, on which they played the sweetest tunes, which enchanted the heart beyond measure." Of Landini, Giovanni da Prato writes: "When singing his own love songs, the blind master Francesco Landini accompanied himself on the portative, so sweetly that there was no one among his listeners who did not feel as if his heart would burst forth from his breast through an excess of joyous excitement caused by the loveliness of this marvelous harmony."

These and many other descriptions indicate not only that music at that time was able to enchant and delight its listeners as much as it does today, but also, and this is particularly important and worth remembering, that musicians of those days were people just as we are today. The style of their performance contained everything in terms of expression and sensitivity of which a human being is capable, but it certainly did not embrace that objectivity which is often demanded today as being particularly stylish, in wrong-headed reverence for and faithfulness to the work. This "objectivity" can result only in a wooden, museum-like sound, but never in full-blooded, living music.

Now that we have reviewed the Medieval instrumentarium and its probable sound, I would like once again to consider the great transition that occurred around 1500. This period witnessed dramatic changes in the instrumentarium and in the sound ideal. Till that time, combinations of sounds from very different kinds of instruments were preferred. These corresponded in ideal fashion to the Burgundian and the complex polyphonic Flemish music, the structure of which could thereby be most beautifully demonstrated. In keeping with the increasing polish of the technique of composition that characterized the period after Josquin, a transition took place to more homogeneous sounds which were better able to express the more harmonically oriented sonority of this music.

And so it came about that the families of instruments (the recorders, gambas, trombones etc.) were built in all sizes, from the bass to treble or discant. This practice became standard for instrumental music of the 16th century and is definitively summed up by Praetorius. Around 1500, several of the Gothic instruments—the rebec, psaltery, portative organ, bagpipes and marine trumpet—disappear from art music. The fiddle is reshaped into the lira da braccio while the gambas and viols assume the shapes familiar to us today. Many wind instruments also begin at this time to gain acceptance: the crumhorns and ranketts, the curved cornetts, the bass shawms and recorders. It is important for us to keep in mind that these instruments now enter into musical practice and so to avoid using them for earlier music. Of course, this is true only for those instruments which have no direct and similarly designed precursors, but which are true innovations.

What possibilities do we have to perform today the music of the Gothic and of the Renaissance? Does it make any sense to try to recreate the original sounds? What has already been done in this field, and with what success? I am firmly convinced that we should do everything in our power to perform this music in a way that keeps as closely as possible to the original. I am quite certain that every form of art creates the perfect means that it requires. By this I mean that the possibilities of composition, of notation and also of rendition (i.e. the instrumentarium and the technique of playing) were absolutely ideal in each period for the music in question. All of the hypotheses citing inadequate instruments, poor intonation, faulty technique, can be refuted. It is very likely that they are based on the fact that most present-day musicians overestimate their own talents. I have already discussed the tonal qualities of early instruments, and, technically speaking, it has been possible using these instruments to produce perfectly any effects which were required. Instrumentalists of our own times, who are very self-assured, are constantly surprised when they hear folk musicians who, using very simple instruments which often closely resemble early instruments, effortlessly master the most unbelievable technical difficulties. It is only possible to evaluate what music can be produced on Medieval instruments after the playing technique of these instruments has been thoroughly studied, with the same conscientiousness that is necessary for mastering a contemporary instrument. Unfortunately, this is almost never the case.

A work such as the flute method of Silvestro Ganassi (1535) proves that musicians of that period were familiar with all the possibilities of this instrument and were able to implement these in ways that appear incredibly sophisticated, from today's perspective. Historical wind instruments which have been preserved, especially recorders, reveal how superbly early musicians were able to tune or temper their instruments. The frequent complaints about bad intonation are probably an indication that one strove for and aurally understood good intonation. If we wanted to describe the musical practice of today, we would have to deplore the poor intonation of many musicians, indeed, of entire ensembles. For purposes of comparison, only the best musicians of each period should, of course, be used. It seems to me that one telling argument against the supposition that musicians in earlier times played badly and out of tune can be found in the works themselves. I cannot imagine that brilliant composers, who themselves were practicing musicians and whose works were doubtlessly intended for their own period, composed their works in magnificent fashion, only to destroy them through substandard performances. To me, such a notion is inconceivable.

Tuning is a field that has received very little attention. A modern equal temperament is not desirable for music of the Middle Ages and the Renaissance. This type of temperament appears harsh and ambiguous when used for such music. In the early stages of polyphonic music, and in some areas probably well into the 16th century, intonation and tuning were based on the Pythagorean system. This system results in a very beautiful melodic structure and absolutely pure, relaxed fifths, fourths and octaves. Only the thirds are too large and are regarded and used as dissonance. The sensuous beauty of the third was discovered around the end of the 14th century. Pythagorean tuning was gradually discarded in favor of pure third tunings, which were described by Henricus Arnaut of Zwolle (c. 1440) and Arnolt Schlick (1511). The melodic quality as a consequence appears somewhat brittle, for the fifths and fourths were no longer pure. But this was the price that had to be paid for absolutely pure thirds and a previously-unimagined euphony. The tonal differences that emerge when we compare various temperaments—e.g. the Pythagorean, the Schlick, the modern temperament—are very great, and any musically sensitive person who hears this kind of comparison must recognize that the music of every style and every epoch sounds far and away best and most convincing when played in the temperament for which it was written.

Musical Instruments in Church and Elsewhere

In the early periods of Western music, the role of musical instruments was subject to repeated change. During the early Middle Ages, sacred music sung by clerics, the direct descendant of ancient (especially Oriental) cult singing, was often accompanied by many musical instruments. In palaces and monasteries, noblemen and monks played organs, flutes, shawms, trumpets and many kinds of percussion instruments during religious services, but later, during the Age of Chivalry, it was wandering artists who played musical instruments. This group was socially scorned and regarded as sinful and dishonorable. (The minstrel had only "the shadow of honor." In order to obtain satisfaction for an insult, he was permitted to punish only the shadow of his opponent.)

Some of the European musical instruments of the Middle Ages developed directly from their ancient precursors (organ, harp, some wind, percussion and plucked instruments), while others were brought to Europe by vagabond entertainers, the Crusaders, or via Moorish Spain from Asia Minor. The lute and many related plucked instruments, many of the winds, and also the strings—or, more precisely, the bow, with the help of which plucked instruments were transformed into stringed instruments—were, as Werner Bachmann has convincingly demonstrated, borrowed from the Orient around the year 1000. Every conceivable type of hybrid form developed as well. The minstrels used these instruments primarily for dance music and as musical background for plays and "mummeries." On into modern times, therefore, the sound of musical instruments was linked to voluptuous pagan sensuality and worldly pleasures which had no place in church. However, even there, one did not want to do without these festive and splendid instruments, and so they were used again and again, even in the face of protest from ecclesiastical authorities. These protests gradually diminished, the general custom being silently tolerated.

Prior to 1500, almost no specifically instrumental music was created, with the exception of dance music. The element of improvisation, playing out of the inspiration of the moment, characterizes the instrumental soloist or virtuoso, as we would say today. When music was to be played by an ensemble of instrumentalists, a frequent occurrence, existing vocal works were arranged by modifying the individual parts through the improvised additions of ornamentation corresponding to the technical possibilities and particular type of playing of the instruments. An independent instrumental style gradually developed from this practice, although the idioms that were typical of certain instruments remained undifferentiated for the time being. Thus, in the 16th century, the form of the instrumental canzona, developed particularly in

Italy by Netherlanders living there, was extended formally and also in terms of sound by the circle around the two Gabrielis in Venice.

The first ricercares, as these canzonas were initially called, e.g. those of Willaert or Palestrina, could be recognized as instrumental music only because they lacked text, since they had been written in the imitative style of the vocal music of that period. However, the masters of the Gabrieli circle had already developed large numbers of clearly instrumental phrases and motifs, a vocabulary of purely musical, textless dialogue, which clearly distinguishes true instrumental music from vocal music. In the first years of the 17th century, works are found with concrete—though never binding—suggestions for scoring, so it is possible to distinguish between typical "wind-like" and "string-like" figures.

Even double and multiple choirs, a special achievement of the Venetian school of composition, which enveloped a church interior simultaneously and on all sides in song (living stereo in the 17th century!), were used in purely instrumental music. Instrumental canzonas were composed in which two or more groups played in a kind of dialogue. These groups were spatially separated; they were also set off musically from each other by the arranging of all wind players in one group, strings in another. Groups were also separated into high and low instruments.

All of these newly discovered possibilities for instrumental music-making were first embodied in vocal music in large polychoral motets by Andrea and Giovanni Gabrieli. To be sure, even prior to this, instruments had been occasionally used to accompany singing voices. But now accompanied singing was something quite different: various groups were used to impart unheard-of color and diversity to this spatial music through the most varied combinations of choruses and solo singers with instruments.

The Great Innovation Around 1600

One of the most radical upheavals in music history took place around 1600. The hallowed order of Western music was suddenly called into question by a bizarre circle of influential students of antiquity, or, more aptly, would-be restorers of antiquity.

Until that time, sacred and secular music, motets and madrigals, basically were polyphonic. They were occasionally homophonic, but primarily they were written polyphonically, in a consistently imitative contrapuntal style. The text could usually not be understood because the words were not sung by the various voices at the same time. Nor was the text the focus of attention; the actual work of art existed in the subtle relationships among the individual independent voices, forming a complex polyphonic structure. These works could be sung using different texts, or they formed, without a text, the basis for purely instrumental music, with the instrumentalists translating them into their respective idioms through variation and ornamentation. This very refined and largely esoteric music can be regarded as the climax and termination of a development that occured over almost two centuries.

Now, suddenly, the "Camerata" of Counts Bardi and Corsi, a circle in Florence with a strongly historical orientation, maintained that the only true music had been discovered. They claimed that Greek drama, the focus of the "research activity" of that circle, had been performed, in antiquity, melodramatically, sung. Because everything that ancient Greek culture had accomplished was regarded as an unsurpassable archetype, it was emphatically claimed that *melodramma*, monody, was the only proper music. As if this were not enough, strict rules were immediately established, e.g. in Caccini's *Le Nuove Musiche*, which held that poetry alone is the mistress of music, and that only certain texts—i.e. those which imitated the classical drama and pastoral plays—were worthy of composition. Finally, all of the polyphonic music in vogue at the time was condemned as barbaric and deleterious to the text.

Of course, a concept that regards language and music as one and the same entity could only come about in a country like Italy, where the language possesses a very melodramatic and song-like quality. Nonetheless, it is a source of the greatest amazement for us today that there were those who wished to simply abandon a highly-developed, rich and flourishing music at the peak of its development, which madrigal and motet actually were at the time, and destroy it in order to install the phantom of recitative singing as the only true music.

The propagandistic writings of the Camerata and its followers, whose numbers grew rapidly, reveal the revolutionary elan with which this task was undertaken. The dogmas of the new orientation were much stricter than the strictest rules of traditional counterpoint, which were under attack. The "new music" was principally monophonic; the melody of language determined its "melos." The accompanying basso continuo was allowed to contribute only simple harmonies in order to underscore certain words, but never should attract "musical" attention. It was held that the manners of speaking of various population segments were to be studied and imitated in the new works. No greater contrast is conceivable than that between what was, at that time, traditional music and the new monody; this is possibly the most radical revolution in the history of Western music.

Nonetheless, traditional music, which was to be destroyed, would probably have been too strongly entrenched, and the new music, which was touted as the only true kind of music, would have been too weak to have brought about this radical transformation, if the greatest musical genius of the age, Claudio Monteverdi, had not recognized the forward-looking possibilities inherent in the new trend. He by no means intended to give up the important achievements of the old style, yet he found ways to form the new ideas of speech-song into the dramatic recitative and the aria, thereby becoming the actual creator of opera. In so doing, he combined all known forms of vocal and instrumental music with the forward-looking ideas of the Florentine reformers without allowing himself to be distracted by their dogmas.

For the choruses of his first opera, Monteverdi used the old polyphonic madrigal, a genre in which he was to remain the unsurpassed master. He drew his inspiration for the instrumentation from the superabundant orchestra of the intermedii (musical intermezzos for theater). By the end of the 16th century, these intermedii had pushed the actual plays so far towards the periphery that the music became the main attraction of the performance. This was due, above all, to the unbelievably abundant orchestration employed. Everything available at the time in terms of sound was offered: all kinds of string instruments, including violins, gambas, and lyres, a multitude of lutes and guitar-like plucked instruments with gut or metal strings, harpsichords, virginals, harps, various types of organs, regals, and an enormous wind section of recorders and transverse flutes, shawms from discant to bass, cornetts and all kinds of brass instruments. This diversity of sound is hardly conceivable today, far surpassing as it does that of the symphony orchestra of late Romanticism. In his *L'Orfeo*, Monteverdi was the last to utilize such an orchestra. This work is thus particularly interesting as it contains the entire tonal palette of the Renaissance as well as the newest ideas of solo singing.

There is no link connecting *L'Orfeo* and the late operas of Monteverdi which have been preserved, since almost all the dramatic works he wrote in the 30 intervening years have been lost. A completely different sound concept dominates in *Il Ritorno d'Ulisse* and *L'Incoronazione di*

Poppea: the colorful intermedii orchestra has disappeared, replaced by an accompanying (continuo) orchestra based on a string group with a few winds and several chordal instruments to accompany the recitatives and arias.

Tonal Aesthetics: Is Ugly Beautiful?

Monteverdi's letters tell us something about his understanding of vocal and instrumental style. Today we basically proceed on the assumption that musical sound should be beautiful, and free of noise interference and mistakes. But I am convinced that the main accent in Monteverdi is on musical truth, on the optimal interpretation of the text, of the words, not simply on tonal beauty alone. No aesthetic limits are imposed in rendering this musical truth in tones. Given what we know of the instrumentarium and about the treatment of the singing voice at that time, we cannot assume that beautiful, absolutely flawless, sound was the ideal. It is often desirable to achieve effective dramatic truth with sounds having a component of ugliness rather than with flawless sonority. It may be again easier today to understand this, since we do not necessarily or constantly strive for absolute tonal beauty in modern music.

It is unfortunate that we are in possession of only a few descriptions, including several from Monteverdi himself, of the ways in which the sounds of the contemporary instrumentarium were applied. However, these few passages are so interesting that it is clear in any case that the beauty of the sound was subordinated to dramatic and musical truth. From the viewpoint of general aesthetics, it is also true that beauty has a much greater impact when it is derived from that which is ugly. This new principle emerged around this time, for we also find it in Monteverdi's treatment of dissonance, which follows completely new principles. The resolution of a dissonance to a consonance was thought to evoke in the listener a sense of relief after a feeling of tension; now a piece could begin with an unprepared dissonance, like a bolt out of the blue—something that had previously been quite impossible! Such an emotional reversal, a sudden change in "affection," is now very consciously introduced. The same element of contrasting effects is also used in the purely tonal realm. This usage was ultimately taken to such extremes that Monteverdi's students occasionally called for special effects in their compositions that would not be encountered again in instrumental pieces until the 20th century. These include bowing behind the bridge of a string instrument, where no specific tone, but only a screeching noise can be created, or knocking with the bow against a string instrument.

The probable reason that we learn little from Monteverdi himself about these matters is that he left very few scores. Normally, he conducted performances of his works; otherwise, he probably left the individual details of performance to the musicians.

We are even less informed about the singers. Yet, as I believe, we can deduce from Monteverdi's remarks that for them text interpretation was also so much in the foreground that it took priority over the beauty of the treatment of the voice. I deduce this also from the fact that bel canto was invented during the last 10 years of Monteverdi's life in reaction to the dramatic speaking song, as if there was a general desire to restore genuinely melodic singing to its proper place. The elucidation of the pure textual truth was probably at times so exaggerated by the singers that they ended up singing incorrectly, and in reaction the pendulum then swung in the opposite direction.

Monteverdi Today

Monteverdi was a scintillating, complex personality who burst the conventions of orthodox music with his brilliant insights. He possessed the majestic self-awareness and self-confidence of genius. Over the course of his long life, Monteverdi lived through several major stylistic changes, the most important of which was the transition from the Renaissance to the Baroque. He himself was in the forefront of all of these stylistic transitions.

It is no wonder that the new style of personal emotions, of grand but restrained style without form, originated in Italy. Among the European peoples, the Italians have the most extroverted temperament, a Southern love of social intercourse, a magnificent language which itself is almost song, and glowing passion. We can understand Italian music much better if we come to know the people, the landscape and the climate of Italy.

When we concern ourselves with Monteverdi and his oeuvre, we must ask a few critical questions: What does his music mean to us, what can it say to us today? Does it have only the exotic charm of "early music," or does it affect us directly? It would be absolutely senseless to come to know and understand this music, to want to perform it as "early music," from the point of view of musicologists or musical archivists. We are contemporary, living musicians, not scholars of antiquity; we can only make music which communicates something to us, music we consider significant. Monteverdi was a passionate musician, an uncompromising innovator in every respect, a thoroughly modern composer.

He was a bitter enemy of everything antiquated, he would have had no sympathy for the renewed interest in "early music." Monteverdi's music is so interesting for us because it can never become "early music," but will always remain vital and living.

We naturally want to learn of the performance practice, the meaning of Monteverdi's performance conditions, but we do not want to flee into false purism, into false objectivity, into misconstrued faithfulness to the work. Nor does Monteverdi himself expect this: he is a full-blooded musician and an Italian as well. Thus, please do not fear vibrato, liveliness, subjectivity, hot Mediterranean air, but please be very afraid of coldness, purism, objectivity and empty historicism. We must understand the genuine musical concerns of Monteverdi and understand how those concerns are reflected in living music. We must attempt as musicians to see with new eyes everything that was current for Monteverdi and will remain current for all times, to reanimate it, to render it with our feelings, our 20th-century mentality—for certainly we do not wish to return to the 17th century. It is very important to study performance practice in order to obtain a real understanding. After all, we must be aware of the range of possibilities in order to be able to select those that are right for us. This means that we must try to understand as much as possible of what it was that Monteverdi intended, in order to discover what it is that we want from him.

Work and Arrangement: The Role of Instruments

Producing an opera today evidently means nothing more than signing on the appropriate singers, a competent conductor, and a stage director—and then realizing the work precisely in keeping with the dictates laid down by the composer. This is not much of a problem: the scores of Puccini, Richard Strauss, Wagner, Verdi, Weber and Beethoven basically contain everything one needs to know. Each note is assigned by the composer to a particular singer or instrument, every one knows exactly when and what he or she is supposed to play or sing. Thus it is possible to discern the work even in the most extreme interpretation.

If a conductor wished to realize a completely different, personal notion of sound in such a work—for example, to ornament the singing voice or to radically change the instrumentation and harmonization—such a departure would not be tolerated, and would be regarded as an atack on a work of art, an unforgivable distortion of the composer's intentions. For example, no one would tolerate a performance of Wagner's *Meistersinger* with an orchestra of pianos, harps, guitars, saxophones, vibraphone, harmonium, celesta and mandolins. It would hardly be possible to convince members of the profession and the public of the artistic necessity of such alterations. The authority of the composer and the inviolability of the work can never be called into question.

The situation in early operas, e.g. works from the 17th century, is quite different. Here we do not merely tolerate an arrangement that intervenes in the work, we accept it as a matter of course, since actually it is demanded by the work itself. The preconditions are manifestly radically different. For this reason, wherever operas, oratorios and other musical works of the 17th century are performed, reference is made to an "arrangement," "musical adaptation," "instrumentation," or however else it may be called. The unbiased listener may frequently ask whether it is not possible to perform these works in an unarranged fashion, just as they were composed. Is it inevitable, particularly in the case of this music, that "arrangers" interpose themselves between the composer and the listener—at a time when almost all classical music and even some pre-classical music can be heard purified of all editorial additions, seeming improvements and retouching? Does the general tendency toward faithfulness to the work, toward respect for the composer, exclude, of all people, the great masters of the 16th, 17th and 18th centuries?

This question does not have a simple answer. To answer it requires an understanding of the historical changes which such concepts as work, composition and performance have undergone. The notion of "faithfulness to the work," which has been elevated over the past fifty years to the status of an indisputable guideline, assumes that every composition, with only very few exceptions, has one single ideal rendition and that consequently a rendition is better the more closely it approximates this ideal. This theory may be valid for some of the music of the 19th and 20th centuries. After all, the composers of this period attempted to define their views down to the minutest detail, in order to keep the arbitrary liberties of interpreters to a minimum. However, total unity between work and rendition in this sense can only happen as a result of creative improvisation, i.e. when the composer and the interpreter are one.

The problem of "faithfulness" with regard to older music is compounded by the fact that our musical training and education has been and is still based primarily on the works of late Romanticism and the early 20th century, i.e. works for which the manner of performance was minutely prescribed by the composer. That the music of earlier epochs was written under different presuppositions, that the relation between work and performance can differ must first be discovered. A dangerous obscuration of these problems occurs because of the notation: as in all handwriting, it conveys an almost magical suggestiveness to the reader and interpreter. Notation, which is almost identical for different epochs, misleadingly suggests certainty; it can cause serious errors in dynamics, in the choice of tempo, in the "emotional" treatment of the individual styles. It can be responsibile for performances of classical and pre-classical music that lack emotion, for expression marks are rare and sometimes completely absent in this music. Upon closer historical consideration, we must recognize that during no epoch did our notation possess that absolute clarity of which so many composers and musicians dream. Is it not surprising and rather disconcerting to think that it is impossible to represent all important details—such as absolute and relative pitch, duration, rhythmical relationships, dynamics etc.—in an unambiguous way? Understanding notation depends on an unwritten convention and agreement between composer and interpreter: it is the key to their reciprocal relationship.

In simple terms, for decades we have read and performed in good faith all of Western music according to the conventions of the time of Brahms. This has resulted in two extreme interpretations which differ in principle, but are based on the same assumptions, even the same mentality, paradoxically enough: either the "missing" marks, dynamics, espressivo, tempi, instrumentation, etc., were added, or music was played "faithfully and objectively," just as it had been written. Our goal, however, must be to discover what is *intended.*

Since in recent years operas of the 16th and 17th centuries have come to be performed more frequently, it may be useful to discuss questions of arrangement, appropriate performance practice, and the various attempts which have been made to answer these questions. When, for all practical purposes, opera was invented around 1600 in Florence, it was assumed that Greek poetry, especially the drama, had been "recited" in a kind of singing, and there was a general desire to revitalize this type of performance. An attempt was made to recite Greek drama and the pseudo-Greek drama of living poets in an authentic way—or so it was thought—and to accompany this recitation on the lute or harpsichord. The correct execution of this newly discovered dramatic solo song was described very precisely, even dogmatically, from the very outset. Up until that point, music had been exclusively measured and polyphonic; now the singer was suddenly expected to proceed only from language itself ("because of the present custom and style in singing where one composes and sings as if one . . . were reciting . . ."). This "speech-song," or monody, was notated more or less in keeping with the rhythm and melody of speech, but at the same time it was constantly pointed out that here there was no metrical accent, but only the inflection of language, and that the notation in 4/4 time represented merely an orthographical necessity. For this singing-speaking, *recitar cantando*, which was supposed to enhance the expressiveness and dramatic persuasiveness of speech, an appropriate type of accompaniment had to be found. Any musically prominent bass, e.g. a counter-melody to the voice line, would have inevitably diverted attention away from language, and emphasized the musical aspect—which was improper, according to the new ideas. A simple chordal type of accompaniment thus came into use. This type of accompaniment for singing was the first important task of the *basso continuo* (thorough bass). In this style, both the execution of the voice part (above all rhythmically) and that of the thorough bass (choice of instrument, of harmony, of rhythm) are possible in many diverse ways, *as intended by the composer.*

Very precise instructions existed for the accompaniment of this recitative, which Monteverdi himself observed as well; only lutes, harpsichord, organ or similar instruments could be used. A cello could be used to reinforce the bass only when the bass line was supposed to be particularly underscored. Only special situations could be emphasized through special instrumentation. This meager accompaniment was also technically necessary, because the recited song was to be executed freely, i.e. without strict rhythm and above all without the scanning meter of accented and unaccented beats.

It goes without saying that the entire "realization," that is, everything that is played on the chordal instruments above the bass, had to be improvised, i.e., freely added. One of the important innovations characterizing the transition in music from the 16th to the 17th century was that the outer voices were suddenly accorded much greater importance than the middle voices. As a result, the actual composition now consisted in the invention of the outer voices, and everything else could and had to be freely improvised by the continuo player. This necessary creative adaptation does not belong to the "work," but rather to performance. This separation of work and performance was an essential and novel feature of the music of that period.

Since a precise instrumentation, as we understand the term today, was customary neither for the continuo nor for the rest of the orchestra, there was a division of all instruments into "fundamental" and "ornamental" instruments. In addition to associative reasons, this division governed the actual use of the instruments. The "fundamental"instruments were suited to execute the thorough-bass, the bass line as well as the harmonies, to fill in and to clarify the harmonic development. This was, of course, done through improvisation. Even in those passages where only "fundamental" instruments are used for accompaniment, the chordal or motivic accompaniment is an aspect of performance, not of composition. The "fundamental" instruments are, as mentioned earlier, the harpsichord, virginal, organ, harp, lute, chitarrone and others.

The instruments on which individual voices could be played were called "ornamental" or melodic instruments, including all of the strings and winds, but also the harp and lute when used melodically, not chordally. Today, the bass line is normally played by one "fundamental" instrument, e.g. the harpsichord, *and* a melodic instrument, e.g. the violoncello. This usage corresponds to the practice of the 18th century. In the beginning stages of thorough-bass music (after 1600), a string or wind instrument (violoncello, contrabass, violone, dulcian, trombone) was often also allowed to play the bass, but only when it had something "to say" in terms of the motif, in terms of movement; the respective "fundamental" instrument alone played the supporting chords laid under the speech-song.

The role of the melodic instruments is a subject of much debate today. Descriptions from the 17th century show that the educational level of the professional musician was so advanced that we could certainly expect him capable of improvising polyphonic movements, probably using simple imitations and uncomplicated harmonies, with slight errors of voice leading being tolerated. Sketches, written notes and perhaps hand signals from the maestro at the harpsichord may well have facilitated fairly orderly playing by a small operatic orchestra. At that time, pleasure was taken in keeping the special features of an art secret, so it seems understandable that no complete sets of performance material, not even all ritornelli, have been preserved written out for all voices. As pointed out earlier, libraries contain only the basic skeleton of the works.

It is thus first necessary to select and distribute the continuo instruments according to the cast and the dramatic situations. It was possible to use them according to two different principles. First, each of the persons involved in the action is always accompanied by the same instrument. Second, a particular dramatic situation is characterized by the sound of certain instruments. The gradations between pure speech-song with very simple supporting chords, to intermediate arioso forms on motivic basses, up to larger aria-like forms, give clear indications regarding the use of ornament instruments. In the speech-song, the fundamental instrument alone provides the simplest possible accompaniment; the listener must not be distracted from the words by the art and fantasy of the continuo player, neither the cello nor the dulcian play along. In the case of arioso intermediate forms, the continuo is executed more richly, but always with improvisation; one or more string or wind instruments play the bass line as a counterpoint to the vocal line. In the larger, aria-like forms, the continuo is, as it were, also performed by the melodic instruments. Here the orchestra participates in the accompaniment. The realization is as simple as possible—it must never distract from the main focus of interest, the singing voice and the bass, but must provide variety in timbre from the purely thorough-bass passages. In addition to these forms, there is the "concitato" (agitated style), which was invented by Monteverdi in his *Combattimento di Tancredi e Clorinda* (1624), an instrumentally accompanied recitative for wild, angry passages.

With regard to selection of instruments, a certain associative symbolism had developed since the intermedii of the 16th century. Tender and subtle effects were associated with strings (in concitato, for anger as well); pastoral and folk-like passages with recorders and shawms; erotic effects with flutes. Water gods, tritons and sounds of the underworld were associated with cornetts and trombones; gods and rulers with trumpets. In a letter Monteverdi explicitly states that if the ocean plays a role, one must of course use trombones and cornetts. The hollow sound of these instruments may well be a very beautiful association for water; in any case, for the listener of that period this must have been self-evident.

One of the most frequently discussed problems related to the performance of early music is the question of improvisation and ornamentation. It appears that too much of a good thing is done in this regard during present-day performances which strive for maximum authenticity. Continuo players display contrapuntal tours de force which are at times very artistic, to be sure, but which are seldom dramaturgically and stylistically appropriate. This is particularly true for music of the early Baroque period. There are numerous treatises on improvisational ornamentation by the singers, yet there are also warning voices of contemporaries, particularly with regard to the works of Monteverdi, that nothing, or almost nothing, should be added to the note text. Indeed, Monteverdi himself wrote out more ornamentation than any other composer of his age. This leads us to conclude that in those passages where he wrote no ornamentation, he wished to have very little of it. In *L'Orfeo*, we find very many written-out ornaments. He wrote one great "aria" of Orfeo both with and without ornamentation; the latter was perhaps intended for a singer who was incapable of performing this difficult ornamentation. Little latitude remains for improvisation or other kinds of freedom for the interpreters in *L'Orfeo*, compared with the late operas that have come down to us. Caccini's rule, which holds that ornamentation may be applied only in passages where it strengthens the musical expression, applies here as well.

Thus it is just as impossible today as it was at the time of Monteverdi to perform an opera written by him or one of his contemporaries without arrangement, without any kind of musical adaptation. After all, every musician today expects to be told precisely what he is supposed to play. As a member of an orchestra, he must routinely interpret works of a variety of stylistic epochs, yet in none of these is he so at home that he can flawlessly improvise counter-melodies. Improvisation today must therefore be written out in those passages where it goes beyond relatively simple ornamentation. The necessity of an arrangement, however, can be easily misconstrued. Monteverdi's contemporaries rarely experienced this type of problem, since almost every musician was an experienced composer and theorist who knew exactly what he had to do. They were not simply instrumentalists or singers, but musicians in the fullest sense of the word. They could compose and express themselves freely using the rhetoric of music, which happily was also what they wanted to do. One could not simply present them with a composition in which every detail of performance was written out and expect them to play it. Creative improvisation was taken for granted; the symbolism of instrumentation was commonly known and needed no explanation. The sparing use of directions in old scores made it possible for all musicians to adapt the work according to their resources and to perform it using the means at their disposal.

The need to arrange a work was thus obvious to those who rediscovered Baroque opera, assuming they desired to perform such historical works in the first place. The range of possibilities in the 19th and 20th centuries, with the music dramas of Wagner and the operas of Puccini in our ears, was of course much broader than during Monteverdi's lifetime, when the only music known was that written by contemporaries. Thus it is possible today, unlike 350 years ago, to transform a Monteverdi opera into a work of the 19th or 20th century through corresponding arrangement and instrumentation. However, we can also try to realize the intentions of the composer by using the resources and possibilities that existed during his lifetime. The main question has remained the same: How is the musical idea best served, how can the *work* best be made understandable for us today?

Work and Performance

In the decades between *L'Orfeo* (1607) and *L'Incoronazione di Poppea* (1642), Monteverdi composed a large number of small dramatic scenes, solos and duets, with and without chorus. He used these to expand his dramatic musical vocabulary, applying it to specific, clearly delineated situations. In terms of scoring alone, these pieces could be performed in very diverse ways, a fact interestingly documented by Monteverdi himself, e.g. in his letter of 21 November, 1615.

> It would be best if the performers were placed in the shape of a crescent moon. At both points a chitarrone and a harpsichord for the continuo, one for Cloris, the other for Tirsi. These two should hold chitarrones in their hands and concertize with both other instruments while they are singing and playing. It would be even more beautiful if Cloris used a harp instead of the chitarrone. Then, when the dance begins after the dialogue, the number of singers should be augmented to make 8, also 8 viole da brazzo, as well as a contrabass and a spinet for the fundament. It would be nice if two small lutes were also included . . .

We can see that a particular performance was given wide latitude, within the framework of aesthetic and stylistic restrictions and, in keeping with accepted convention.

The form in which the two late operas of Monteverdi have come down to us has been frequently described as sketchy. The vocal parts are complete, and they have a bass line with occasional figures. A few short ritornelli have three parts (in the Venetian manuscript), four parts (in the Neapolitan manuscript) or five parts (in the *Ulisse* manuscript in Vienna). There are some remarks such as "violini" or "tutti gli stromenti," in passages where only voice parts and bass are notated. This type of writing should not be described as sketchy; it defines the *work,* the composition. It remains for us to deal with the question of a suitable *performance.*

A brief historical review may help to clarify some basic assumptions. It is very unlikely that the manuscripts were used for performances, even though they show traces of use. It is much more likely that this wear is due to copying and to occasional perusal, rather than to weeks of rehearsing and actual performances. Many other opera "scores" of the middle and second half of the 17th century exist in Venice, and most are similarly arranged. Several contain notes on orchestration, a few contain empty staves in some passages between the voice and bass, sometimes with a few notes, e.g. in the first measure of an aria. It is noteworthy that no performance materials exist, despite the fact that, at the very least, several continuo parts, parts from which the singers studied, and orchestral material would have been indispensable for even the most basic kinds of performances.

In France as well, operatic scores were similarly written and printed from the mid-17th to the mid-18th century. Here, however, many orchestral parts have been preserved, a fact indicating that instrumentation was a matter of *performance*. The various performance materials of one and the same work can thus differ considerably in instrumentation and part-writing. What was customary in France from the middle of the 17th to the middle of the 18th century appears to have been true of Italy only during the second third of the 17th century.

The fact that only the French performance materials, and not their Italian counterparts, have been preserved could be due to differing approaches to the role of the conductor, the *maestro*. The French evidently were indifferent to the uses to which their version would be put, while the Italians seem to have jealously guarded their ideas and may well have destroyed all material, once it had been performed.

The meaning of the very simple notation of these "opera scores" can be easily discerned. At the beginning of the 17th century, the opera was still a very young genre. It soon became fashionable at courts that lionized the arts, and characteristic styles and types of performances developed in various regions. Opera houses sprang up everywhere. Every leading princely court established an opera and the first purely commercial operatic enterprises were founded in Venice. Each of these wanted to play the same successful and well-known pieces, although under widely varying conditions. The greatest orchestral and technical resources were to be found at the imperial court in Vienna, while several of the Venetian opera companies had to keep a close eye on their budgets. If a composer was interested in having his works performed at several locations, he had to write them down in such a way that they could be adapted to local conditions by the respective maestro. For this reason it was important to leave as much leeway as possible. The same work could be performed at one court by a large orchestra which clothed it in magnificent sounds, while at a different location it was staged with only the most essential accompaniment. The critical point was that the changes could only affect the sound quality, the musical garment. It could not represent a serious alteration of the composition as such, but might amount to a richly varied execution of the basso continuo. The work is therefore complete, even in the simplest realization. Works notated in this way could thus be played in a minimalist version with one harpsichord and four strings, but they could also be adapted to meet all requirements and conditions, this being one of the tasks of the respective maestro.

This great freedom that the performing musician enjoyed in intervening in a formative way in the work of a composer can be explained by the following consideration. As a creative artist, the composer by no means received the adulation in the 16th and 17th centuries that has come to him since the 19th century. This phenomenon can be observed in all the arts. It used to be true that even the greatest painters frequently did not sign their paintings—they often merely made a basic sketch, leaving the execution to their apprentices. A similar situation existed in music as well. A composer like Monteverdi, who at times had many students, perhaps discussed the overall concept with the librettist and himself wrote out key phrases, but only sketched the rest, leaving the final touches to his most famous student, Francesco Cavalli. (This may also be one of the reasons Cavalli's handwriting is found again and again in the late operas of Monteverdi, a fact which has given rise to doubts concerning Monteverdi's authorship.) From my perspective as a musician, it is not all that important whether all 120 measures of the concluding duet of *Poppea* are by Monteverdi himself, or whether he only sketched the idea of the passacaglia, with Cavalli then seeing to the ultimate execution. Even if it should happen to be in part the product of the workshop, this final duet loses nothing of its beauty as a result. This workshop element indicates that the composer regarded certain details of the execution of his work as being of secondary importance. Thus we come once again to the conclusion that the arranger, the performer who himself is involved in shaping the work, is indispensable in the realization of the piece.

An additional and not unimportant point concerning the explanation of the framework-like notation of these works is the social situation of the artists of the period. There was no such thing as copyright—every composer had to expect to see his significant and beautiful thoughts filched and published by others. Composers may have attempted to protect themselves against pirated editions by taking care not to use great precision in writing down their ideas. This surmise is supported by the fact that *L'Orfeo,* which is preserved in a printing that was authorized by the composer, is precisely notated. On the other hand, the late operas were not printed.

Very few years after the premier performance of *Ulisse,* the librettist stated that this opera could no longer be performed because the master, who was the only one who knew exactly how it should be performed, had passed away. A new arrangement would be too costly and difficult. Why should it have been so difficult, if the two lines of the score, singing voice and bass, really represented the complete opera? I think that the difficulty had to do with the fact that, in this case, the composer was identical with the performer. He could use his authority ad hoc to determine instrumentation and manner of performance.

We might imagine the progress of an operatic performance in those times as being similar to the way in which a half-improvised musical is performed today: only a sketch is prepared, the composer notes chords and one or two melodic turns, a counter-part, etc. This is written down in the briefest form and distributed. Intelligent and creative musicians can perform even an opera with such instructions, but such notes are never preserved in a library. Instead, they are discarded after the performance because they were intended to be used, and could be used, only for this particular performance. It is therefore probable that a performance, which, after all, represents a considerable creative portion of the work itself, disappeared with the respective performers. In Venice, many operas were performed every year during the carnival season—Cavalli wrote 45 operas in the space of 30 years—, but no performance material exists for any of them. All we have are the skeletal scores, although these are heavily annotated.

Once these premises are clarified, questions arise about the realization of a specific work. In my opinion, a musical or cultural "updating" must be ruled out here. In practical terms, such an updating would result in the creation of a *new* piece, one inspired by the work of Monteverdi. But Monteverdi's operas are autonomous as works of art and perfect in themselves, as are all great masterpieces; nothing need be improved or altered. The work itself contains the key to its own realization. Monteverdi's talent for music drama, which is comparable only to that of Mozart, the translation of his understanding of the text into sounding movement and gesture, together with his written remarks, must remain the guideline for every performance.

Bach and the Musicians of His Age

Johann Sebastian Bach brought the baroque principle of "musical discourse" to perfection. His traditional education in a many-branched family of musicians and his personal predisposition and inclination enabled him to become a composer who perfected that which already existed. Bach did not open up new horizons, despite the originality of his ideas. Nonetheless, he was equally successful and talented in each of the three roles which he held throughout the course of his peaceful career: organist in Arnstadt, Mühlhausen and Weimar; musician, concertmaster and maestro at the courts of Weimar and Köthen; Kantor and music director in Leipzig. If the circumstances of his life had led him to a large Catholic court or to an independent civic position (a development he would have welcomed), he would undoubtedly have become the greatest opera composer of his time. His abilities and interests include every conceivable field of musical creation.

Rhetoric formed the basis of all his work. Yet, although rhetoric formed the essential foundation of all baroque music from the time of Monteverdi on, for Bach it represented much more than an accepted stylistic convention of the period. It is a known fact that Bach consciously designed his works on the basis of rhetoric: as far as he was concerned, "music that speaks" (i.e., according to the rules of rhetoric) was the only form of music. The rhetorician Birnbaum, a friend of Bach, writes: "He is so perfectly aware of the aspects and advantages that a piece of music has in common with the art of rhetoric that one not only hears him with great pleasure when he focuses his conversation on the similarity and agreement that exists between both; but one also admires the adroit application of the same in his works." His circle of friends, predominantly university professors of German philology and rhetoric, reveal through their personal accounts his intense, life-long preoccupation with this material. Bach completely exhausted all possibilities in music as it existed up until his time in terms of formal aspects, harmony, expression and melody. Because of this immeasurable richness, Bach formed the basis of every new development to come.

Since his pieces were worked through to the smallest detail, emotionally as well as rationally, he was the only composer of his time who repeatedly had to break down the barriers between "work" and "performance," barriers which were such basic determinants of baroque music. He prescribed every detail that could be imagined at the time relating to the execution of his works by the interpreter, especially in connection with articulation and ornamentation. He was obliged to do this because his clearly worked out view of his oeuvre left no latitude for the interpreter. To Bach, ornamentation was meaningful only when it strengthened expression, when it was necessary and possible only in one particular form.

Of course, this meant that Bach had to abandon the old principle of the autonomous, creative interpreter. His works, especially the more complex pieces, could be so distorted by even slight misunderstandings on the part of the performers that he believed he could trust only his own interpretation. Bach's prescribed ornamentations reveal the well-founded distrust he felt toward his interpreters. A very authoritarian attitude on the part of the composer appears here for the first time. By depriving the interpreter of his chief perquisite, the possibility of ornamentation, Bach once and for all eliminated the borderline between work and performance which had been of such great importance. Composers of later generations followed him in this direction: the performing musician no longer played a role in shaping a work.

Musicians were unwilling to accept their new status, however. A description has come down to us of a public controversy which depicts the pros and cons in an illuminating way. In this dispute, Johann Adolf Scheibe, a maestro and writer on music, took the part of the disenfranchised musicians, while Bach was represented by his friend Johann Abraham Birnbaum, professor of rhetoric in Leipzig. Scheibe criticized Bach's manner of composition (*Der Critische Musicus*, Hamburg, May 14, 1737):

> By now Herr Bach is the most distinguished musician in Leipzig . . . His dexterity (on the organ) is astounding, and it is hard to believe that it is possible for him to cross and extend his fingers and his feet so strangely and so nimbly, making the broadest jumps without playing a single wrong tone, or distorting his body by such energetic movement. This great man would be the object of admiration for entire nations, if he possessed more pleasantness and if he did not remove every natural element from his pieces through their bombastic and muddled nature, obscuring their beauty through an over-abundance of art. Because he judges according to his own fingers, his pieces are extremely difficult to play; for he demands that the singers and instrumentalists reproduce through their throats and instruments whatever he can play on the clavier. But this is completely impossible. *All ornaments, all little embellishments, and everything that one understands to belong to the method of playing, he expresses with actual notes;* this deprives his pieces not only of the beauty of harmony, but also makes the singing quite difficult to listen to.

Later, when the public debate was well underway but before Scheibe had admitted authorship of the anti-Bach polemic, he attacked the master in the area in which he truly dominated. According to Scheibe, the basic reason for Bach's "errors" was the fact that "this great man" had "not informed himself sufficiently of the sciences which are required of a learned composer." He was insufficiently "concerned with the rules derived from poetry and rhetoric . . . which are so necessary in music." Scheibe denies Bach's knowledge of rhetoric, of all things, something for which Bach was famous all over Europe. It is of course no coincidence that Bach's champion, Birnbaum, was a rhetorician.

Birnbaum responded in January 1738: "Unbiased Comments on a Dubious Passage in . . . *Der Critische Musicus*," dedicating this extensive and well-founded answer to Bach himself! We may assume that Bach's own ideas are reflected in the comments of his friend.

> The man has yet to be born who has the very special good fortune to please everyone . . . It does not require much perusal to find more than one reason for this. On the one hand, there is a lack of fundamental insight into the things which are praised or blamed. Judgment is passed on things one does not understand. On the other hand, one is blinded by overly biased emotions. Such a judgment always represents a violation of truth. Stubborn but corrupted taste here sets forth precepts for reason. Whatever agrees with this taste is alone found to be praiseworthy: what is contrary to it, on the other hand, is rejected as totally wrong. One is seduced by the general judgment of the world. One speaks more in keeping with the pre-conceived opinions of others than from one's own conviction.

Birnbaum reacts to Scheibe's anonymous attack because "the love of truth and a special reverence for this truly great master of music . . . obligate me to defend his honor . . . The author of this writing praises the 'Herr Hofcompositeur' in one passage, but in another he criticizes him all the more sharply. Upon closer inspection I have found the praise accorded him imperfect, the errors attributed to him unfounded."

In brilliant language, Birnbaum condemns the clever tone in which Scheibe sought to humiliate Bach, by calling him a "Musicant" (a derogatory term) and not a "Virtuoso" or "great composer," as extraordinary artists were normally called. "The 'Herr Hofcompositeur' is a great composer, an unparalleled virtuoso on the organ and the clavier, but he is by no means a 'Musicant.' " Birnbaum is irritated that a "knowledgeable" connoisseur of true musical perfection like Scheibe praises Bach's technique, of all things. "Why does he not extol the astonishing number of unusual and well-executed flashes of inspiration; the modulation of a single theme through all keys." Bach's learned champion now turns to the direct attacks, first addressing the reproach of a 'lack of pleasantness.' His words are a plea on behalf of contrast in harmony and against a pleasant smoothness: "A remarkable passage from the English *Spectator* could be used almost by itself to disprove this charge. This passage points out that music is intended to please not just tender ears alone, but all those who can distinguish between a harsh and pleasant tone, i.e. who know how to use dissonances appropriately and to resolve them skillfully. True amenity of music results from the joining and alternation of consonances and dissonances without destroying the harmony. Music demands this by its very nature. The different emotions, feelings of sadness in particular, could not be expressed without this alternation which is in keeping with Nature itself."

Birnbaum also brilliantly refutes Scheibe's reproach that Bach's music is bombastic and confused:

> What does the term 'bombastic' mean when applied to music? Should it be understood to mean approximately the same as that type of writing which is called bombastic in rhetoric, in which the most magnificent adornments are lavished on inconsequential matters, thereby revealing their insignificance more clearly than ever? . . . Merely to think such a thing, let alone to say such a thing, of the 'Herr Hofcompositeur' would be the crudest slander. This composer does not waste his magnificent embellishments on drinking songs and lullabies, or on foolish little trifles of gallantry. In his sacred works, overtures, concertos and other musical pieces, the ornamentation is always appropriate to the main theme . . . What does the term confusion mean when applied to music? One must inevitably turn for help in understanding this term to that which is called confused in the first place, if one wishes to divine the general intent of the author. What I know is that confusion connotes something which possesses no order, the individual parts of which are so strangely admixed and intertwined that it is impossible to detect where each element actually belongs . . . But wherever the rules of composition are observed in the strictest possible sense, there order must inevitably be found. Now I certainly hope that the author does not believe that the 'Hofcompositeur' violates these rules. It is certain that the parts in the works of this great master of music are led [i.e., are contrapuntal—ed.] in a wondrous way, but without the slightest confusion. They progress in similar or contrary motion, as is necessary. They leave each other and at the appropriate time join together once again. Each part can be distinguished from the others, though often they imitate each other. The parts are disjunct and conjunct without the slightest irregularity as they outdo each other, so to speak. If executed in an appropriate manner, nothing is more beautiful than such harmony.

In this quote from Birnbaum, we are probably hearing Bach's own views of the meaning of his polyphony, the characterization of the individual voices, and their interrelationships.

And now on the concept of nature and art.

> The laudable attempts of the 'Herr Hofcompositeur' are aimed at presenting to the world this natural aspect with the help of art, in a most magnificent outward form. But this is precisely what the writer does not wish to admit. He states expressly that the 'Herr Hofcompositeur' obscures the beauty of his pieces by an overabundance of art. This sentence is contrary to the nature of true art, which is really what is under

discussion here. The essential concern of true art is to imitate nature and, where necessary, to assist nature. If nature imitates art, then that which is natural must indisputably shine forth everywhere among works of art. Consequently, it is impossible for art to remove the natural aspect from those things in which it imitates nature, and this holds for music as well. If art assists nature, then its intention is solely directed at preserving it, indeed, improving it, but not destroying it. Many things are extremely malformed in nature, but receive the most beautiful appearance once they are shaped by art. Art thus bestows on nature the beauty it lacks and enhances the beauty it possesses. The greater the art, the more diligently and carefully it works to improve nature, the more perfectly the beauty it has created will shine forth. Consequently, it is impossible for the greatest art to obscure the beauty of an object. Should it then be possible for the 'Herr Hofcompositeur' to be able, even with the greatest art he uses in the elaboration of his musical pieces, to deprive them of their natural element and to obscure their beauty?

The Baroque concept of nature and art is clearly expressed here: unformed nature is the raw material for the beauty which it acquires only after being shaped by the tools of art. The garden is thus much more beautiful than wild nature, the geometrically clipped hedge lovelier than the natural tree.

Birnbaum also rejects Scheibe's criticism of the difficulty of Bach's pieces, which "only he himself was able to play." Bach "does not act inappropriately in judging according to his fingers while composing these pieces. His conclusion can be none other than this: what I have been able to achieve by means of diligence and practice must be attainable by anyone with a modicum of natural talent and dexterity. And so for this very reason, the pretext of impossibility disappears as well. Everything is possible, as long as one has determination and diligently strives to transform one's natural abilities through untiring effort into skillful dexterity."

And as far as Scheibe's harsh criticism of Bach's practice of writing out the ornamentation is concerned, Birnbaum regards this practice as

a necessary wisdom on the part of a composer. On the one hand, it is certain that that which is called method (of ornamentation) of singing and playing is almost universally approved and considered pleasurable. It is also undeniable that the method pleases the ear when introduced at the correct place, but uncommonly insults the ear and ruins the primary melody when inappropriately applied. Experience also teaches us that one usually leaves the application of ornamentation to the arbitrary decision of the singers and instrumentalists. If all were adequately instructed in what is truly beautiful in the method, if they knew how to apply this method only where it could serve as an actual *ornament and special emphasis* for the main melody, then it would be a superfluous thing for the composer to prescribe one more time in written notes what they already know. But since very few have enough knowledge of this, they ruin the main melody through an inconsistent application of their methods, and indeed even introduce passages which have nothing at all to do with the actual structure of the piece (something which could easily be misconstrued as a mistake on the part of the composer). Therefore, any composer, certainly including the Herr Hofcompositeur, is justified if he points those going astray into the right direction and at the same time takes care to preserve his own honor by prescribing a correct method in keeping with his intention.

The obvious inability of performers to improvise ornamentations corresponding to the content and value of Bach's music is mercilessly exposed here. Only the composer himself can do justice to the demands inherent in his work.

If by way of experiment we remove the prescribed ornamentations from an instrumental work by Bach (an adagio from a solo sonata for violin, perhaps, or the flute part to "Aus Liebe will mein Heiland sterben" from the *St. Matthew Passion*) and try ourselves to invent ornamentation, then we will see how correct Birnbaum was, unfortunately. These pieces, these parts *must* be ornamented, but no other musician since Bach's time has possessed the power of Bach's imagination. All other attempts are doomed, in view of Bach's own natural and solely correct ornamentations. Bach was right—even if the musicians of his day did not wish to admit it.

Performance Traditions

In the performance of early music, tradition is as formative a factor as the manuscript of the work itself. Through countless performances over the course of decades and centuries, each piece of music undergoes a formation which in time acquires almost a definitive character. All of the many interpretations copy each other, adding up to an "authentic" form which cannot be circumvented in more recent performances. The possibilities of interpreting the major works of musical literature in various ways without encountering objections are very narrow and are becoming ever narrower, at least insofar as the elementary formative characteristics such as tempo and dynamics are concerned. Deviations from this traditional interpretation (for example in a Beethoven symphony or one of Bach's Passions) is felt as a shock by the listener—tradition being regarded as a kind of refinement, a crystallization of the conclusive interpretation, confirmed by years of testing.

A clear distinction must be made between works which have been performed in an unbroken line from the period in which they were written up until today, and other works which disappeared from concert programs for a shorter or longer period of time. The compositions of Beethoven, for example, have been played uninterruptedly since their first performances; the tradition of rendition, therefore, can be traced directly to the composer. In such cases, traditional opinion is probably correct. The traditional interpretation born of many performances undoubtedly possesses a high degree of authenticity.

However, Mendelssohn's performances of Bach's oratorios were a completely new beginning after many decades of silence. Romanticism, the style of his age, was vigorous and spirited, and there was no dutiful feeling that Bach's works should be performed as he had intended. Instead, an attempt was made to "purify" the Baroque compositions, which were generally regarded as "bewigged" and old-fashioned, and to render them in keeping with the modern Romantic style. Even the instrumentation was changed to achieve the symphonic sound then in vogue. Our own interpretation of Bach is based on these first revivals from the first half of the 19th century and is linked to them by an unbroken chain of performances. It is clear that such a tradition is less valuable than one which refers back directly to the composer. Nonetheless, there is no doubt that over the course of more than 100 years of efforts concentrated on the work of Bach, from Mendelssohn to Furtwängler, standards and fundamental truths have been found which represent at least the experience of several generations of listeners.

At no time has more attention been conscientiously paid to the artistic legacy of the past than is the case today. We no longer want to interpret the interpretations of past decades, the old arrangements (Bach-Busoni, Bach-Reger, Stokowski and many others), because we do not consider a two-fold interpretation—by the arranger and the performing artist—to be necessary. Today we are prepared to accept only the composition itself as our source and to represent it on its own merits. In particular, we must attempt to hear and to play the masterpieces of Bach as if they had never been interpreted, as if they had never been shaped or distorted in performance. We must attempt an interpretation which ignores the whole Romantic performance tradition. All questions must be raised anew, with only Bach's score itself accepted as the crystallization of a timeless work of art in a time-linked form of expression. Our resolve to ignore the performance tradition should of course not be allowed to lead us to an artistic anti-position, where everything is intentionally done contrary to custom. It is certainly possible that a newly-obtained result may correspond to traditional practice. The upshot is that we must approach the great masterpieces by pushing aside the lush growth of traditional experience and interpretation, and once again begin from the beginning.

The Concerto

The Baroque concept of concerto is often confused with the solo concerto of the 19th century, although the two forms have little more in common than their name. Originally, at the beginning of the 17th century, concerto had the same meaning as "sinfonia," or "concentus," a harmonic blend of sounds, or the instrumental ensemble which plays the music. The term comes from "conserere" or 'bringing together.' However, since the time of Praetorius, "concertare" (rivalry or competition) has been cited as the origin of the term.

Even though it is etymologically wrong, this second derivation undoubtedly better characterized and even influenced the form of the late Baroque concerto than the first term, which simply describes a harmonic design. The Baroque concerto is not a solo piece with dominant soloist and accompanying orchestra, even though today it is often taken as such. The essential feature of the concerto is the dialogue, the contest among different groups of sounds. Thus a concerto can be a chamber piece for three instruments or an orchestral work for 50 musicians; the only requirement is that it be based on the dispute-like alternation of musical expression which typifies this form. The tutti passages in which all participants, including any soloists, together make the same statement provide the formal framework—and such passages must exist even in concertos with trio scoring. The "concertizing" can occur among several soloists or between soloists and ripieno players ("ripieno" means all players, a better term for the given orchestra) or within the orchestra.

The most important technical means used to clarify these forms of statement and reply are articulation—the distinct pronunciation of musical speech—and dynamics. In the 18th century, much was written about articulation in the sense of musical rhetoric. Therefore we can easily recognize even today how a musical motif is intended and how it should be played.

The role played by dynamics is less familiar to us. Because the composers of the Baroque age wrote virtually no dynamic marks in their works, and because some of the most important instruments of that period (organ and harpsichord) could be played louder and softer only in steps, and also because several formal characteristics of the music itself appear to imply this, it was long believed that dynamics were always used "in terraced fashion," in steps, abruptly and without gradual changes. Even though a very small part of this theory is true, nonetheless, consistently applied, it destroys musical continuity and makes it impossible to play music that "speaks." In the old descriptions, very pronounced dynamic nuances intended to clarify the musical expression are often mentioned, even in the smallest space, even on individual notes.

In the concerto form, the great dynamic differences are found between solo and tutti, with the tutti playing forte and the solo piano, in principle. The soloist who dominates and triumphs over the orchestra is completely alien to this style. This view, which contrasts with that of today, is also reflected in the instruments. In the Baroque period, instruments of different sizes were built within each family: larger, louder ones for the full orchestra or ripieno, smaller instruments with a delicate and noble sound for solo playing. In certain passages of some solo concertos, the soloist is supposed to be covered by the full orchestra, his part at that point being inessential and almost inaudible. We might recall in this context that a musical interpretation in which all details of a score are clearly audible is quite questionable in many instances. A tone certainly need not always stand out from the overall texture in order to have a meaning. It can add a nuance which, while not fully audible, would be missed if it were not there. However, it can also be true that the complete overshadowing of a singer or instrumentalist can have a distinct musical purpose intended by the composer.

Bach's violin concertos were not written for virtuosos. Much more difficult and spectacular solo pieces for violin exist, some written by Bach himself. He was moved to write his extremely difficult solo sonatas and suites for violin through his acquaintance with the best German violinists of this period, Johann Paul von Westhoff and Johann Georg Pisendel. Vivaldi's solo concertos inspired his own violin concertos. Although Bach clearly uses the new Vivaldi form, he avoids the violinistic niceties of his model, in order to far surpass this model in terms of musical richness and expression. The orchestral setting intended by Bach was as small as that used for the Brandenburg concertos. An interpretation such as that used for violin concertos of the 19th century, in which the soloist is allowed to dominate the orchestra, is incorrect for the music of Bach. Here the soloist's role is not that of a brilliant virtuoso, but rather that of the lead singer of a chorus. In this way a dynamic situation emerges which makes both the dialogue form as well as the solo-tutti interplay comprehensible, as has already been said: the solo passages are piano, the tutti passages forte. These concertos ideally embody the concept of dialogue-like concertizing, and even occasionally take the form of friendly disputes.

To be sure, in solo concertos of the Baroque period the slow movements are often conceived as instrumental songs or even as arias. Here the orchestra actually becomes an accompanying instrument and the dialogue takes place in an imaginary way, between the soloist and the listener being addressed. The accompaniment is usually very simple; in Bach's concertos it can even include an ostinato bass part. Since a constant ostinato motif requires an unchanging rhythm, while the violin solo, apparently unconnected to it, hovers freely in space, the soloist is here called upon to perform in the Baroque rubato style: "playing the notes somewhat faster or somewhat slower, with expression." It is precisely described in the old treatises, including that of Leopold Mozart:

> Many who have no idea at all of good taste do not want to adhere to the evenness of the beat when accompanying a concertizing voice; rather they try to defer to the principal part ... but when one accompanies a true virtuoso worthy of the name, then one must allow oneself neither to speed up nor slow down, which the soloist, through the prolongation or anticipation of the notes, is able to do very skillfully and movingly; but rather accompany everything in the same type of movement. Otherwise the accompaniment would destroy that which the soloist wanted to create. A skillful accompanist must therefore be able to judge a concert player. He certainly may not 'give in' to a true virtuoso, otherwise he would ruin his tempo rubato. But what is meant by the 'stolen' tempo can be demonstrated better than it can be described ... And it does not go according to the beat, for he plays in a recitative fashion.

This is a very concrete description of the ideal accompaniment for a soloist who is playing, or singing, in free rhythm. Present-day musicians are always surprised to learn that the effort to follow the soloist's lead with great sensitivity, which is usually regarded today as pefect accompaniment, was thought of as exactly the opposite in the 18th century! With this kind of accompaniment, one transfers the rubato of the soloist to the entire sound, thereby defeating it. Such fluctuating tempi are a sign of poor accompaniment, since the soloist can unfold his subtle art of "too-early, too-late," a floating "approximation" or "je ne sais quoi," as was said at that time, only against the background of a steady tempo. In rhythmical terms, therefore, non-accompaniment is actually the ideal type of accompaniment.

The Gamba Sonatas—Idiomatic Sound or Ad Libitum

It is very interesting to examine on the basis of Bach's chamber music how important or unimportant a particular timbre was for the composer, why a work was intended for a particular instrument and not for another. Just a few generations before Bach, the musical realization of a composition was left completely to the performer, and even at his time there were still many works in which a flute solo, for example, could just as well be played on an oboe or a violin. As long as the special technical possibilities or the particular tonal qualities of different instruments were not consciously applied by the composer, such an "ad libitum" arrangement is completely legitimate.

Bach's music is particularly difficult to comprehend in this regard, especially because he never followed strict and clearly understandable principles which can be invoked once and for all, but rather in each new case found a new solution which often deviated considerably from earlier ones. Bach wrote many works whose musical substance does not call for a certain instrument in technical or melodic terms. In many of his other compositions, the playing technique of the instruments is hardly considered, but their tonal qualities are essential. Finally, there is also a series of compositions in which the tonal *and* technical possibilities of the instrument were fully utilized. Bach's adaptations of the works of other composers and also of his own compositions for other instruments provide particular insight here. Aside from the compositions for instruments with limited practical ranges or with clearly limited musical vocabulary (such as the trumpet and horn), a great number of compositions for keyboard, string and woodwind instruments nonetheless exists, in which the tonal *and* technical idioms are so clearly established that it would be impossible to replace the particular solo instrument with a different one. For example, the fifth Brandenburg Concerto is a true harpsichord piece. An adaptation such as Bach frequently undertook for violin and other harpsichord concertos would be completely inconceivable for this work. Similarly, several sections of the solo sonatas and suites for violin and violoncello were written entirely in the language of these instruments. Most of the wind and string solos in the oratorios and cantatas also belong in this category.

Bach appears most frequently to have had in mind specific instrumental timbres, which may well have been particularly important to him. Thus without any technical necessity and even without utilizing its specific possibilities, he uses a violino piccolo for the first Brandenburg

Concerto and a retuned (*scordatura*) violin for the G Major Trio Sonata, BWV 1038. In each of these cases he was clearly interested *only* in the particular sound that was thereby achieved.

His use of the viola da gamba presents a similar case. At the time of Bach, this instrument was in the process of being displaced as the noblest and most respected solo instrument, although it was still in fashion, particularly in France. Marin Marais and Antoine Forqueray, the great French gamba virtuosos and composers, had just written their most important works, in which the musical, tonal and technical possibilities of this instrument were exploited to the fullest. We can safely assume that Bach was familiar with these works. Nonetheless, like most of his German predecessors and contemporaries, he continued to use the gamba above all because of its tonal possibilities.

It appears that the German composers may have viewed the gamba in quite a different light than the British or the French, who had made the gamba the most distinguished and highly developed solo instrument together with the lute and the harpsichord. (The Italians almost completely ignored the gamba in favor of the violin, and wrote next to nothing for it.) With the exception of August Kühnel and Johann Schenk, who borrowed from French models, German composers such as Heinrich Schmelzer, Johann Kaspar Kerll, Dietrich Buxtehude, Georg Philipp Telemann and George Frideric Handel wrote for the gamba just as for any other melodic instrument. They were interested solely in the special sound of the instrument. "The sound of the gamba, delicate and slightly nasal, like the voice of a diplomat," writes Le Blanc in 1740. Telemann made an exception in the first part of his Parisian quartets and wrote somewhat in the manner of the French gamba virtuoso Forqueray, for whom this part was intended.

Bach definitely followed the German tradition in his treatment of the gamba. Technically speaking, his numerous gamba solos in the cantatas and the St. John Passion could be performed just as well on other instruments; the composer calls for the gamba here exclusively because of its particular sound and the associations it evokes. One exception is exemplified by the gamba solo in the St. Matthew Passion (bass aria: "Komm, süsses Kreuz"), in which the gamba is used entirely in the manner of the French virtuosos.

Bach's three gamba sonatas are thus gamba music in quite a different sense than the sonatas and suites of Marais and Forqueray. In Bach's gamba sonatas, the gamba and the harpsichord are completely equal partners which must perform a mostly strict three-part texture in such a way that the gamba plays one and the two hands of the harpsichord player the other two parts. This composition technique, which Bach also used in his violin sonatas, was quite unusual at that time. The special feature is not so much that the harpsichord plays a completely composed two-voice part in place of the customary general-bass, but rather that the principal and secondary voices are evenly distributed between both instruments, which means that the gamba must often accompany the harpsichord.

Bach originally wrote the first of the three sonatas for a completely different setting, i.e. as a trio for two transverse flutes and basso continuo. In the flute version, the two upper voices lie in the same register, the bass part is figured, as in all trio sonatas, and is performed with improvised harmonization. In the gamba version, the composer sets the part of the second flute one octave lower, without any major changes, as the gamba part; the part of the first flute and the bass now form the harpsichord part, without added chords. In this version, the pure three-part writing naturally has a much greater impact than in the harmonized flute version. This is very likely also the reason underlying the selection of the instrument—for, with the best of intentions, this revised flute trio cannot be regarded as an idiomatic gamba piece. The composition demands delicate and sensitive instruments with fine dynamics, qualities possessed by both the transverse flute and the gamba. The gamba is probably particularly well-suited to be a middle voice, through the octave transposition, because it is easier to adapt than any other instrument. It is interesting and may demonstrate the meaning of the Italian "tempo" marks at the time of Bach, which were used primarily as directions for expression, that the third section of this sonata is marked "Andante" in the gamba version, and "Adagio e piano" in the flute version.

The second sonata, in D major, is perhaps the most "gambaesque." Even though it does not call for any kind of chord technique, the technical demands imposed on the player by the two allegro movements are typical of the gamba. The strict three-part structure is abandoned in certain places in favor of a solo accompanied by a continuo, which allows the gamba to move into the foreground with greater soloistic importance. Nonetheless, in order to underscore the equality of the partners, the large gamba cadenza accompanied by the harpsichord in the last movement is preceded by a smaller harpsichord cadenza, accompanied by the gamba. In this sonata, the sound of the gamba is obviously so very much a part of the composition that it is difficult to imagine this music played on other instruments. If we hear the sonata played on a cello or a viola, the harpsichord seems to be an alien element. I can find no reason for this other than that Bach intuitively "custom designed" the sonata for this instrument.

The third sonata in G minor has an almost concertante character. Its structure is much more complex than that of the other two sonatas. The guess has frequently been hazarded that it originated from a concerto. I regard it more as an experiment to try to continue the direction of the second sonata to an extreme, with the contrast of continuo-obbligato in the harpsichord part corresponding approximately to a concertante solo-tutti contrast, just as in the slow movement of the Fifth Brandenburg Concerto.

In a formal sense, therefore, the three sonatas are based on each other, rather in the manner of a cycle. The first is a pure three-voice piece in which each of the three voices is absolutely equal to the others; the second treats the gamba somewhat more in an idiom that is purely its own (although how this happens cannot be explained), and the three-voice texture is replaced in very few places by a solo accompanied by continuo. In the third sonata, the newly-invented, intermittently concertante manner of composition is further expanded, with the *form* receiving absolute priority ahead of the *technique* of the solo instrument. Thus this sonata may well have been composed with a view to playability, but without particular consideration for the special gamba technique.

These three sonatas were intended by Bach expressly for gamba and harpsichord. They are most easily played on these instruments in a musically plausible way, since the necessary balance between the voices exists a priori. The gamba sound is set off sufficiently from the harpsichord, but it also blends in a particularly felicitous way with the sound of the harpsichord, so that both the necessary unity as well as the necessary differentiation of sound can most readily be achieved. These are unusual works, especially with regard to their instrumentation and sonority, since they really are gamba music only in terms of indefinable psycho-acoustic qualities. Such an approach to instrumentation may well have been possible only in Germany, where the solo gamba was regarded as a somewhat exotic instrument. With his impressionistic instrumentation, Bach looks far beyond his own time.

The Cantatas—At the Center of Bach's Work

In studying the works of Bach, it is impossible to distinguish between "occasional pieces" or "commissioned works" and those which were close to his heart. Thus his cantatas are in every respect the equal of his most famous compositions—the *St. Matthew Passion,* for example, to remain in the sacred vocal style. I have never felt that Bach worked in a routine manner, that he repeated himself in his works. And when one has the opportunity, as we have had over the course of many years, to perform and to record one cantata after the other, one is thunderstruck—even after recording over 100 cantatas—at how a human being could produce such an overpowering abundance of compositional originality and inspiration. I must say that each new cantata, each new aria is still an adventure, an exciting discovery for us; there is no trace of routine, of repetition. I know of no other composer who constantly traverses the entire outermost gamut from strictest counterpoint to the most expressive romanticism. For this reason, it makes no sense to me to dig up second-class works of second-class composers, or even to repeat and repeat first-class works, so long as no adequate interpretations exist for these magnificent compositions.

We felt that the time was right to present Bach's cantatas anew, as his central body of work, in consistent interpretations utilizing the best resources available to us. In addition to calling on the most advanced knowledge of the performance practice of Bach's time, this meant that we had to utilize the correct tonal means in an appropriate way. No other composer demands such a rich and complex instrumentarium, nor places such great stress on subtle tonal symbolism as does Johann Sebastian Bach. We are well-acquainted with the difficulties he constantly encountered in the formation of his orchestra. The fact that he nonetheless constantly called for the most unusual combinations reveals the importance that he ascribed even to apparently trivial aspects of instrumentation. Many problems have not been solved even today. Indeed, we do not even know all of the instruments which Bach calls for in his cantatas. Nonetheless, solutions are being found, some of which may remain hypothetical for the time being, thereby motivating our successors to produce more definitive results.

Our rendition of Bach's cantatas is an attempt to interpret them in a way that is meaningful in terms of today's world. The classical symphony orchestra, no matter how it is constituted, has really no similarity to the colorful orchestra of Bach, and the modern choral society, no matter how great its virtuosity, bears no resemblance to the transparent choir of boys and young men of the Bach cantatas. We do not regard this new interpretation as a return to the long-vanished past, but rather as an attempt to free this great early music from its historical tonal amalgamation with the classical symphonic sound and to find our way to a truly modern interpretation based on the more transparent and characteristic early instrumentarium.

The Wind Instruments in Bach's Cantatas

When we study the scoring and the designation of the instruments in Bach's cantatas, we notice that many different names are used for wind instruments, in addition to the usual designations for the string instruments, which we transfer relatively nonchalantly into our modern nomenclature (there are a few exceptions, which can easily become a trap). The meaning of these names for wind instruments is difficult to determine and in some cases has not yet been definitively decoded. We must assume that in the 18th century, terms were not used with the pedantic scrupulousness that today is universally called for, an attitude probably influenced by the strict definitions of terminology used by modern bureaucrats and lawyers.

It is customary to begin every essay with a definition of terminology and then to hold strictly to that definition. In the 18th century, ultimate linguistic clarity was not a particularly important consideration; strict logic and convincing analogy had not yet become established criteria, at least in the scores of the time. Several examples follow. Today, the instruments are clearly listed at the beginning of a given score line or in the title of a given score. In those days, a score specification could designate the instrument, or the player, or a manner of playing, or a particular range on an instrument. Thus the expression "clarino" can mean that a high trumpet part is involved. (The fourth octave of the natural trumpet, i.e. from c" to c''' was designated as clarino. The musicians who mastered this range were the clarino players; today we would call them the first trumpets.) But "clarino" could also signify that the first trumpet must play here (also possibly a violin; see p. 000), or that another instrument (perhaps a horn) is played here in the fourth octave (the clarino register), or that a slide trumpet (probably played by a first trumpet) must be used, etc. etc. Little information is found in the treatises of the period concerning these questions. After all, at that time every musician knew the answers and was unaware of the problems which would cause us so many difficulties 250 years later. Nor could our systematic and scientific way of thinking have been anticipated. It is therefore extremely questionable to use our methodology to approach treatises which reflect an entirely different kind of thinking.

At this point I would like to discuss the wind instruments Bach calls for in the cantatas BWV 1 to 70, and to try to clarify just which instruments were meant. Some questions will inevitably remain unanswered, and several hypothetical solutions will be offered. I believe that, in some cases, the instrument was not as important to the composer as it is to us today. A designation such as "corno" (a point to which we shall return later) can imply a direction to play the part "on a wind instrument customarily used and suited for cantus firmus reinforcement," which could be a zink (cornetto), a slide trumpet, a horn, or a soprano trombone— very likely the composer regarded each of these possibilities as equally good. Even if Bach had had a very specific instrument in mind, the equivocality of the written designation could still be explained. After all, he wrote for particular musicians whom he knew personally, and therefore he knew which instruments they would use. It is even possible that Bach occasionally adopted the name that a given musician used for his own instrument.

The most frequently called-for wind instrument is the oboe, usually correctly called by its French name "hautbois" by Bach. It appears in almost all of the cantatas, with the exceptions of 4, 18, 51, 54, 59, 61. Yet even this apparently unmistakable designation is not unambiguous. At the time, there were a number of oboe types, both in terms of design (shape and materials used for the bell, shape of the instrument) and tuning (instruments of differing sizes were built, in the keys of c', a, f). Each of these types could bear one or more designations which differed from region to region, but every type of oboe could also be simply described as such, and the player himself had to know or determine the specific instrument intended. However, several general principles can be inferred from this apparent chaos. "Oboe," "hautbois" and "obboe" all mean an instrument suitable in its tuning for the given part; either the normal oboe in C' (tonal range c' to d''' without C-sharp') or an oboe in A (such as the oboe d'amore). It is possible to recognize the intended instrument by the following factors: the voicing, range, key (pieces written in flat keys are very difficult to play on an A major instrument), the soloistic use of C-sharp' (which could not normally be played on the standard oboe), and by the context of the work. (When a *particular* kind of oboe is required just before and after, it must also be used in the intervening piece, since the same musicians played all types and therefore needed some time to change instruments.) Then as now, the player had to recognize which instrument of the oboe family he had to select.

When Bach wanted the special sound of a specific type of instrument, he always designated the instrument precisely, e.g. "hautb. d'amore" or "hautb. da caccia." It is therefore incorrect to regard every oboe in A as "oboe d'amore" or every oboe in F as "oboe da caccia."

In terms of instrumentation, Bach used the oboe primarily to add texture, playing in unison with the violins. This blending of sound, which can be realized only with Baroque oboes and Baroque violins since modern instruments always remain distinct in sound, is the true tutti sound of the Baroque orchestra. In these violin-oboe parts, tones frequently occur which can be executed on the violin, but not on the oboe. These tones were either produced by means of a trick or two, or the players transposed them an octave, or omitted them entirely. One example is the C-sharp' on the normal oboe. To be sure, this tone occurs occasionally, but very seldom, in the old fingering charts (the c' key was half-covered); but in practical terms it cannot be executed even in this way. By manipulating the key one can set it up for C-sharp' or c', although a rest of about one bar is necessary for this adjustment. In "colla parte" the C-sharp' was therefore omitted; in the solo it does not appear in a rapid alternation with c'.

The real *oboe d'amore* ("hautb. d'amore," "hautb. d'amour"—tonal range a-b," without A-sharp or B-flat) has a subdued, very sweet sound because of the way in which it is designed, largely due to its spherical bell. It is today notated as a transposing instrument, i.e. the player views the notes not as tones, but rather as fingerings (corresponding to the normal oboe in c'). Bach ordinarily writes using actual ("concert") pitch notation: the player must finger the same notes differently on each instrument. Occasionally, particularly in the case of solos, Bach writes transposing parts. We can assume that in so doing, he was directly addressing the wishes and habits of the players.

As an a instrument, the oboe d'amore sounds best and most natural in the sharp keys. At that time, the wind instruments were not chromatic, i.e. with half-tones that sounded and were playable evenly; rather, they were built around a functional scale, here A major. The further a key is removed from this functional scale, the more "difficult" it sounds. This is an important aspect of the characteristics of keys.

We shall deal more extensively with the *oboe da caccia* in a later section. For this instrument as well, Bach occasionally writes a transposed part, occasionally in concert pitch notation. It is definitely a solo instrument (Cantatas 6, 16, 27), used above all in very soft, subtle passages and frequently in unusual and "impressionistic" combinations of instruments, with horns (Cantatas 1, 65), and recorders (Cantatas 13, 46, 65).

Many cantatas call for a "taille." This is a tenor oboe in F (in French music of the 18th century, "taille" or middle means a middle voice, customarily the third, whether it is intended to be sung or played on a string or wind instrument). Bach always means "taille d'hautbois" when he specifies "taille" (although the full name never appears). This instrument is not used for solos, but only to double the singing voices or the string instruments. Bach used the term "taille" already in the early cantatas he wrote in Weimar. The use of the term does not connote a particular type of instrument, but rather a register, as we have said. It would therefore be wrong to translate taille as oboe da caccia, since any F-oboe could then and can still be used as taille, while the oboe da caccia represents a very particular type of oboe in this range. Of course, this instrument can also be used as "taille."

Bach occasionally calls for "flauti," which are always *recorders* in F' (tonal range f' to a'''). As with all wind instruments, he uses the tonal range to the limits of what was playable at the time. When Bach was in Leipzig, this instrument was already dropping out of fashion. However, Bach continued to use it for particularly subtle sound combinations: in Cantatas 13 and 46 with oboe da caccia; in Cantata 25, three recorders in the orchestra; in Cantata 39, two recorders in the orchestra and soloistically in a soprano aria; in Cantata 46 with strings; in Cantata 65 with horns and oboe da caccia.

The *transverse flute* is always specified by Bach as "flauto traverso" or "traversière" (tonal range d' to a'''). Although it became a fashionable instrument in the first half of the 18th century because of its "empfindsam" (sensitive) possibilities of expression, Bach used it relatively infrequently, in comparison with the oboe, for example. It is primarily used as a solo instrument, for tender affects or sparkling virtuosity (Cantatas 8, 26, 55) or for indistinct, impressionistic sounds (Cantatas 30 and 34 with muted violins).

The *bassoon* (tonal range B-flat to g' without C-sharp) in the 18th century was often added as a contouring instrument to the bass groups of pure string orchestras. Since it did not need to be specifically mentioned, it appears relatively seldom in Bach's scores. But there are various indications that Bach normally used this instrument even in pure string ensembles (without oboes). Several bassoon parts have been preserved from such cantatas. In addition to this function of strengthening the bass group—for which the Baroque bassoon with its woody, "brushing" sound is very well suited—Bach occasionally used this instrument to deviate slightly from the bass or to embellish the bass (Cantatas 31, 42, 63, 66). However, it is very probable that in arias with two or three solo oboes the bassoon player (who was present in any case, since he plays in the tutti parts of the cantatas) was supposed to execute the bass soloistically with the organ—without violoncello.

The situation with the brass instruments is much more complicated than with the woodwinds. An example might serve to clarify this observation. In Cantata 48, the original *score* calls for "tromba," the original *part* for "clarino," the title *cover* of the manuscript "corno": three different designations by Bach for one and the same instrument! The music itself indicates that it had to be a slide trumpet, since the required tones could not be played on a natural instrument (trumpet or horn). Evidently with "tromba," even without "da tirarsi" a slide trumpet was meant; "clarino" means, as already mentioned, not an instrument, but rather the register of the natural instrument above the 8th partial tone (for the horn as well as the trumpet). By association, the clarino player, i.e. the first trumpeter, can also be meant, perhaps indicating that he should also play another instrument, e.g. the violin (Cantatas 31 and 43, concluding chorales). "Corno" was probably a general expression connoting a large number of wind instruments which were not more specifically described, i.e. trumpet, horn, slide trumpet, cornett, etc. (Even today, in the English-speaking world musicians still call almost all wind instruments "horns.")

The ordinary *natural trumpet* in B-flat, C, D and F is notated as a transposing instrument by Bach (tonal range c to d''', transposed respectively.)

The natural harmonic series

also represents the playable tones, with the 7th, 11th, 13th and 14th partial tones being "impure," i.e. too low. These errors were at times compensated for by first-class musicians with embouchure; at other times, the resulting tones, which sounded somewhat unnatural, were used for affective purposes. This made all the more sense since the natural trumpet with its *pure* major triads musically embodies the ideal baroque proportion (4:5:6 represents the ideal triad and symbolizes the Holy Trinity). This instrument was therefore expressly reserved by law for great festivities, personages of high rank, and cities with special privileges. The listeners of that time were so familiar with the natural harmonic series that they immediately recognized the slightest deviation; the composer therefore could vividly illustrate a disturbance of the divinely established order of things by using the false natural tones. (Unfortunately, the ability to make this kind of association no longer exists). Thus Bach uses the *bad* tones in order to underscore the expressiveness of emotive terms: for example, in the bass aria (No. 7) of Cantata 43, the word "Qual," torment or agony, on a b'-flat, the much too low 7th partial. Occasionally Bach also calls upon the embouchure artistry of his trumpeters in order to produce intermediate tones, e.g. b', c-sharp'' and g-sharp', not always for a desired effect, but sometimes also in order to expand the otherwise all-too-simple "trumpet tonality."

The *horn* (in C, F, B-flat, C; tonal range essentially as in the trumpet) was used by Bach especially for gentle, romantic portrayals of nature ("Wie schön leuchtet der Morgenstern," Cantata 1, or for the wandering of the magi from Saba, Cantata 65). In such cases, he usually designates it as "corno da (di) caccia" or "corno parforce," but sometimes simply as "corno." The notation is always transposed, so that in Cantata 1, for example, one can recognize that F horns are intended, although the concept "corno" without an addition can also stand for other instruments, such as slide trumpet or cornett. In such a case, however, it would not be notated transposed and is not restricted to the natural tones.

Even when the horn instrumentation is clarified in this way, important questions remain, such as that of pitch. For example, in passages for C horn it cannot be determined on the basis of the score whether this involves a high or low horn (sounding as notated or an octave lower). This question cannot always be answered directly in musical terms, because the tonal *impression* of wind instruments quite often deviates by one octave from the sound that is actually played (e.g. Cantata 65). Thus high C horns sound extremely high in the second ledger line octave: so high, that this special effect must be required by a particular emotion conveyed by the piece. Even today, these questions have not been definitively resolved. Unsolvable problems relating to playing technique also arise as a consequence. Thus horn players can hardly blow higher than a″ employing the mouthpieces normally used today, no matter what type of horn is used. But it is certain that at that time one could play somewhat higher by using a *trumpet* mouthpiece. This technique of "clarino" horn-playing has not been revived, however, and must be learned from trumpeters. (Very promising experiments are underway in this connection.) The horn is then brought closer to the trumpet, not only in terms of register, but also in terms of tone. Further discoveries about late Baroque instrumental skills can thus still be expected. "Clarino," too, can mean a horn, as in Cantata 24. Here the register indication "clarino" was used for the horn, as in the final chorale, for which an F horn is clearly required. The third movement is written for a B-flat instrument. This horn part was probably originally played using trumpet technique and a corresponding mouthpiece.

Bach very frequently used the *slide trumpet,* which he designated as "tromba (or corno) da tirarsi," for chorale cantus firmi. Several trumpets from the 17th and 18th centuries are still extant in which the tubing to which the mouthpiece is attached can be lengthened telescopically by three half tones. Chromatic scales can be played on these instruments from about a on, so that they can be used to perform almost all chorale melodies. Whether Bach's trumpeter had such an instrument at his disposal or whether he played these parts on a B-flat or E-flat trombone (with trumpet mouthpiece) cannot be ascertained at this point. The latter is certainly possible, since the trombones of the time had the same bore as the trumpet and were occasionally used as trumpets, which was expressly prohibited, by the way, for reasons of social class distinctions and privileges. There are only a few genuine solos for this instrument (Cantata 46). Not all parts for slide trumpet are unambiguously characterized; thus in Cantata 48 the instrument is called clarino, corno and tromba (all three designations original). Clarino probably refers to the high register which required a first trumpeter. In the case of corno (a general name for a suitable wind instrument) and tromba, we must mentally add the words "da tirarsi," since it is clear from the music that this is called for. In Cantata 60, a corno part is notated in D, i.e. transposed. Here, too, only a slide trumpet can be meant because of the notes called for; this was possibly an instrument in D. Remarkable and still unexplained is the untransposed notation of the final chorale of this cantata.

Trombones were used by Bach in the traditional way to reenforce and add timbre in contrapuntal 4-part writing, i.e. in choral parts without obbligato instruments. (Cantata 25 is an exception. Here the trombones, together with recorders and cornett, play a four-part chorale in cantus-firmus fashion, within a large, contrapuntal choral setting.) Bach sometimes calls for four trombones, sometimes three trombones and cornett, as a traditional upper voice in four-part wind writing. This distinction seems meaningless, since "cornetto" is occasionally written above the first trombone *part* in a 4-part trombone setting. This can be explained by the fact that the cornett routinely played the upper voice in a trombone chorus, without this having to be specifically mentioned. Aside from this, the highest part of these movements may go up to g″, far surpassing the normal range of even the alto trombone; it would have to be played, if not on the cornett, then on a discant trombone, which had almost completely dropped out of use at that time. Nonetheless, both types of instrumentation (with cornett or discant trombone as upper voice) seem legitimate to me, since the composer likely wanted the usual and familiar wind sound.

By the time of Bach, the role of the *cornett* (tonal range a to a″ [d‴]) had been reduced from widespread use as a solo instrument to that of a wind discant in chorale settings. It was probably played only by town pipers. The official and specific name "cornetto" appears in only a few cantatas. Very frequently, however, the ambiguous term "corno" may have been used to signify this instrument. (In some sources, the cornetto, "Zink" in German, is simply called "corno.") In Cantata 68, *both* terms appear. For cantus firmus reenforcement, only an instrument not restricted to the natural tones can be used. The horn is thus ruled out, nor is it a typical cantus firmus instrument, since it was mostly used for solos. Only the cornett and the slide trumpet, therefore, remain as possibilities.

Bach's "Oboe da Caccia" and its Reconstruction

Even during his lifetime, Johann Sebastian Bach was noted for being much more interested than other composers in musical instruments, their design and sound, as well as in questions of hall acoustics. His sons and students frequently described his special knack for quickly recognizing and evaluating the acoustical qualities of any room. It was said that when Bach viewed a church interior, he could immediately determine the ideal location and optimal disposition for a new organ. The most important organ makers of his time consulted with him on their work and at times showed him their new instruments for his evaluation. Gottfried Silbermann, for example, demonstrated his newly invented Hammerklavier or pianoforte for Bach. Bach encouraged the conception, but found the results unsatisfactory, an observation which offended the self-assured Silbermann, but which also led him to undertake decisive improvements. After a hiatus of several years, he produced an instrument capable of handling all of the demands placed on it. All the obituaries published on his death described Bach as the "inventor" of the viola pomposa, a fact to which great importance was attributed.

From all this it can be seen that Bach had an unusually intense interest in the actual sound of his music, and that instrumentation occupied an extraordinary place in his mind—for the period. No other composer in the 18th century was able to evoke such subtle and complex combinations of sounds from the relatively simple instrumentarium of the day. However, no other composer entrusted such extreme tasks to so many different instruments. Even today, neither musicians nor musicologists know in every case which instrument was actually meant. This uncertainty is particularly notable in the case of wind instruments such as corno, tromba, corno da tirarsi, clarino, lituus, oboe da caccia, etc. Of course we cannot interpret these terms with the strictly defined nomenclature of the 19th and 20th centuries in mind. In our own day, the worst mistakes may well be caused by the fact that Italian or Latin names used by Bach are simply translated literally (e.g. corno = horn). In order to understand the instrumental terminology used by Bach, we must take a "baroque" approach to nomenclature.

In Bach's Leipzig cantatas, after 1723, and oratorios, a new name suddenly appears which was hardly known to music up until that time: "oboe da caccia." (Occasionally the oboe group in hunts was thus designated. Thus the Zedler Lexikon 1732: "Hunt-hautbois are not only used during a major hunt as a change from the shouting and calling in the forest; but every morning and evening with their pleasant music they attend in an appropriate setting the master of the hunt." But this was a functional designation, not the name of an instrument.) The instrument first introduced by Bach is evidently, like the "taille" discussed in the previous chapter, an oboe in F. However, while the "taille" appears solely in tutti passages, the "oboe da caccia" is definitely a solo instrument. There are no solos designated "taille" and almost no tutti passages with the designation "oboe da caccia." However, one cantata with a "taille" part contains an aria designated for "oboe da caccia." All of the tenor oboes in F might have been called "taille" at the time, but the oboe da caccia was a special form, whose special sound inspired Bach to the composition of solo music.

After our Concentus Musicus had given a few concerts and made several recordings (cantatas, *St. John Passion, St. Matthew Passion*), for which we had used different kinds of tenor oboes as "oboe da caccia," we began to have some doubts. It was highly improbable that Bach had designated taille solos simply by "oboe da caccia." Bach must therefore have known a particular instrument that existed in Leipzig, or perhaps even inspired its invention. In order to identify this instrument, we could use only the music written for it and its name, but no kind of documentation.

"Da caccia" could only signify an instrument that had something to do with the hunt. However, Bach's actual use of the instrument is absolutely contradicted by this derivation—none of the solos is in any way related to the hunt, e.g. written in typical 6/8 hunting motifs or even simply with a brisk, open-air feeling. Rather, they are all particularly sensitive, thoroughly tender and gentle; the frequent combination of the instrument with the extremely soft transverse flute also points to the same conclusion (*St. Matthew Passion:* "Er hat uns allen wohlgetan," "Aus Liebe will mein Heiland sterben;" *St. John Passion:* "Zerfliesse mein Herze"). What could "da caccia" have been, therefore, if not the sound of the instrument?

As chance would have it, we came across a remarkable instrument in the Museum of Musical Instruments in Stockholm: evidently a tenor oboe in F, but bent in a semicircle and outfitted with a brass bell. This instrument looked like a large hunting horn; the bell had the same form and was also held at hip level, just like a large hunting horn. Amazingly enough, the name of the instrument maker "Johann Heinrich Eichentopf, Leipzig 1724" was engraved on the instrument. It had thus been built by the very man who may well have been the most famous maker of wind instruments in Leipzig at the time. Since Eichentopf also made brass instruments, he might have been inspired to equip a woodwind with a brass bell. Given Bach's notorious interest in instrument making, it is quite clear that at the very least, he must have known Eichentopf and his instruments. It would be hard to believe that this was simply a coincidence. During the relevant years, a Leipzig instrument maker builds tenor oboes which deviate markedly from the traditional. The instrument, normally built in a straight line, is bent in a semicircle, given a bell like a horn and covered with leather. At the same time, Bach composes numerous solos in Leipzig for an instrument that he calls the "oboe da caccia" and which had never before appeared in music. Such an unusual designation for an instrument could certainly only have been employed if the musicians were familiar with it. Naturally, the musicians in Leipzig were familiar with Eichentopf's newest instruments, which he may have played himself, as has always been customary among instrument makers.

This exciting combination of a woodwind and brass instrument in Stockholm could unfortunately not be tested musically because it had split beneath its leather covering and so was not completely airtight. Nonetheless, it was possible to thoroughly examine it and note its dimensions. It turned out that a second similar instrument, built the same year by Eichentopf, was located in the Museum for Musical Instruments in Copenhagen, but again, unfortunately, could not be played, so was simply examined and measured. We were, therefore, not dealing with a unique curiosity, since at least two instruments had been preserved to the present. Eichentopf's instrument was evidently copied by other instrument makers, for instruments from the first half of the 18th century which also have the characteristic semi-circular bending and the leather covering can be found in various museums. To be sure, they are not equipped with metal bells, a specialization that probably only the versatile Eichentopf could afford; but their wooden bells, unlike those of the straight tenor oboes, are extremely large and shaped in imitation of metal bells. Even the typical black interior coat of paint found in horn bells is present.

We were convinced that if the instrument was musically convincing as well, we had finally discovered Bach's "oboe da caccia." It could, after all, not simply be a particularly appealing form of the tenor oboe, but rather a fairly rough and unwieldy instrument had to become a flexible and sweet-sounding solo instrument.

We had the Eichentopf instruments copied right down to the minutest technical details. This slavishly blind precision was crucial, for we had no idea how they should or would sound. A few days before the recording session for the *Christmas Oratorio,* they were ready; all the participating musicians, but particularly the horn players who were to play them, were won over immediately. We are now certain that we have redis-covered the true "oboe da caccia." Oddly enough, the instrument is easier to play than its "straight" predecessors. The broad metal bell gives a fine metallic shimmer to what is actually a dark tone. This instrument possesses great dynamic flexibility. The musicians must of course still gain experience with this instrument, until all of its possibilities can be completely explored. Yet even in the form of our early experiments, it represents a great step forward. The alto aria "Willkommen will ich sagen" in Cantata 27 was the first true solo to be played and recorded on this instrument.

Bach's Use of "Parody"

Words and music are intimately linked to each other in the works of Bach in a manner reminiscent of the early 17th century in Italy. (See the chapters "The Great Innovation Around 1600," "Monteverdi Today" and "Work and Arrangement: The Role of the Instruments".)

This incredibly direct interrelationship is of the greatest importance for musicians. We do not isolate the musical aspect from the text, nor do we simply try to make beautiful music using more or less appropriate words. Rather, we visualize an ideal combination of words and music and an ideal interpretation, which, in the case of Bach, often takes place on several levels. This means that the singer sings a text, while the orchestra comments on this text. The orchestra does not simply accompany the text, but interprets it and explains it in accordance with the meaning that Bach wanted to convey. The idea of the sermon therefore underlies this type of music. To be sure, this kind of sermon possesses a multi-faceted quality, a simultaneity of verbal statement and musical-rhetorical interpretation; even the element of gesture is contained as it was in the old music drama, in a way that is inconceivable in speech alone. However, the ability to maintain this multi-faceted quality presupposes careful analysis on the part of the interpreter. Each instrumental part must receive its own rhetorical shaping, which often diverges from the sung text. Only in interaction does the meaning of the text—usually a moral and pedagogical meaning—reveal itself.

This intimate interrelationship between music and words has often been doubted by musicologists who point to Bach's frequent use of "parody"—the retexting of one and the same composition from a secular to a sacred version (e.g. *Herkules am Scheidewege, Christmas Oratorio*). By the way, the parody technique had been used 100 years earlier by Claudio Monteverdi, one of the most vigorous champions of intimate word-tone relationships. Monteverdi's *Pianta della Madonna,* for example, is a reworking of the *Lamento d'Ariana.* As later in the works of Bach, a perfect adaptation takes place through the most subtle rhythmical and melodic modifications. Nonetheless, I believe that a unity exists between the original secular version and the final sacred version, a unity which holds true for Bach as well. Interestingly enough, Bach's parodies always move from the secular to the sacred, never the reverse.

The practice of reworking the text of a piece in order to be able to reuse its musical substance is frequently encountered in the history of music. Many of the Protestant hymns of Luther's age were based on well-known secular songs, often "hit tunes" having a very explicit content, which were made "church-worthy" through the use of a sacred text. Such techniques were consciously used to encourage the congregation to participate in the singing of hymns in church.

Bach's approach to closely coupling music and text became widely known and formed the focal point for heated debates. After all, this practice raises the question of a valid, meaningful link between words and music in a quite radical way. We know that during the Baroque era, music was understood as speech in tones; that musical and textual affects always had to coincide. This was particularly true in Bach's case. Some over-emphasized Bach's role as a musical preacher, an interpreter of evangelical teachings, which in turn led others to categorically deny this aspect of his work, claiming that his music had no relationship at all to the text because he was constantly reworking and parodying his pieces. He was described by some as a spiritual preacher, by others as a Kapellmeister interested solely in absolute music and indifferent to religious or denominational concerns. The dedication of the Mass (Kyrie and Gloria from the *Mass in B Minor*) by the Protestant Bach to the Catholic King of Saxony is often cited as an example, since it contains an offer to write any kind of sacred or secular music.

Cantata 30a provides a particularly interesting example. Bach composed it on September 28, 1737, as a work of homage dedicated to Johann Christian von Hennicke, Lord of Wiederau. It was probably performed nine months later, on June 24, 1738 in Leipzig, as the sacred cantata *Freue dich, erlöste Schar*. It is interesting to note that the performance dates of the secular piece and its sacred counterpart closely coincide (e.g. in the case of the *Christmas Oratorio*). Since both versions were typically written by the same poet (in this case, Christian Friedrich Henrici-Picander), it seems likely that both the secular and the sacred cantata were jointly conceived from the outset. This intention naturally places the process and its value in quite a different light. It certainly makes a great difference if musical material is simply reused due to the press of time, or whether the composer had both texts in mind from the beginning and designed the first with an eye to the second, sacred version. This could also explain the remarkable and often-noted fact that the sacred second version, the parody, is artistically more convincing and consistent than the original secular version, even though in a few instances the original text may still shimmer through the musical interpretation. It must certainly be discouraging for a composer of Bach's stature to invest all his genius and effort in an homage cantata which is to be performed for a single occasion and never used again. Thus it is more than understandable if the composer had the second, final version in mind while he was composing the original work. This process is greatly facilitated if a talented and experienced text writer is available who knows the plans and ideas of the composer and is able to respond to them.

The Baroque concept of God and the Baroque attitude toward a ruler were so deeply intertwined, and hierarchical thinking so entrenched, that an identification of the two figures did not seem blasphemous. God was the greatest ruler, so to speak, but the distance between a king or his regent and normal mortals was so great that the gap between one's own bourgeois person and the prince was felt to be unbridgeable. (From the Baroque age onward, royalty lived in magnificent, church-like palaces which bore no resemblance to the dwellings of their subjects.) The king was also a "higher being." At the court of Louis XIV, church-goers were obliged to sit with their backs to the altar, facing the king, as though God could be reached only through the intercession of the king, himself a "demi-god."

So it is quite natural that the same jubilant chorus was used to introduce both the homage cantata and the cantata for the feast of St. John. The first chorus is in the form of a stylized bourrée-rondo, with the first two verses recurring three times as Bourrée I, twice varied, and interrupted by the remaining three verses. The mood of the first group is jubilation, that of the second a more neutral exposition. Both texts are identically constructed. If we compare the entire texts of the two cantatas, we note that even the recitatives are worked as precise textual parodies, a convincing indication for the hypothesis suggested above: that the two works had been jointly conceived from the beginning.

It is all the more remarkable that Bach did not carry out this original plan—a plan must have existed, otherwise Picander would not have taken the trouble to design the texts in identical fashion—but wrote completely new music for the second version, despite the precise correspondence in text. It appears he did not feel that they corresponded sufficiently closely. In order to keep the recitatives convincingly true to the text, he had to compose them anew, after all. In the first recitative, the correspondence goes so far that the festive portion of the secular version "Dein Name soll geändert sein" is set for four voices, which would make much more sense in the sacred version "Es freuet sich wer immer kann"; it was probably composed with an eye to this. Nonetheless, the details of the interpretation of the words ultimately did not meet the demands Bach placed on the sacred cantata; therefore, in this case he did not resort to parody.

English translation on pages 66–71 taken from *Johann Sebastian Bach Cantata Texts, Sacred and Secular* by Charles S. Terry (1964). Reprinted by permission of New Holland (Publishers) Ltd., London.

Kantate »Freue dich, erlöste Schar«, BWV 30

Chor
Freue dich, erlöste Schar,
Freue dich in Sions Hütten.
Dein Gedeihen hat itzund
Einen rechten festen Grund,
Dich mit Wohl zu überschütten.

Rezitativ (Baß)
Wir haben Rast,
Und des Gesetzes Last
Ist abgetan.
Nichts soll uns diese Ruhe stören,
Die unsre liebe Väter oft
Gewünscht, verlanget und gehofft.
Wohlan, es freue sich, wer immer kann,
Und stimme seinem Gott zu Ehren
Ein Loblied an,
Und das im höhern Chor,
Ja, singt einander vor!

Arie (Baß)
Gelobet sei Gott, gelobet sein Name,
Der treulich gehalten Versprechen und Eid!
Sein treuer Diener ist geboren,
Der längstens darzu auserkoren,
Daß er den Weg dem Herrn bereit'.

Rezitativ (Alt)
Der Herold kömmt und meldt den König an,
Er ruft; drum säumet nicht
Und macht euch auf
Mit einem schnellen Lauf,
Eilt dieser Stimme nach!
Sie zeigt den Weg, sie zeigt das Licht,
Wodurch wir jene selgen Auen
Dereinst gewißlich können schauen.

Arie (Alt)
Kommt, ihr angefochtnen Sünder,
Eilt und lauft, ihr Adamskinder,
Euer Heiland ruft und schreit!
Kommet, ihr verirrten Schafe,
Stehet auf vom Sündenschlafe,
Denn itzt ist die Gnadenzeit.

PART I

1. Chorus
Come, rejoice, ye ransomed souls,
Joyful sing in Zion's dwelling!
Ever faithful, ever sure
Is God's promise. From His store
Grace and love for us are welling.

2. Recitative
Content is ours! The law's avenging
    load is now
withdrawn. Nor shall our blessed
    peace be broken,
which in His love Almighty God ordained and
planned in our cause. 'Tis well! Rejoice! I say,
whoever may, and raise to God's
    high praise and
glory a joyous lay, as, with the choirs above,
we tell our grateful love.

3. Aria
Now praise ye the Lord!
    With thankfulness name Him
Who truly performeth and faileth us ne'er!
His trusty servant hither cometh.
Foretold, he swiftly 'fore Him runneth,
And will the way of God prepare.

4. Recitative
The herald comes and doth his Lord announce,
He calls; so tarry not! Make no delay, but take
your eager way! Haste, hasten Him to meet! He
shows the way! He is the Light! To pleasant
pastures man He leadeth, where heavenly grace
the soul receiveth.

5. Aria
Come ye sinners, wayworn, tearful!
Come rejoicing, be not fearful!
'Tis your Savior, hear His cry!
Come, ye wandering sheep, to meet Him;
Rise from slumber, haste to greet Him;
Lo! the hour of grace is nigh.

Kantate »Angenehmes Wiederau«, BWV 30a

Chor	1. Chorus
Angenehmes Wiederau	Pleasant fields of Wiederau,
Freue dich in deinen Auen!	Happy be and make rejoicing!
Das Gedeihen legt itzund	For new honor's to you paid,
Einen neuen, festen Grund,	Fresh renown is on you laid!
Wie ein Eden dich zu bauen.	Here New Eden is uprising!

Rezitativ (Baß)
2. Recitative

HICKSAL: So ziehen wir
In diesem Hause hier
Mit Freuden ein;
Nichts soll uns hier von dannen reißen.
Du bleibst zwar, schönes Wiederau,
Der Anmut Sitz, des Segens Au;
Allein,

LE: Dein Name soll geändert sein,
Du sollst nun Hennicks-Ruhe heißen!

HICKSAL: Nimm dieses Haupt, dem du nun untertan,
Frohlockend also an!

[Fate] Within this pleasance here,
with good intent,
we four appear nor yet from it shall aught
expel us. E'er wert thou,
lovely Wiederau, a
spot of charm, fertility. But now—

[All] No longer shalt thou so be known. As "Hennicke's
Rest" henceforth thou'rt famous.

[Fate] Thus greet thy lord, to whom thou subject art,
with loyal and gladsome heart:

Arie (Baß)
3. Aria

HICKSAL: Willkommen im Heil, willkommen in Freuden,
Wir segnen die Ankunft, wir segnen das Haus.
Sei stets wie unsre Auen munter,
Dir breiten sich die Herzen unter,
Die Allmacht aber Flügel aus.

Right welcome! All hail! We take thee rejoicing.
May blessing attend thee, new lord of this land!
Here fields are green and loving greet thee,
Here hearts are warm and burn to meet thee,
And wings to soar thou may'st command.

Rezitativ (Alt)
4. Recitative

ÜCK: Da heute dir, gepriesner Hennicke,
Dein Wiedrau sich verpflicht',
So schwör auch ich,
Dir unveränderlich
Getreu und hold zu sein.
Ich wanke nicht, ich weiche nicht,
An deine Seite mich zu binden.
Du sollst mich allenthalben finden.

This happy day, right honored
Hennicke, Wied'rau
homage pays. I swear also, that everlastingly
most true to thee I'll be. I'll not withdraw,
I'll e'er be near, close at thy side
will ever hold me,
and friendly shalt thou ever know me.

Arie (Alt)
5. Aria

ÜCK: Was die Seele kann ergötzen,
Was vergnügt und hoch zu schätzen,
Soll dir Lehn und erblich sein.
Meine Fülle soll nichts sparen
Und dir reichlich offenbaren,
Daß mein ganzer Vorrat dein.

Everything the heart can wish for
Everything that gives thee pleasure,
Be for evermore all thine!
Nothing in my store's denied thee,
Here's my word, let it decide thee;
Thou art lord of all that's mine!

Choral
Eine Stimme läßt sich hören
In der Wüste weit und breit,
Alle Menschen zu bekehren:
Macht dem Herrn den Weg bereit.
Machet Gott ein ebne Bahn,
Alle Welt soll heben an,
Alle Täler zu erhöhen,
Daß die Berge niedrig stehen.

ZWEITER TEIL
Rezitativ (Baß)
So bist du denn, mein Heil, bedacht,
Den Bund, den du gemacht
Mit unsern Vätern, treu zu halten
Und in Genaden über uns zu walten;
Drum will ich mich mit allem Fleiß
Dahin bestreben,
Dir, treuer Gott, auf dein Geheiß
In Heiligkeit und Gottesfurcht zu leben.

Arie (Baß)
Ich will nun hassen
Und alles lassen,
Was dir, mein Gott, zuwider ist.
Ich will dich nicht betrüben,
Hingegen herzlich lieben,
Weil du mir so gnädig bist.

Rezitativ (Sopran)
Und obwohl sonst der Unbestand
Den schwachen Menschen ist verwandt,
So sei hiermit doch zugesagt:
Sooft die Morgenröte tagt,
Solang ein Tag den andern folgen läßt,
So lange will ich steif und fest,
Mein Gott, durch deinen Geist
Dir ganz und gar zu Ehren leben.
Dich soll sowohl mein Herz als Mund
Nach dem mit dir gemachten Bund
Mit wohlverdientem Lob erheben.

6. Chorale
Hark! a solemn voice is calling
In the desert loud and clear,
On the ears of men is falling
Bidding them God's way prepare.
Make His path before Him straight,
Haste to meet him, be not late!
Let the valleys all be rended,
And the mountain tops be bended!

PART II
7. Recitative
Remember, Lord, my Savior true,
    the oath that
long ago unto our fathers' sires Thou swearest,
and show their sons that still for them Thou
carest! So will I ever Thee adore, O God most
loving; yea, do Thy word
    and keep Thy law, in
piety and fear of Thee e'er dwelling.

8. Aria
Ne'er will I cherish—
Else may I perish!—
What dost to wrath Thee, Lord, provoke!
Ne'er will I grieve or vex Thee,
But with my heart confess Thee,
Whose eyes on me so loving look!

9. Recitative
Alack, I know how weak is man,
    and how his frailty
mars God's plan. Yet let me now
    my vow up-raise;
So sure as doth each morning rise, so long as day
succeeds the day that's past, so long will I too,
firm and fast, O God, in Thy good grace, live for,
and only for, Thy glory. Thee, Lord, I'll praise
with heart and mouth, remembering e'er
    Thy gracious
oath, and of Thy love rehearse the story.

Rezitativ (Baß)

SCHICKSAL: Und wie ich jederzeit bedacht
Mit aller Sorg und Macht,
Weil du es wert bist, dich zu schützen
Und wider alles dich zu unterstützen,
So hör ich auch nicht ferner auf,
Vor dich zu wachen
Und deines Ruhmes Ehrenlauf
Erweiterter und blühender zu machen.

Arie (Baß)

SCHICKSAL: Ich will dich halten,
Und mit dir walten,
Wie man ein Auge zärtlich hält.
Ich habe dein Erhöhen,
Dein Heil und Wohlergehen
Auf Marmorsäulen aufgestellt.

Rezitativ (Sopran)

ZEIT: Und obwohl sonst der Unbestand
Mit mir verschwistert und verwandt,
So sei hiermit doch zugesagt:
Sooft die Morgenröte tagt,
Solang ein Tag den andern folgen läßt,
So lange will ich steif und fest,
Mein Hennicke, dein Wohl
Auf meine Flügel ferner bauen.
Dich soll die Ewigkeit zuletzt,
Wenn sie mir selbst die Schranken setzt,
Nach mir noch übrig schauen.

6. Recitative

It shall be always my delight, with all my care
and might safe to protect thee;
for thou'rt worthy,
and 'gainst all envious might
I'll hold and shield
thee. For ever in the days to come Thou'st my
protection. I'll spread the rumor of thy fame,
and it disperse abroad in every nation.

7. Aria

I will uphold thee,
Wath ever o'er thee,
Thou art the apple of mine eye.
I'll tell thy just promotion,
Thy doing and high station,
Writ large on stone for all to see!

8. Recitative

Inconstancy, I must admit,
is oft with me unwelcome
knit. But still a promise I do make: so often as
each day doth break, so long as night doth follow
after day, I promise you, brave Hennicke,
thy good-will
to pursue, thee on my broad wings
onward bearing.
Not until dawns eternity my task completed shalt
thou see, in heaven when thou art seated!

Arie (Sopran)
Eilt, ihr Stunden, kommt herbei,
Bringt mich bald in jene Auen!
Ich will mit der heilgen Schar
Meinem Gott ein' Dankaltar
In den Hütten Kedar bauen,
Bis ich ewig dankbar sei.

10. Aria
Haste, slow moments, hither fly!
Waft me straight to heaven's pasture!
There will I, 'neath angels' eye,
To my God an altar raise.
'Neath the spreading tents of Kedar
I'll give thanks to God on high.

Rezitativ (Tenor)
Geduld, der angenehme Tag
Kann nicht mehr weit und lange sein,
Da du von aller Plag
Der Unvollkommenheit der Erden,
Die dich, mein Herz, gefangen hält,
Vollkommen wirst befreiet werden.
Der Wunsch trifft endlich ein,
Da du mit den erlösten Seelen,
In der Vollkommenheit
Von diesem Tod des Leibes bist befreit,
Da wird dich keine Not mehr quälen.

11. Recitative
Be patient! The long expected day must
surely now be close at hand, when man from
every ill which this imperfect life doth menace,
and holds us bound and powerless,
    released shall
be and find a solace. One day, his lot shall be
to stand among the
    ransomed mortals in never-
ending bliss, from death's dread scourge and
tyranny released, and care-free enter heaven's
portals.

Chor
Freue dich, geheilgte Schar,
Freue dich in Sions Auen!
Deiner Freude Herrlichkeit,
Deiner Selbstzufriedenheit
Wird die Zeit kein Ende schauen.

12. Chorus
Come, rejoice, ye ransomed souls!
Joyous sing in Zion's dwelling!
Your salvation now is come,
Your contentment now is won,
And shall know no term or ending!

Arie (Sopran)
Eilt, ihr Stunden, wie ihr wollt,
Rottet aus und stoßt zurücke!
Aber merket dies allein,
Daß ihr diesen Schmuck und Schein,
Daß ihr Hennicks Ruhm und Glücke
Allezeit verschonen sollt!

Rezitativ (Tenor)
R: So recht; ihr seid mir werte Gäste!
Ich räum euch Au und Ufer ein.
Hier bauet eure Hütten
Und eure Wohnung feste,
Hier wollt, hier sollet ihr beständig sein!
Vergesset keinen Fleiß,
All eure Gaben haufenweis
Auf diese Fluren auszuschütten!

Arie (Tenor)
R: So wie ich die Tropfen zolle,
Daß mein Wiedrau grünen solle,
So fügt auch euern Segen bei!
Pfleget sorgsam Frucht und Samen,
Zeiget, daß euch Hennicks Namen
Ein ganz besondres Kleinod sei!

Rezitativ (Sopran, Baß, Alt)
Drum, angenehmes Wiederau,
Soll dich kein Blitz, kein Feuerstrahl,
Kein ungesunder Tau,
Kein Mißwachs, kein Verderben schrecken!
CKSAL: Dein Haupt, den teuren Hennicke,
Will ich mit Ruhm und Wonne decken.
K: Dem wertesten Gemahl
Will ich kein Heil und keinen Wunsch versagen,
Und beider Lust
Den einigen und liebsten Stamm, August,
Will ich auf meinem Schoße tragen.

Chor
Angenehmes Wiederau,
Prange nun in deinen Auen!
Deines Wachstums Herrlichkeit,
Deiner Selbstzufriedenheit
Soll die Zeit kein Ende schauen!

9. Aria
Haste ye moments, an' ye may,
Cease to move, or turn ye backward!
But mark! this do I ordain:
Henn'cke's glory and his fame,
Happiness and joys unnumbered,
Shall forever constant stay!

10. Recitative
All hail! Right honored guests, I greet ye! I
welcome you to pastures pied! Here pleasant
mansions build ye, here make
    your home securely,
and here remain content at my side! Your bounty,
pray, dispense, and shower your gifts
    and send increase
upon these meadows spread around ye!

11. Aria
Just as I'm my waters lending,
Wied'rau's harvest store extending,
Do ye too add your virtues rare!
Nourish every fruit and flower,
Show the world with all your power
That Henn'cke's name's beyond compare!

12. Recitative
[Time]   So, henceforth, happy Wiederau,
nor lightning's stroke, nor thunder's
rouse, nor sudden cold, nor thaw, nor famine,
nor worse, needest fear ye!
[Fate]   Thy brows, distinguished Hennicke, with palms
of fame and glory decked be!
[Fortune] And from thy worthy spouse nothing let be
withheld her heart's desiring!
[All]   Their peace and joy, whom their most sov'reign
lord promotes this day, our hearts be ever
constant hoping!

13. Chorus
Pleasant lands of Wiederau,
Happy be in all your doing!
Fruitful seasons never cease,
Nought of ill disturb your peace,
While in space the world's enduring!

If we compare the texts of the choruses and arias, we find such a close correspondence that it is almost embarrassing to see these words of praise and homage directed both at Christ and at the parvenu Hennicke. In the first chorus, the correspondence is total. In both cases, the first aria is a greeting of welcome; in the sacred version it is directed to John the Baptist. Here we might consider the possibility that the chain of triplets in the first part corresponds better to the word "Freuden" (joys) than "Name"—on the other hand, the panegyric is very convincingly expressed. In the second aria, the composition is already completely geared to the sacred version, and the secular piece is simply an anticipation of the material, as it were. The unusual character of the total sound, the restless, veiled effect, is appropriate for each phase of the sacred text; it is much less convincing as an expression of happiness in the homage cantata (the exclamations on "schreit" [shout] then lie on "sein" [be], etc.) The same is true of the third aria, where perfect correspondence between text and music is achieved only in the sacred version. The strong accents at the forte entrance of the orchestra on "hassen" (hate; "ich will nun hassen") depict "ich will dich halten" (hold) much less forcefully. In the fourth aria, the text correspondence is almost identical in both cases. The rising interval leaps before the fermata (measures 44/45) can probably be understood both as an interpretation of "rottet aus und stosst zurücke" as well as the impatient pleading "bringt mich bald in jenen Auen." The following recitative and the aria of the Elster were not taken over into the sacred cantata, so the comparison can be sustained only for the last recitative. Here no correspondence can be recognized, aside from the fact that both versions end with a soothing arioso, so that the contrasting effect of the final chorus—a slightly changed da capo of the entrance chorus—is displayed to the fullest advantage.

No evidence of the carelessness as to the unity of words and music that nowadays is often imputed to Bach can be sustained here. On the contrary, Bach's approach even to the secular work (which after all satisfied the needs of only a single day), the way in which he arranged it with a view to its ultimate use as a St. John cantata, clearly demonstrates the conscientiousness with which Bach treats these "double duty" compositions. The secular version thus had something of the nature of a preliminary study.

The First Performance of the
St. Matthew Passion
by the Concentus Musicus

Seldom does a frequently-performed work cause completely new strings to resonate in a performing musician. More typically a particular work is presented in very similar fashion, sometimes a bit better, sometimes not quite so well. Beautiful performances remain in our memory, but are not distinguished in essential aspects from all the others.

When we prepared Bach's *St. Matthew Passion,* the ensemble was somewhat larger than for the works of Bach that we had previously given because of the double choir, and we were joined by several musicians from Holland and Belgium. Every one of us had played the *St. Matthew Passion* many, many times—the first oboe, violin, viola, cello, organ—at the annual performances that are customarily presented during the Easter season. None of us expected a cataclysmic experience to flow from yet another performance of such a well-known work, despite the fact that we were playing it for the first time on original instruments.

We had begun rehearsals well in advance. During these rehearsals we frequently remarked on how unfamiliar we actually were with the work, although each of us was able to play his part almost by heart. The small orchestration (three first violins, three second violins in each of the two orchestras, and only one player on each of the other parts) and the clear articulation of the early instruments with their varied tone colors allowed the complicated polyphonic writing to emerge in a way we had never heard before. Almost of their own accord, the individual voices took on a completely new character, each for itself but also in combination with the other instruments.

We had often doubted the meaning of the finely differentiated articulations which Bach calls for in the parts written in his own hand and in his score, since they are usually drowned out in a magnificent mishmash of harmonic sounds. Now we were able to see how each individual musician could again take pleasure in his own eloquent, well-articulated playing, because every line "spoke," and the interweaving sounds of the instruments as they played with and against each other suddenly became meaningful. As with every great piece of music, the results of our efforts, which are so often written off as historicizing, became clear once again. What we accomplished was not the revival of an historical sound, not a museum-like restoration of sounds belonging to the past. It was a modern performance, an interpretation thoroughly grounded in the 20th century. As musicians, we find that the best instrument is the one whose sound and technique aid and inspire us in our interpretation. In our eyes, the Baroque orchestra is such an instrument. It constantly provides us with new ideas and fills our ears with a fresh world of sound, the richness of which seems suited for conveying the riches contained in the music of Bach.

Since the chorus was present only at the last rehearsals prior to the recording session, we were quite curious to learn how it would affect our newly-found tonal balance. Even the positioning of the performers was unusual. We placed both choirs and orchestras opposite each other at the ends of the room, and thus actually reproduced the true two-choir effect Bach called for in his final version of the *St. Matthew Passion*. As we played the opening chorus for the first time, we were all enchanted. Since the time of Bach himself, the *St. Matthew Passion* had certainly never been performed with such small choruses and orchestras, yet the work retained all of its monumentality, its grandeur. The large, high-ceilinged hall resounded from all sides. Questions and answers of the faithful and the daughter of Zion swirled back and forth: "Sehet—wen?—den Bräutigam—seht ihn—wie?—als wie ein Lamm." Never before had we so intensely understood the meaning, including the musical meaning, of this stupendous dialogue. Then when four boys and the organ superimposed the chorale "O Lamm Gottes unschuldig" like a silver thread on the steadily progressing choral movement, we understood for the first time the meaning of the new balance: The choral parts are the sole carrier of the musical action—the chorale must never be allowed to drown it out nor to deprive it of its transparency. Instead, it must add another, higher dimension to intensify the reality of the chorus.

The material that has come down from Bach proves our assumption correct. Bach's autograph score brings the chorale—without a text—in the right hand of the two organs, as it were, illuminating from a distance the meaning of the Passion drama enacted in foreground by the chorus. (In those days, these chorales were generally known, so that the composer could use the melody as a "text reference.") Bach did not write this score until about 1740, after he had performed the *St. Matthew Passion* several times, i.e. each time *without* the sung chorale. Only about two years later did Bach write, mostly in his own hand, complete performance material for the work, and *only* in this material do we find a part for ripieno sopranos, in which this chorale text appears. At the time, Bach probably had a somewhat larger group of boy sopranos and wanted to use them as ripieno singers. He normally considered them capable only of chorale singing. There could not have been more than three or four boys.

In any case, our experience in the earlier orchestral rehearsals, i.e. that the familiar *St. Matthew Passion* revealed itself as an exciting new work through this orchestration and interpretation, now was confirmed with the addition of the chorus. Again and again during the recording sessions using original instruments and a small orchestration, the suspicion was voiced that the "monumentality" of the piece was being manipulated; that the sound was "cranked up" by the audio engineers. It was thought that such a small chorus and orchestra, especially one using early instruments, could never result in such a full sound, a sound that was quite powerful, in its own way. We never even considered such a manipulation, because it was never needed. Of course, the size and the acoustical properties of the hall must correspond to the tonal means. If the space is carefully and appropriately chosen, and it was so for this *St. Matthew Passion,* then the impression is just as monumental as in the usual performances with large orchestras, only the sound is much clearer and much more transparent.

In the case of the *St. Matthew Passion,* we were worried that we might not be able to adhere to our principle of performing each work as if we had never played it before, indeed, as if it had never been performed before, because of the powerful associations that each of us had with this piece, based on a great many performances. But then it happened, spontaneously, beginning with the sound of the orchestra and the wonderfully transparent sound of the boys' and men's choir: the *Passion According to St. Matthew* became completely new for us. We had never played it nor heard it before—there was nothing with which we could associate it.

The *St. Matthew Passion:* History and Tradition

Each year before Easter when we hear the oratorios Bach composed on the passion of Christ, we hardly recall the fact that this music is almost 250 years old and that, even in his wildest dreams, the composer could not have expected that his works would live so long. In those days, music was still being written for particular occasions. It *had to be new,* it had to captivate the listener by surprising and novel turns of phrase. A particularly important work might be performed again after a few years, since the listener could certainly not grasp every detail the first time around. Nonetheless, after very few performances the work was ultimately consigned to the archives. Bach's *St. Matthew Passion* was performed under his direction about three times during his lifetime, and thereafter gathered dust in the archives for almost 100 years. Mendelssohn studied the score and was so overwhelmed by the grandeur of the music that in 1829 he performed the *St. Matthew Passion* in Berlin. This was the first time the piece had been presented since Bach had last performed it.

We should not think of Mendelssohn's performance as a revival in keeping with Bach's own interpretation. The musical life of Romanticism was much too pervasive and Mendelssohn himself much too creative a musician to allow this to happen. His performance transposed this great work of the Late Baroque period into the musical world of Romanticism. This Romantic tradition can be clearly felt in most present-day performances, especially in the way the conductor shapes the sound of the orchestra. A truly Romantic orchestral sound is usually heard in modern performances of this work. Despite the beauty and the persuasive quality of such an interpretation, we sense that essential aspects cannot be expressed in this way.

The contemporary musician must surely ask himself if there is really no other way to honestly come to terms with the works of Bach than by rendering them in the style and with the resources of late Romanticism. It seems absurd that today, in the final third of the 20th century, we insist on interpreting and hearing a work of 1729 in the spirit and with the musical resources of 1870. Other approaches must exist which better correspond to our own time. Since no binding musical idiom exists today which would allow the *St. Matthew Passion* to be transferred fully into the sound and spirit of our own age, only one other approach remains: We must bypass the completed historical development of Romanticism and late Romanticism and return to the sound and spirit of the original.

It is frequently pointed out that Bach had to struggle to bring about his Leipzig performances in the face of inadequate resources. And it is further claimed that these inadequacies should not be repeated today in performances that are "true to the original." Bach's letter to the Leipzig city council, "A short but very necessary plan for a well-situated church music," is truly a heart-wrenching document, not because Bach had to make do with such inadequate means, but because only with the greatest difficulty was he able to assemble even the truly minimal (according to today's standards) forces needed for his performances. We are never led to believe that he would have preferred to have more musicians or singers than he called for, but it is obvious that he truly needed an irreducible minimum of performers. But again and again he was forced to carry on with even fewer singers and players than he thought necessary.

His complaint about the quality of the musicians must also be seen through Bach's eyes. In Köthen he had conducted an ensemble of brilliant soloists. The town musicians of Leipzig were certainly not as capable of meeting his exacting artistic demands, with the possible exception of the leading artists. However, it is known that Bach always adapted his compositions to the performers who were on hand. If he did not have a first-class chorus to work with, he wrote in a very simple choral style, but when he had first-rate performers, he demanded the utmost from them. Birnbaum, the professor of rhetoric, wrote (Leipzig 1739) in response to criticism focusing on the difficulty of the works of Bach: "But, since the Herr Hofkompositeur is certainly not so fortunate as to be able to perform his pieces at all times with real virtuosos, he attempts at least to make those who are not yet virtuosos into virtuosos by accustoming them to pieces that are somewhat more difficult; on the other hand, when this is not possible, he takes the necessary care to design his works according to the abilities of those who are to perform them." Writing in a playable and singable way was the accepted policy of composers at that time, since mistakes were never ascribed to the performers, but always to the composer.

In support of this position, Hindemith expressly demanded that the works of Bach be played with the resources for which they had been written because they were absolutely optimal. The views of H. J. Moser, the Bach singer and musicologist, coincide: "Demands placed on the voice, which appear to us unusual, are actually based on Bach's great familiarity with the voice and what it can do. Since, like all composers before Beethoven, he did not create with a completely free imagination, but rather empirically, in keeping with the abilities of the musicians who were available to him (to be sure, however, undoubtedly to the fullest extent of their abilities), it is very likely that Bach's vocal works are realistic portraits of his vocal interpreters." We therefore must be careful not to place Bach with the composers of the 19th century who composed more with an eye to the future and not in relation to an actual performance. Bach's sacred works were written for specific performances, for specific situations, if not in terms of quality, then at least in term of quantity.

The questions of the formation of the ensemble and the instrumentation are inevitably linked to each other. During the last 250 years instruments have been so profoundly changed in sound that an instrumentation which is ideally balanced when 18th-century instruments are used gives a totally distorted tonal image with modern instruments. It is therefore not only a question of a small ensemble, but also of the appropriate instrumental balance and timbre.

It is difficult to imagine that this work, which we have heard so often magnificently performed by 150–200 singers and instrumentalists, is actually chamber music, insofar as the number of performers is concerned. It is not easy to grasp that the piece forfeits nothing of its grandeur when it is played by only a few performers, that its many facets and its richness receive much greater prominence with a smaller orchestration. The musical unity of arias and choruses can be achieved only by a small ensemble. It may be that when recourse is made to the means used during Bach's time, the listener will initially be disappointed by a lack of "monumentality." But must the grandeur of such a work be expressed through masses of sound? Is it not possible that the clear transparency, the better balance between vocal and instrumental means convey the grandeur of this composition even better, because it is more appropriate? A satisfactory relationship of chorus to orchestra, of winds to strings, can be achieved with the original instruments and a boys' choir. We are convinced, and have observed in countless performances, that the balance is correct in all details, without a need for technical intervention. When the piece is played by a typical "modern" symphony orchestra, which is in reality not modern at all, since it is the unchanged hundred-year-old orchestra of late Romanticism, the string section spreads a tapestry of sound over everything, so overwhelming that the meticulous instrumentation of the first chorus is drowned out. It seems that we are listening to Brahms, and in fact Brahms was greatly influenced by these sounds. This Romantic image of Bach's Passions has enchanted generations of listeners since the first revival by Mendelssohn in Berlin at Easter, 1829. So it is not easy today for either the audience nor the musicians to circumvent these experiences and to return to the time when this music was first played.

Of course we know that, even with all our original instruments and boys' choirs, we cannot completely transpose a performance of the 18th century into present day terms, which would be a colossal piece of busywork for practical musicology. Nor do we wish to do so; too much music history has happened in the meantime. Present-day musicians and audiences have grown up musically with Beethoven, Brahms and Stravinsky; they so play and hear the works of Bach with quite different ears than the musicians and listeners who were Bach's contemporaries, familiar only with Buxtehude, Kuhnau and Reinken. We wish to arrive at a 20th-century interpretation based on the resources of the 18th century. As musicians, we would never play on authentic historical instruments of the 18th century if they provided no advantage beyond their authenticity. In reality, however, they offer us the richest tonal and technical stimulation, which constantly influences our interpretation. This is the only and the real reason why we are so insistent on performing on original instruments. It is the free decision of the performer to perform a work in optimal fashion, not simply the antiquarian's dream of recapturing the sounds of a bygone age. For us, the sound and the musical substance are combined in ideal fashion when original instruments are used, so the selection of these instruments is not the decision of an antiquarian, but a decision of living musicians. We understand *musically* why certain combinations of sounds must result in strange and irregular colors on the wind instruments, which please us much more than the smooth regularity of the modern instrumentarium when employed in making this music.

Similar criteria obtain with regard to the sound of the chorus. Not that a chorus of boys and men sings better, technically speaking, than a mixed chorus, but it is much more suitable for this music in terms of sound, and this is why we perform Bach's great oratorios with a male chorus whenever possible. Even the most beautiful female voices do not blend in such an ideal way with early instruments as do the voices of boys. The objection could be raised that we view the music too much from a physical aspect, from its sound. We know, of course, that even the finest and most subtle tonal differences do not alter the musical substance. For the musician, the question of sound is nonetheless decisive, because the tones, the voices, the instruments act to stimulate and inspire the music-making and thus profoundly—if almost imperceptibly—affect performance.

An interesting and relevant question concerns the solo singers who were available to Bach for his performances. The question has to do with whether or not a perceived divergence between actual resources and an ideal conception has been incorrectly posited. We know that for his passion oratorios, Bach used only male soloists: boys for sopranos and possibly for altos, men for altos, tenors and bass. The opinion is occasionally voiced that it is impossible for young boys to exhaust the expressiveness of this music. It must be remembered, however, that there have always been children gifted with great musical talent, who achieve a completely natural and quite adequate musical expressiveness at a very early age. Moreover, in those days the male voice changed three to four years later than it does today, which meant that Bach could count on having soprano soloists who were 17 or 18 years old, whereas boy soloists today are 11 to 14 years old, at most. It is equally clear that different vocal qualities are associated with boys' and womens' voices, so a completely different tonal balance between the singer and the accompanying instruments is involved.

The two alto parts in the *St. Matthew Passion* are of critical importance, but are also problematical. It is very likely that Bach wrote these parts, which require extraordinary breath control, not for boy altos, but rather for men. At that time the falsetto, the head voice of the baritone, was still used as a matter of course as *altus*, i.e. a *high* male voice. It has been customary at all times and everywhere in the world to use these ranges of the human voice, not only in places where women were not permitted to sing for religious reasons, but also because of the unique charm and the special tonal color of this vocal register, which can be achieved in no other way. A well-known example is yodeling in alpine folk music, where reaching the high notes is considered especially "masculine."

Bach wrote his sacred cantatas for his pupils at the St. Thomas School, who were often joined by singers and musicians of the Telemann Collegium musicum. Soprano falsetto singers are thought to have sung with this collegium from time to time, and Bach may have intended that his demanding solos such as "Jauchzet Gott in allen Landen," be sung by such singers. The male alto voice is much leaner and more transparent than the female alto, because it is a high, not a low, voice. Thus it also corresponds ideally to the boy soprano.

The major difficulty in assigning the solo parts is finding singers for the three bass soloists—Christ, solo arias and solo singers of the first chorus, solo arias of the second chorus—whose voices differ appropriately in terms of tone. Although the tonal range of the three bass parts is exactly the same (G or A to e'), the words of Christ consistently cover the entire tonal range, while the soloist of the first chorus, who also sings the words of Peter, Pontius Pilate and Judas, does not sing lower than d until late in the second part of the work. Pilate sings for the first time below this d (to the G) in the recitative "Was soll ich denn machen mit Jesu, von dem gesagt wird, er sei Christus?" The singer who sings the part of Christ must therefore have the lowest, darkest voice, the bass singer of the second chorus the next highest, and the soloist of the first chorus the brightest voice. It certainly makes sense that of all nine soloists, Christ must form the base, the fundament. This also corresponds to the Baroque theory of proportion, in which the fundamental tone symbolizes the *Unitas,* or God. Today it is unusual to hear the evil-doers—Judas, the high priest and Pilate—higher, i.e. more in the baritone range, than Christ. The association: low bass=black villain, which comes from 19th century operas, is certainly the reason behind this shift.

In terms of text, Bach's *St. Matthew Passion* operates on three levels: the Biblical passages, Picander's contemplative contributions and the Protestant chorales which always had been sung during Lent. Bach incorporated these chorales into his work in order to symbolize the congregation's participation in the events of Christ's passion. The biblical text is sung by an evangelist-narrator, so long as it is not in direct speech and assigned to a crowd or to one of the acting characters.

At the time of Bach, the accompaniment of recitatives was subject to rules which were familiar to every musician, but which are largely unknown today, so that present-day interpretations often deviate greatly one from another, a difference which goes far beyond "differences in interpretation." For example, the organ and the cello never sustained the bass tones in the recitativo secco. The notation in long note values was an orthographic convention; the harmonic relation between the singing voice and the bass (which sounded after the attack of the chord only in the imagination of the listener) is evident in the notational apparatus. As a result of this general practice of playing each new chord only briefly, the words could be easily understood. As late as 1774, Jean Baumgartner writes in his violoncello method: "There are two kinds of recitatives, recitativo accompagnato and the usual recitativo (secco) . . . It is against the rules to sustain the tone in this type of accompaniment. One must pause until the bass note changes."

This performance style, which is described in many other sources as well, clearly distinguished recitatives from arias. The former were supposed to be performed as natural and clearly understandable speech song, which was of primary concern to the composer. Even Heinrich Schütz declared: "The evangelist does not dwell longer on one syllable than one ordinarily does in slow, understandable everyday speech." The organ was not permitted to illustrate the message of the text of the recitatives by changes of register. Only a stopped diapason was used to accompany the recitatives and the arias set for chamber music.

The different ways in which the evangelist's recitatives are written in the score and in the organ part are very striking. This difference often gave rise to confusing speculation. The score was written after 1741, the voices evidently shortly thereafter. Now it is a principle of musicology to regard the latest source as the documentation of the composer's definitive intention. Here, the way in which the parts were written was regarded as a correction of the score. Since Bach had lived with this work for more than 15 years, it is unlikely that he wanted to introduce such a decisive change. It would also be hard to believe that he suddenly wanted to introduce a new style of recitative accompaniment in the *St. Matthew Passion*, of all works. In all of his sacred and secular cantatas, and in the *St. John Passion*, he notated the recitatives just as in the *score* of the *St. Matthew Passion* (following page).

Now, as we have said, in the recitatives each new harmony was played only *briefly*. In the *continuo part* of the *St. Matthew Passion*, therefore, Bach for once notated what was supposed to be played, not, as in the score, the usual orthographically-correct long bass notes. He probably wanted to ensure that the almost imperceptible differences in the cello part between the evangelist's recitatives, which was to be played with short notes, and the recitativo accompagnato of Christ's recitatives, which was to be sustained in full note values, did not lead to confusion. Thus, in the recitatives, there is no difference at all between the original scores of the *St. Matthew* and the *St. John Passion*. This difference is found, confusingly enough, only in modern editions, because the manner of notation in the parts is incorrectly regarded as a correction made by Bach.

The most obvious differences between traditional performances and the attempt to return to the sources have to do with tempo and articulation. At the time of Bach, it was hardly necessary to indicate tempo markings at the beginning of individual movements because certain tempos were always associated with particular musical forms, meters and types of motion, which were known to every musician. There is an inclination today to construe the absence of tempo marks as implying total freedom for the interpreter, which is incorrect. The tempo differences are greatest in the different interpretations of the central passage of the work, "Wahrlich dieser ist Gottes Sohn gewesen." These words, spoken by the Roman centurion who was converted as a result of the events which occurred at the death of Jesus, are understood by Bach as a confession of faith by the congregation. For this reason, the double chorus writing is suspended here, as in the chorales. All interpreters appear to agree that this is an important passage, but frequently try to do it justice through an extreme retardation. The tempo differences of various performances are consequently more than doubled.

If the musical premises of the time of Bach are thus used as the basis for present-day performances of his works, this leads, as we have seen, to important deviations from the still customary Romantic performance tradition. Even within the framework of the dramatic action, the impact on the listener is much greater if Baroque rhetoric, which inspired the music emotionally, determines performance, and not Romantic pathos. This applies even to the chorales, the correct performance of which, one would suppose, had been established as the result of centuries-old church practice. Here, too, performances which are based on the Romantic tradition try to superficially exhaust the content of the text, as if it were a musical painting, although even the text itself has a much more intimate and profound effect in simple strophic execution.

Mozart Was Not An Innovator

How puzzling the music of Mozart is! All motifs, parts of phrases, entire phrases—everything that we could term his musical vocabulary—seem familiar to us. All composers of his time spoke this same "language." Mozart was not an innovator in his art, as were Wagner and Monteverdi; he did not want to reform music. In the tonal language of his time he found the resources to say and express everything he wanted. Everything that we believe we recognize as "typical Mozart" is also found in the works of his contemporaries. Mozart's personal style of composition cannot be defined, it does not distinguish itself from the style of his age—except by its incomprehensible greatness. Without inventing or using the musically unprecedented, the completely novel, he could, employing the same resources as any other composer of his age, convey insights with his music as no other. This puzzles us: We cannot explain it, nor can we understand it.

Like all composers of the 18th century, Mozart wrote only for his contemporaries, and among these only the "true connoisseurs." He was fully aware of "showmanship," something he could use to evoke swift applause from a less well-educated audience, and which he by no means scorned, so long as it was not accomplished at the cost of his intentions. The relatively small circle of musically trained connoisseurs comprised his true audience. Mozart's music addressed itself to this group, and his intention was to be understood by them. And he knew that he was understood by this group, by this audience. The desperate feeling of the artist who is not understood by his own age, who offers composition after composition to an uncomprehending world—perhaps in the hope of finding understanding in a later age—was never the lot of Mozart or his art. On the contrary, it is likely that the richness of his music could be fully understood only by his contemporaries. It must have hit the nerve, stirred, aroused and transformed them.

Subsequent generations could no longer comprehend his art in its entirety, because new movements and styles, which directly addressed the feelings, followed the intense and complicated dramatic vocabulary of Mozart's tonal language. Aside from general musicality, no musical training was needed to "understand" the new music of the 19th century.

Mozart: Size of Orchestras

Mozart occupies a unique position in present-day consideration of musical classicism. The typical notion of Viennese classicism runs something like this: *Beethoven,* a wild, powerful untamed genius who burst every conventional form, *is the center.* All other composers either lead to him (Haydn and Mozart) or they continue his tradition on which they are grounded (Brahms). *Haydn,* the trailblazer, who explored the possibilities inherent in symphonic forms and who occasionally achieves "almost Beethovenesque" power and grandeur in his later symphonies. *Mozart,* the sensitive youthful genius who always remains within the scope of Appolonian harmony. No harshness, no great contrasts are found in his music. It can be played with a small orchestra. Everything is natural and possessed of perfect harmony. Great emotion, great dynamism in performance would disrupt this harmony, is romantic and therefore un-Mozartian. *Schubert,* on the other hand, is regarded as a pure romantic and lyricist. Great contrasts are not called for in performing his music, but for different reasons. He is not a "dramatist"; Beethoven-like power is not his forte.

This familiar division, found in a great number of variations, is much more nearly incorrect than it is correct. Given the multiplicity of legitimate possibilities of interpretation, it is impossible for such preconceptions to express *only* incorrect opinions, but everything about this view is badly distorted and not infrequently wrong. A composer need not be a dramatist in the sense of having a knack for the theater in order to express "dramatic" contrasts in music. Schubert is certainly not an operatic composer, so in this sense he is not dramatic. Nonetheless, his scores call for more "dramatic" outbursts than those of any of his contemporaries. If we study Schubert's handwritten scores, not those editions which were smoothed and toned down by the circle around Brahms, we find extreme crescendos from ppp to fff, which immediately collapse, without a transitional diminuendo, to the softest ppp. Schubert's accents, which he often prescribes in a very sophisticated way for the various groups of instruments, are the most abrupt that were written in his time. The instrumentation using trumpets, horns and trombones, typical of Schubert but not at all "normal" for his time—in addition to the woodwinds—underscores these extreme dynamics. We should remember that the brass instruments of the time did not possess the full round sound of present-day instruments. They sounded sharp and blaring when playing fortissimo.

Schubert's scores are full of garish dynamics; his music always reminds me of E. T. A. Hoffmann. Among and between these explosions, the effect of the tender, infinitely lyrical passages is extremely sensitive and moving. With the exception of chamber music players, modern interpreters ordinarily follow the old Schubert edition that was "tempered" by Brahms. They even smooth out any remaining harshness and fear. The Schubert image that most music lovers cultivate is based on an infinite number of such performances. I believe that a hypothetical original Schubert performance—which has never taken place, sadly enough—would be immediately and indignantly rejected as "un-Schubertian." "After all, Schubert is no Beethoven!"

The same holds true of Mozart. His music as performed today embodies the highest level of serene, light-hearted harmony. Praise is reserved for interpretations characterized by Elysian perfection, meaning no tension-involving tempos. These, as well as dynamics, must be absolutely "natural." No conflict, no despair: This music is reduced to a wise smile and soothing, perfect harmony. An interpretation that ignores this hallowed convention is "un-Mozartian," for (again) it moves Mozart too close to Beethoven.

For me, however, Mozart's music is so perfect because it not only contains all these elements, but conveys infinitely more. It encompasses the fullness of life, from heartfelt anguish to the purest joy. It expresses the bitterest conflicts, often without offering a solution. It can be shockingly direct when it shows us our reflection in a mirror. This music is much more than beautiful. It is "dreadful" in the ancient sense of the word: sublime, all-seeing, all-knowing.

Mozart's contemporaries, who knew his work primarily through his own interpretations, clearly felt that this music was different from anything else they had ever heard. The intensity of musical and emotional statements carried the listener to his utmost limits: anything more would be unendurable. Again and again we find comments made by musically knowledgeable contemporaries, even by his father, which point to the excessive demands made on his listeners. Mozart was told that he should write "easier" music with a less complicated elaboration of the individual voices—that it was difficult to follow and understand his music, that he should not go so far in his harmonies (hard, dissonant tensions), etc. Despite universal admiration for his genius—few critics doubted that Mozart was the greatest composer of his time—these opinions reveal a certain dismay at the unsettling effect of his tonal language: could and should music convey such things?

But others accepted and even understood Mozart's tonal language, although they may have found it shocking. His G Minor Symphony is described as "fiery, deeply felt, passionate, awesomely beautiful . . . fanciful." This symphony was "the great portrait of a passionate soul which ranges from melancholy to the sublime." These two comments were written about 12 years after Mozart's death. Even in the following generation, which, after all, was forced to come to terms with Beethoven, similar criticism is still voiced. Hans Georg Nägeli, for example, the

Zürich philosopher and musicologist, delivered a series of lectures on music in Stuttgart and Tübingen in 1826 (Mozart would have just turned 70). Mozart, Nägeli claimed, had an excessive love of contrast; he was "the most styleless of the outstanding authors," he was "both shepherd and warrior, sycophant and hothead . . . soft melodies frequently alternate with sharply cutting tonal interplay, grace of movement with impetuosity. Great was his genius, but also great [were] his genial errors of creating effects through contrast." It was "unartistic . . . when something can be made effective only through its opposite . . . This stylistic nonsense can be pointed out in many instances in many of his works."

I regard Nägeli's criticism as a classic example of rejection based on understanding. The differences reside in the differing approaches to the question of what music is all about. Similarly, I view the negative criticism of Eduard Hanslick 50 years later as by no means the errors of an ignorant critic, but rather as well-founded expressions of a highly-qualified expert who proceeds from premises which I do not share. I find Nägeli's criticism marvelous, not because I share it, but because from it I can recognize the effect that this music still had at that time. However, I do believe that Nägeli's opinions are based more on the scores than on specific performances. On the other hand, I am convinced that had Nägeli only known Mozart's works from present-day performances and had never seen the scores, he would never have come to such an assessment.

Mozart's works do in fact contain everything that Nägeli condemned. The protagonists, be they the characters in his operas or the imaginary ones of his instrumental music—are indeed all things at the same time: shepherd and warrior, sycophant and hothead. They are likeable and repulsive, according to the position from which they are viewed or illuminated at a given moment. They are real human beings possessing all of the conflicting qualities of human nature, not schematic, two-dimensional figures—and it is this quality that makes them so alive, so frighteningly real. Not good or evil, harsh or loving, but everything at the same time. Soft melodies alternate with cutting answers—the musical dialogue rests on the greatest contrasts: a moving plea is swept aside by a thunderous and heartlessly brutal "Nein!"

"Chiaro-oscuro," the black/white contrast, which in music normally refers to dynamics, was recognizably one of Mozart's greatest strengths. He used it, much more comprehensively than his contemporaries, for expressive contrasts. In any case, one thing was still clear at the time: if the juxtaposition of the harshest contrast was rejected in music for aesthetic reasons, then the music of Mozart also had to be rejected, because it was constructed around just this kind of dialogue. It is by no means "stylistic nonsense," but a highly artistic means of causing something to "take effect by means of its opposite." To be sure, this technique was not used during Mozart's lifetime with the same matter-of-factness as today; it was shocking in those days. During his lifetime, Mozart's tonal language was rejected by conservative aesthetes due to its crassness. Today, through the work of several generations, this tonal language has been flattened, smoothed out, sweetened and harmonized in a way that cannot be explained on the basis of Mozart's scores. Yet today, just as during Mozart's lifetime, one is startled when one encounters his works in their almost unknown original form. They speak a dialectical language which has again become thoroughly relevant today.

Clearly, this smoothing-out mentioned above was based in part on the late Romantic sound ideal, in which we commonly indulge even today: a soft, full, dark string sound, with an admixture of the greatest possible number of dark-timbred wind instruments. The dynamics are undulating and not graduated; clarity and transparency are sacrificed to this sound and these dynamics. The playing technique (in the case of the strings, one very often plays on low strings in higher positions) and the sound of the present-day orchestral instruments contribute their share. In the wind instruments, the attack (the first characteristic moment in the forming of the vibration of the tone) was shortened as much as possible, which reduced the specific quality, the distinguishing characteristics of the individual instruments and timbres. The resulting tone, which is almost free of dissonant overtones, blends with the dynamic swell of the strings. A characteristic blaring of the brass instruments is possible only at a very loud fortissimo and is therefore almost never used in Mozart.

At the time of Mozart, string players restricted themselves as much as possible to the lower positions; only for the high passages did they shift to the required position on the top string. The instruments thus sounded brighter and more distinctive. The woodwinds sounded more reed-like, the brass instruments much leaner and more colorful. As natural instruments, the horns and trumpets were much longer than the valve instruments of today—which meant that their sound was more colorful and richer in overtones. But they also had a narrower bore, especially in the region near the bell, and were hammered more thinly, so that they produced blaring sounds even in a medium forte dynamic. Every forte attack of the brass together with the kettle drums, which were then played with ordinary wooden drum sticks, had the incisive effect of an engraving—heroic, aggressive or triumphant; the sound was never merely one color, as is the case with the orchestra of today.

And so it is clear that when the music of Mozart is played by the so-called modern orchestra, the sound qualities of the Mozart orchestra must be known in order to achieve sounds and transparency that are in keeping with the work. Some particularly unsuitable instruments must be replaced by more appropriate ones: horns (F horns) and trumpets (preferably also low F trumpets), which are as long as possible, with bells which are hammered out as delicately as possible, mix very well with the other winds and strings. The orchestral trombones of today, which are designed for a completely different kind of music, are especially ill-suited for Mozart's special sound. I have had good luck with early instruments and reproductions. This is the only case in which a mixture of historical and modern instruments seems to work well. This may be due to the fact that the trombone of 1800 is not so extremely "historical"; after all, instruments with a similar bore are used in popular music even today. Bassoonists should try to bring out the reed-like or string-like sound of their instruments through the use of corresponding reeds, so that it blends with the sound of the cellos. The sound of the modern bassoon tends to be hollow and isolated. Clarinetists should definitely rediscover the rich color gradations of the various instruments. Mozart wrote for G, A, B-flat, B and C clarinets. I conducted the Overture to *Die Entführung aus dem Serail* using C clarinets and would not gladly do without this fresh color.

Closely linked to the problems of instrumentation is the question of adequate orchestration. When we say "Mozart orchestra" or "Mozart orchestration" today, we think of a smaller ensemble. The orchestrations of the age of Mozart, however, were extremely varied, much more varied than the most extreme orchestrations today. On November 4, 1777, Mozart wrote from Mannheim: "The orchestra is very good *and large.* On each side ten to eleven violins, four violas, two oboes, two flutes and two clarinets, two horns, four cellos, four bassoons and four contrabasses, plus trumpets and kettledrums." This number corresponds roughly to a mid-sized "Mozart orchestration" today, although there are a few interesting differences: the first and second violins are equally strong in number. (Today, the second violins usually have two fewer players.) This equality appears very sensible and necessary when we recall that Mozart often called for the second violins to play very important counter-melodies in a lower register, which can be brought out clearly only with some difficulty.

The small viola group is surprising, as it is in all of the orchestra rosters of the time. In view of the very essential part-writing for violas, we can understand this only if we assume that the sound of the violas of that day was much stronger than that of today's instruments. And this was the case: violas came then, as they come today, in the most varied sizes. The smallest viola I own was built in 1805, and its body is 37 cm long. (By way of comparison, a violin is approximately 35 cm long). The largest, from the 17th century, is 56 cm long! Today a viola with a body length of 41 cm is considered a large instrument; in orchestras, smaller instruments are played almost exclusively. At the time of Mozart, very large violas with a powerful, sonorous sound were usually played in the orchestra. Unfortunately, almost all of these instruments were made smaller during the course of the 19th century; they were brutally cut in order to make them easier to play. With the disappearance of the very large viola, an important and interesting color vanished from the string section.

The number of oboe, flute, clarinet and horn players corresponds to what is customary today. The four cellos balance well with the violins, also by today's standards. However, their sound is considerably strengthened and contoured by the four bassoons (!) and four contrabasses which double their part. The bass fundament was thus certainly more powerful than we are accustomed to today. Yet it would be senseless to try to imitate these conditions with the instruments of today's orchestra. The bassoons of today do not blend with the sound of the cello, and completely different solutions must be sought if we hope to realize the original sound even to a limited extent.

On April 11, 1781, Mozart wrote from Vienna: ". . . the Symphony went magnificently and met with every success. There were 40 violins [probably 20 first and second violins, respectively]—the wind instruments all doubled [!]—10 violas, 10 contrabasses, 8 cellos, and 6 bassoons." From this description, it is clear that the previously mentioned relationships of violins-violas-cellos-bassoons-contrabasses are maintained even in this gigantic orchestration. It is also clear, however, that Mozart desired the largest possible orchestration, including doubling of the winds. Today this would be denounced as a great sacrilege against the "true Mozart tradition."

Clearly, the orchestrations available to Mozart could differ greatly. The smallest was 3,3,2,2,2 in 1787 at the Prague Opera for *Don Giovanni*; in the Vienna Opera: 6,6,4,3,3 in 1782 for *Entführung*; in Milan: 12,12,6,2,6 in 1770 for *Mitridate* (the two cellos were reenforced by four bassoons); in Vienna for several benefit concerts: 20,20,10,8,10 after 1781. By way of comparison, a few figures for Haydn: in Eisenstadt and Esterháza: 3,3,2,2,2 from 1760 to about 1770, later there were four more violins; in 1794 at the King's Theater in London: 12,12,6,4,5 (here too, the woodwinds were doubled).

When we look at these figures, we see that the characteristics of the orchestra at the end of the 18th century do not correspond in any way to the doctrinaire opinions which have been formed about it. Interpreters who for reasons of taste play Mozart's works with double-sized wind sections and very large string sections are condemned today as lacking style. Actually, in this case only the attitude of the critic should be condemned, because he is usually not really interested in serious knowledge, and acts correctly or incorrectly in a rather haphazard way. We are safe in saying that, with few exceptions, the largest possible orchestra was desired, and that after the string group had reached a certain size, the winds were automatically doubled. However, this was probably true only for certain passages.

If we study the occasions at which the various orchestrations were used, we will observe that the size of the performance hall and its acoustical properties were the decisive criteria for determining the size of an ensemble. It is not possible to say that one work was conceived for a large orchestra, another for a small orchestra. For example, Mozart's Salzburg Symphony in C major (KV 338) was played in that city with a very small orchestra, but it was performed in Vienna under Mozart's direction with an orchestra that was four to five times as large. Does the first performance of Beethoven's "Eroica" in the Viennese Palais Lobkowitz indicate that this work was conceived for a tiny chamber orchestra? Does the incredibly small orchestration for Haydn's "Creation" at its first performance in the Palais Schwarzenberg indicate that Haydn wanted to have the work performed in this fashion?

I know both halls well; even a very small ensemble sounds very loud and booming there because of the dimensions, the spatial geometry and the marble panelling of these rooms. In a "normal" concert hall, a very large orchestra must be used to achieve a similarly live, quickly responsive sound. The acoustical differences that characterized the locations of Haydn's various performances in Esterháza and London were recently calculated. This study revealed that the actual sound impression obtained in the large London hall with a large orchestra was very similar to that evoked in the small halls of the palace with the small court orchestra.

Most listeners have a wrong notion of the difference in volume obtained from orchestras of different sizes. Six violins do not sound twice as loud as three, but only 10% louder! Only an unrealistically large violin section actually sounds twice as loud. Enlarging the string section does not result simply in a more intense sound. To put it differently, even a precise attack of a section is never perfectly together. Through the minimally staggered entrance of the individual instruments, a soft, very intense attack comes about in the ideal situation, because the colors of each individual entry do not occure precisely together, but come one behind the other, thereby enriching the overall attack. The impression of a rich sonority therefore emerges. This miniscule, initial "imprecision," which should never be perceived as such, is veiled by good, slightly resonant acoustics, so that, in terms of physics, the "overall sound of the strings arises in time segments of overlapping lengths and . . . underscores . . . character and color in lively fashion. Therein lies in essence the reason why several instruments on a part produce considerably more lustre than does an individual instrument" (Fritz Winkel).

Mozart's Use of "Allegro" and "Andante"

Not many composers have been as concerned as Mozart with clearly indicating their ideas and wishes with regard to the tempos of their works. This concern can be seen in the unusually large number of different tempo marks which Mozart uses in his music. We find at least 17 different gradations of adagio, more than 40 gradations each of allegro and andante, etc. We also observe that Mozart attempts to use the same tempo marks for exactly the same tempi—often for emotional effects as well—over a relatively long period of time.

In order to clarify some of these marks, I will list them in order, from slower to faster:

Andantino sostenuto (walking, slightly restrained) i.e., even slower than andantino, which is already close to the adagio, used by Mozart primarily for sad pieces;

Andantino (slight walking motion);

Andante ma Adagio 3/4 (moving forward, but quietly)—always seems to be added during the working process to delineate a tempo in both directions;

Andante un poco Adagio 3/4 (walking, but somewhat quiet);

Andante ma un poco sostenuto 6/8 (walking, but holding back somewhat);

Andante ma sostenuto (walking, but holding back);

Andantino grazioso (somewhat moving ahead, graceful);

Andante moderato 3/4 (moderate walking)—Mozart used this marking for his German songs;

un poco Andante 3/4 (moderate walking);

Andante Maestoso 3/4 (majestic, walking);

Andante 3/4 (walking, in the sense of moving forward, not too slowly);

Andante grazioso 3/4 (gracefully walking—could be with a slight spring);

un poco più Andante (somewhat faster—no matter what tempo was previously indicated);

più Andante (faster);

Andante con moto (moving, walking);

Molto Andante C (with great urgency);

Andante agitato (excitedly walking).

There are several other andante terms, but above all there are numerous subdivisions for each of the designations in different kinds of meter; here, the distinction between C and ₵ must have been especially important to Mozart.

Now a few allegro gradations used by Mozart. (I translate allegro as "fast," although Mozart calls it "gay" in his songs, because it by no means describes only happy movements.)

Grazioso un poco Allegretto (graceful and somewhat fast);

Allegretto ma moderato 6/8 (somewhat fast, but moderate);

Allegretto maestoso 3/4 (somewhat fast, majestic);

Allegretto C (somewhat fast)—this tempo is very close to the Andante with which Mozart not infrequently links it verbally, e.g. Andante piutosto Allegretto, where "piutosto" can be translated as "rather" or "somewhat";

Allegretto vivo C (somewhat fast and lively);

un poco Allegro 2/4 (somewhat fast);

Allegro moderato (moderately fast);

Allegro comodo (comfortable [but] fast);

Allegro maestoso C (majestic, fast)—almost always prescribed for dotted rhythms, a sign of majesty;

Allegro aperto C (open allegro)—this hard-to-define concept seems to imply a certain naivete, an easy intelligibility. There is nothing to hide, no secret. The tempo is somewhat controlled;

Allegro vivace C (lively, fast)—in movements marked vivace, the liveliness refers to the figures in small note values, which should not be played too quickly, so that they may be enlivened in detail. This originated in the first half of the 18th century;

Allegro risoluto C (energetic, fast);

Allegro (merry, cheerful)—the meaning of the Italian vernacular is always decisive for a term, even though in many movements allegro simply means "fast," without reference to the emotional quality;

Allegro spiritoso (witty and gay)—here the actual meaning of allegro is heightened by the adjective "spiritoso";

Allegro vivace assai (fast and quite lively);

Allegro assai (rather fast, or sufficiently fast)—for some composers, very fast as well;

Allegro con brio (spirited or fiery);

Allegro agitato (agitated, restless, excitedly fast);

Molto Allegro (very fast)—in Mozart's usage, this is the fastest allegro tempo, approaching presto.

Even though we might argue about the precise ranking of certain intermediate stages, e.g. allegro vivace, allegro spiritoso and others, it is clear from this selection just how pedantically and minutely Mozart distinguished among various tempos. That these nuances were important to Mozart and are not at all coincidental is proved by the corrections that he frequently made in the tempo marks in his manuscripts, changes which seem so insignificant that they hardly imply any differences to most modern musicians.

In the final analysis, we are forced to rely on comparative approaches for Mozart's music, i.e. we must compare all passages which have the same tempo marks. Some of these demand by their nature a certain tempo, which helps to reveal Mozart's system. Sometimes, particularly in the operas, the relations and thereby the precise meanings can be derived from the larger interrelationships, such as extended accelerandos or ritenutos. Sometimes, as in the case of the Haffner Symphony K. 385, the composer explains in words what he means. Mozart wrote to his father on August 7, 1782: "The first allegro (allegro con spirito C) must be quite fiery—the last (presto C) as fast as possible." But such an investigation neither can nor should be divorced from the musical event. A sense of musicality, an instinct for music, should ultimately rule out the type of mistakes which could arise from purely theoretical consideration.

As an example, Mozart's great G minor symphony K. 550, could be cited. The first and last movements of this work were originally both marked allegro assai ¢. The composer later corrected the mark of the first movement to molto Allegro ¢. Mozart evidently considered it important to point out very clearly the difference in tempo of the two movements. It is also obvious that the two designations had to represent clearly different tempos—otherwise, the correction would not have been necessary. The question of whether allegro assai ¢ or molto allegro ¢ means the faster tempo cannot be answered definitively on the basis of linguistic consideration alone. Even in the 18th and at the beginning of the 19th century, this was a debated issue. Although there was never a doubt concerning the meaning of "molto" ('very'), "assai" also could and can still be translated as "very," but, like the French "assez," it also meant "rather" or "sufficiently". Thus it was frequently used to indicate just a slight acceleration or underscoring of "allegro." This usage is found around the beginning of the 18th century in Sébastien de Brossard's *Dictionnaire de musique,* 1703, and is still found 100 years later in Beethoven, who writes "ziemlich geschwind" ('rather fast') above "Allegro assai."

In his *Dictionnaire de musique,* published in 1767, Rousseau assumes a very polemic stand in opposition to the views of Brossard: "Assai is a comparative adverb associated with tempo words; presto assai, largo assai, which mean very fast, very slow. The Abbé Brossard typically misinterpreted this work by replacing its true and sole meaning with '. . . a meaningful, moderate measure of the slow and of the fast.' He thought that 'assai' means 'assez,' [and he was right—Author]. Thus we can admire the singular quirk of this author, who for his vocabulary preferred a language which he did not understand to his mother tongue."

Back to the G Minor Symphony. Since molto allegro ¢ is Mozart's fastest allegro, the first movement must be taken faster than the last. This is also confirmed by musical arguments based on the work itself. The eighth notes of the violas in the first movement evidently do not establish the tempo; the movement actually begins only on the upbeat, with the violins, basses and violas representing an excited, trembling g minor sound which is "suspended" in the room and is audible shortly before the beginning of the movement proper: this calls for a very fast tempo. Unlike the rhythmical and emotional aria of Cherubino "Non so più" (which is probably marked "allegro vivace C" only because of the diction called for by the text), the first theme consists almost exclusively of appogiaturas, which convey a mood of haste and restlessness. There is no feeling of peace, of harmonic and melodic relaxation.

Thematically, the final movement is not only derived from the minuet, but is also related to the bourrée, a dance movement, which is then executed in sonata form. The dance begins quite correctly and strictly. The first and second parts of eight measures each are repeated (they are not repeated in the reprise), and only thereafter, after measure 23, does the dance develop into a sonata movement. Furthermore, each of the two dance parts is divided strictly into two-measure segments; in terms of in musical choreography, the solo pair (couplet) is answered by the tutti chorus. This strict formality should probably also be reflected in a moderate tempo. It does not allow for the abandoned frenzy of a presto finale. The melodic and rhythmic ostinato of the forte passages and the fervor of the second theme (measures 71–101) can be represented much more convincingly in a controlled tempo.

The tempo corrections can also be taken to mean that Mozart wanted to warn against an ordinary, accented eight-note allegro in the first movement, but also against a cheap finale effect based on speed alone. The desired differences in effect can be achieved even if the actual tempos are very similar.

There is one other argument I consider important for the meaning of these tempo relations. Mozart's last three symphonies, which he wrote in July 1788 in one outpouring of creativity without a commission and apparently without an overt reason, seem to me to comprise an intimately linked cycle. In this context, the G Minor Symphony has a retarding effect as concerns its tempo, i.e. each movement is metrically somewhat slower than the previous one. In the "Jupiter" Symphony which concludes the cycle, the reverse is true: here each movement is somewhat faster than the previous one, a composed accelerando to the finale, as it were. The ♩ in the first movement, the ♪ in the second movement, the ♩ in the third movement and the ♩ in the fourth movement are all somewhat faster, respectively.

In order to understand the composer's tempo intentions it is not enough to know the tempo-words, since their meaning has changed repeatedly over the course of the centuries. Instead, we must attempt to understand these designations as they were understood at the time of composition. This is especially important, of course, in the case of designations whose meaning has changed so much that we cannot recognize a called for acceleration or retardation without precise

95

historical knowledge. Andante, for example, is normally viewed today as a slow tempo, so that molto andante means very slow and più andante even slower. However, andante, a concept which has been in use since the end of the 17th century, simply means walking, signifying a moderate, somewhat swinging, tempo, something along the lines of not dragging, of moving ahead. In association with other tempo words, it means an acceleration (e.g. largo andante—a largo in a walking tempo). Andante had still another meaning, which was only indirectly related to tempo. It designated movements with walking basses in eighth notes, where these are to be played evenly ("égale"—in contrast to "inégale"). This form, however, is no longer used by Mozart.

It is very important to know where the andante is found in Mozart's palette of tempos, and above all whether modifications accelerate or retard this tempo. For Mozart, as generally in the 18th century, andante is still included among the faster tempos. Thus andantino, "a little andante," like meno andante, signifies slower; più andante or molto andante mean faster.

It was precisely at the time of Mozart that the change in meaning began which transformed andante into a slow tempo, a shift which reversed the significance of these modifications. Around 1813, Beethoven wrote to an English "melody-supplier": "If andantinos are included in the melodies you send to me in the future for composition, I would ask you to indicate whether the andantino is intended to be slower or faster than andante, since this expression, like many others in music, has such an imprecise meaning that andantino can at times approach the allegro, but at other times be almost an adagio." In 1833, Carl Gollmick wrote in his critical terminology: "The literal translation of andante to mean walking has resulted in serious misunderstandings. Andante belongs definitely to the slow tempos . . ." It is clear that the meaning accepted today had already asserted itself, and concern was felt that it could be misunderstood in accordance with the old usage of the 18th century.

Today this meaning has been reversed. Andante is understood in its 19th century meaning as a slow tempo; so the faster andantes of the 18th century are played too slowly. I would like to clarify these tempo relations by using two examples from compositions by Mozart. Movement 4 of the choruses and entr' acte pieces from *Thamos, König in Ägypten*, contains a musical dramaturgy closely related to the text, in which the tempos also play a role, for the piece is a melodrama. On the basis of text fragments inserted by Leopold Mozart, we can use the libretto to reconstruct the exact relationship between text and music. At the beginning Allegro 3/4 stands, an excited introduction: the audience has just witnessed the betrayal of Pheron and Mirza. This section ends (measures 22–29) with a strange, pounding rhythm of the strings ♩♪ ♪ | ♪ ♪ | ♪ in piano. The stage direction in the libretto reads: "Sais comes out of the house alone . . . , looks around to see if she is alone." The music thus portrays the anxious beating of her heart. Now, in a fermata measure, she says: "No one is here. The doors of the temple are closed. Nothing will hinder my intention." Five measures of Allegretto 2/4 follow, fresh and decisive—Sais intends to make a vow. Twenty-eight andante measures follow; at this passage Leopold Mozart writes: "Has second thoughts." In the libretto, "nachdenkend" or 'pondering' is written. Here, andante is a tempo retardation in relation to the allegretto which clearly explains the new emotion: "But can I carry it out? Is Sais her own woman?" As the piece progresses, a vision offering encouragement emerges from a kind of invocation to her dead father: "Yes! You hear me! My intention is strengthened once again. You yourself, yes, you, have inspired my resolve." And now comes the "più andante" of measure 63: "I! the tool of traitors? . . . No, it (the scepter) shall remain in his hands!" Here she recovers her former resolve, but her mood is more heroic than at the beginning—più andante is clearly an acceleration. The following measures (73–79) are closely linked thematically with the middle part of the first andante (measures 40–42), and the text is solemn in both places. This passage is marked più adagio, or slower. This comparative adverb can refer only to the previous tempo, i.e. slower than the preceding (but by no means implying a particularly slow kind of adagio). Thus the più adagio merely reestablishes the andante—the tempo before the acceleration in measure 63, which is also confirmed by the thematic relationship. (From our standpoint today, it would have been more natural for Mozart to have written andante once again, instead of più adagio. However, since this designation was understood at that time more as a relative tempo marking, which expressed acceleration more likely than retardation, he only had the options of più adagio or meno andante.) After six measures, five allegretto measures follow with the same themes that appeared at the beginning. There it was "nothing will hinder my intention"—here it is "Yes, it shall be so!" The piece ends with an adagio prayer: "Sun, I dedicate myself to you as your priestess."

I have specially selected this piece because many different tempos are juxtaposed, in the smallest space and with unusual textual clarifications, and because in present-day performances these relationships are frequently misunderstood and misrepresented as their opposite.

Allegro 3/4	Allegretto 2/4	Andante	più Andante	più Adagio	Allegretto	Adagio
fast	a little slower	even slower	faster	slower	faster	slow

Present-day interpretation retards più andante as compared with the andante, so that from the allegro on a steady retardation takes place, to the very slow più adagio, which can be justified neither in musical nor in dramaturgical terms. This misunderstanding is based on an inappropriate understanding of tempo words.

Another example: a whole array of similar relational problems can be found in the second finale of *Le Nozze di Figaro,* as in most of Mozart's finales.

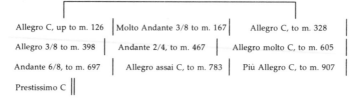

Allegro C, up to m. 126	Molto Andante 3/8 to m. 167	Allegro C, to m. 328
Allegro 3/8 to m. 398	Andante 2/4, to m. 467	Allegro molto C, to m. 605
Andante 6/8, to m. 697	Allegro assai C, to m. 783	Più Allegro C, to m. 907
Prestissimo C ‖		

The entire finale is constructed in C, i.e. in four-quarter time—not in alla breve ₵. This is important because in very fast tempos, an error at this point destroys the entire scheme of emphasis. (This happens all too often, unfortunately, e.g. in the overture to *Figaro,* which is clearly written in and intended to be played in presto C, but is almost always played in ₵, i.e. much too fast, something for which the tempo-sensitive listener pays the price at the prestissimo C conclusion of the second finale.) The molto andante 3/8 in this finale is usually taken much too slowly, resulting in a stiff minuet, instead of subdued, ironic laughter. For Mozart, molto andante is simply faster than the andante, not slower! The text of the count thus more closely approximates a speaking tempo. Furthermore, the parallelism of the thematic and rhythmical structure of

Su - sanna

(measures 122–125 of the Count and Countess),

Si - gnore

(measure 129 of Susanna) and

Su - sanna   son   morta

becomes clear only by a corresponding linkage of the tempos; the second allegro after measure 167 must be just as fast as the first, in principle. In the allegro 3/8 at the entrance of Figaro, the eighths should be just as fast as during the previous allegro, which makes the basic pulse— two-eighths as compared with three-eighths per beat—slower and thus more rustic; this is a country dance, after all. The response to it is a courtly, measured gavotte in andante 2/4: the scene belongs once again to the count. Up to this point, this is the slowest passage in the finale. In the greatest contrast to it, the allegro molto C follows, at the entry of the blindly raging gardener Antonio; this is the fastest passage to this point. The final intensification begins in a menacing way with the andante 6/8.

The last scene (measure 697) begins allegro assai C, i.e. within the framework of this finale as well we find the juxtaposition of allegro molto (measure 467) and allegro assai; here too, the former must be faster. The rhythmic structure ♩ ♫ ♩ ♫ is identical, but the situation is different. In the previous instance, the mood was naked rage, but now it is one of cleverly considered intrigue; moreover, room is needed for the intensification of the final acceleration. This is marked più allegro C—faster—and begins with the mockery of Marcellina, Basilio, Bartolo, the Count and the desperate confusion of Susanna, the Countess and Figaro, and ends in a breathless prestissimo C—but not ¢.

The fine tuning within the medium tempos and the care that Mozart took in describing them can best be studied in the accompagnati, the orchestral recitatives, e.g. in the accompagnato of Ilia and of Idamante after Aria 19 ("Zefiretti lusinghieri") in the third act of *Idomeneo*. It begins *andante* with a weaving movement of the violins. Idamante has realized for the first time that Ilia loves him. The movement of the strings should not be too slow, as it represents imaginary daydreaming. Ilia is encouraged by the vigorous, dotted-rhythm orchestral interjections which are accelerated to *molto Andante;* whereupon she says tenderly: "I will say it again, I love you." At this point the tempo sinks (in staccato cantabile) to *Larghetto.* The following duet begins Un poco più Andante, or slightly faster, than the Larghetto.

Clearly it is imperative to properly understand the meaning of the basic tempos in a given period or for a given composer, in order to correctly understand the desired retardations or accelerations. Unhappily, the modifications in tempo are today usually undertaken precisely the other way around: instead of accelerating, the conductor retards at molto andante, finds no meaningful relation to the larghetto and so begins the duet much more slowly.

The sequence from slow to fast that is customary today therefore looks something like this:
Largo—(molto) Adagio—(più) Andante—Andantino—Allegretto—Allegro—Presto.
At the time of Mozart and in his circle, especially the mid-range tempos lay elsewhere:

The correctness of these gradations is confirmed when we note that Mozart occasionally uses the terms Andantino and Larghetto for the same piece: the one in the work itself, the other in his hand-written *Catalogue of All My Works . . .*

From Minuet to Scherzo

Dance movements, particularly the minuet, have been the cause of serious tempo-related problems, because hardly a musician today envisions a real dance when he plays such a piece. Viennese musicians in particular do understand just how great the difficulties here actually are, because in later dances—e.g. the polkas and waltzes of the Strauss family—they have developed an unerring instinct for the correct tempos and tempo modifications. Nothing is prescribed, yet every good Viennese musician understands and feels precisely how fast, with what swing, with what kinds of emphasis he has to play, but he also knows where a certain style calls for deviations from the beat. Composers were able to take this knowledge for granted, and these insights have been preserved in Vienna as something natural and obvious for almost 150 years. The same approach must also be adopted for minuets and other dances of the 18th century.

To return to Mozart's works, his symphonies and chamber music contain many minuets which suggest a certain tempo due to their harmonic and rhythmic structure. When a given trio, seen in isolation, "demands" a completely different tempo, intuition comes into conflict with (supposed) knowledge, since it is thought that the tempo of a minuet and its trio must basically be the same. Here we evidently lack the sure instinct of the 18th-century musician, on which the composer was able to rely.

At this point, I would like to try to minimize to some degree the seriousness of this problem and to relieve us musicians of some of our uncertainty by tracing the historical development from minuet to scherzo. Like most dances, the minuet originated in folk music and its social rise to a court dance was accompanied by a noticeable slowing of the tempo. As an exotic country dance from the Poitou (Branle à mener de Poitou), the minuet arrived at the court of Louis XIV around 1650; he danced it in public for the first time in 1653 to a composition by Lully. So auspiciously introduced, it soon established itself and became the most important of all court dances. From the beginning it was a sophisticated couple dance, which could also be "performed" solo. The often complicated steps were quickly choreographed by dance masters so there soon were countless ways of dancing a minuet, and such high demands were made that very few people succeeded in finding recognition as accomplished minuet dancers.

Now I would like to list chronologically several sources for the tempo of the minuet:

1. 1688, Lange, *Methodus*, Hildesheim: "Rapid French dance . . ."
2. 1700, Johann Kuhnau, *Clavierübung:*". . . that one ordinarily treats the gigues and minuets somewhat briskly . . ."

3. 1703, Sébastien de Brossard, *Dictionnaire:* ". . . very merry and very fast . . ."
4. 1737, F. David, *Méthode nouvelle:* ". . . The minuet, the chaconne, etc. require a measure in three rapid beats."
5. 1739, Johann Mattheson: ". . . in a minuet, moderate merriness is aimed at . . ."
6. 1740, James Grassineau, *A Musical Dictionary:* ". . . The minuet is a dance form with very fast and short steps . . ."
7. 1742, Jean Baptiste Vion, *La Musique pratique:* ". . . three slow beats: these are used in some faster arias, for the chaconne and the minuet, etc . . ."
8. 1752, Johann Joachim Quantz, *Versuch:* ". . . A minuet is played liltingly, and the quarters are marked with somewhat heavy, but short, strokes of the bow; on every two quarters comes a pulse beat."
9. 1766, Lacassagne, *Traité general:* ". . . The minuet is a piece of music with three more or less brisk beats . . ."
10. 1777, Jean Jacques Rousseau: ". . . elegant and refined simplicity."
11. 1789, Daniel G. Türk: ". . . The minuet, a well-known dance piece of a noble, charming character, is played moderately fast in 3/4 time (less frequently in 3/8) and is performed pleasantly, but without embellishments. In some places, minuets are played much too quickly when they are not intended to be danced . . ."

Of these examples, numbers 1, 2 and 3 probably mean a very fast tempo, counted in one; 4, 5, 6, 8, 9 a somewhat slower tempo, in three moderately fast beats; 7, 10, 11 a slow tempo in three beats. It should be pointed out that in 6 the dance steps, not the tempo, are described, and these are so complicated that a less than skilled dancer would most likely have wanted them to be played slower.

The retardation in tempo with the passage of time is quite obvious. It reached its peak in what is probably the most famous of all minuets, i.e. that in Mozart's *Don Giovanni*. Here the slow, measured tempo results from that of the other dances which are played at the same time. This minuet, in its rigid tempo, became for us the prototype of the minuet in general. It thus was responsible for countless errors in the choice of tempo and, because of all too frequent repetitions of this error, ultimately for a shift in the tempo feeling. This minuet is the end point of a development that took place over the course of almost 150 years. It was composed at a time when the minuet as a dance form had already gone out of fashion, but had been transformed, in sonatas and symphonies, into an art music movement. It was also used as an ironic quotation to conjure up by-gone Baroque affectations. With its severe tempo problems, the minuet was treated imprecisely and ignorantly by scholars as well. But there are some indications—a few of which I have already quoted—which can help us to classify the large number of preserved minuet compositions and to play them in a natural tempo.

It is noteworthy that Brossard's important quote of 1703, "The tempo is always very merry and very fast" as late as 1777 incites Rousseau to a polemic refutation: ". . . On the contrary, the tempo is more moderate than fast and one could hold that the minuet is the least merry of all of the dances in use today." The character of the minuet had simply undergone decisive changes in the interim. Nonetheless, and this appears particularly important to me, the very fast minuet was never totally forgotten over the course of the 18th century: at the same time that the minuet was slowing down, the passepied came into fashion as a very fast relative of the minuet. The passepied was beat in 1, and the running three-eighths rhythm was interrupted from time to time by heavily accentuated hemiolas:

We will return to this point somewhat later.

At the same time that Rousseau was describing the slow minuet as the only legitimate tempo, Charles Burney complains in his travel journal of an all-too-fast minuet resembling a crude gigue which was probably a passepied. In 1780, Diderot writes very correctly in his *Encyclopédie* that both fast and slow forms of the minuet are danced; he uses formulations similar to those of Brossard and Rousseau, but links the two together in an amicable and objective way.

A propos this change in the minuet's tempo, I would like to relate an anecdote Saint Simon tells about Louis XIV. Louis supposedly was accustomed to dancing twelve minuets each evening before retiring for the night. In advanced age, when he had become corpulent and ponderous, he ordered the minuets to be played much more slowly (and therefore also composed differently!), and so the new, slower tempo soon became fashionable.

If one reads all these descriptions indicating that very few minuets of the 17th and 18th centuries had tempo marks, one might ask how the musicians were able to recognize whether a fast, moderately paced or slow minuet was intended. Purely musical criteria must have existed which were so clear for contemporary musicians that the composer could dispense with a more detailed indication. It has always been customary in dance music to leave the tempo to the musicians, an approach which works wherever the living link to the corresponding dance form has not been broken. After three generations this practice continues to work today for waltzes and polkas (though only in Vienna!), and it worked in the case of the minuet in the 18th century.

Before I discuss the musical criteria from which the correct tempo can be deduced, I would like to point out that all descriptions of the dance agree that in the minuet, two measures always belong together in terms of the dance, i.e. that each group of steps combines two measures into a kind of overriding 6/4 time. This characteristic is "built into" every good minuet and should be clear in any competent performance. There are quite a number of ways of accomplishing this: first: the first measure is stressed and the second fades away, etc.; second: the same thing, shifted by one measure; third: the first measure has an up-beat crescendo while the second diminishes; fourth: the same, reversed. In the stylized minuets of string quartets and symphonies, the composers often injected irregular shifts of these schematic progressions.

Critics from the 18th century to today have complained that a "frivolous" dance movement such as the minuet properly belonged only in a suite, but had been introduced into the symphony since the time of Stamitz and Haydn. Burney writes around 1777: "Are there really so many galant symphonies for which a minuet is appropriate? Does it not usually offer too much contrast to the other movements, to blend into a whole? If this is true, one must be even more dissatisfied with the more recent German composers who use them even in their quartets and trios. An abuse that has been pointed out by connoisseurs for some time . . ."

It does not seem to me that Mozart's symphonies in three move-ments, the "Paris" Symphony, for example, are more serious than his four-movement symphonies containing minuets. But it is very clear to me that an entirely new element enriched the symphony and string quartet as a result of the substantial minuets of Mozart or Haydn. All conceivable colors of that palette of expression contained in the three "sonata" movements—allegro-adagio-allegro—could certainly be exhausted; however, the minuet introduced a quite new component—body-related. In the conventional three sonata movements, the musical effect is achieved through a stylized dialogue derived from rhetoric; in the minuet, the effect derives from the element of pantomime. Like no other medium, this dance-like body language is able to portray the eter-nal opposites of reality and dream, of sturdy vitality and the most heart-felt emotion, of courtly gravity and folkloristic merriment and senti-mentality. No other form was as well suited for this as the minuet; none offered such a wide range of possibilities.

The minuet thus became a substantial symphonic movement, in terms of length as well. At the time of Mozart, the minuet was normally played after the trio, again with both repeats. This practice is not only evident in many notes written by Mozart, but also in the writings of other con-temporary composers who always expressly mentioned it at those places where they wanted the reprise *without* repetition; "menuetto da capo senza repliche." Daniel G. Türk writes in his keyboard method in 1802: "Minuetto da capo, this signifies that the minuet should be played again from the beginning, with the prescribed repetitions, i.e. just as the first time, unless ma senza replica is expressly stated . . ." This repetition underscores the meaning of the minuet and the symmetry of the group.

I would now like to concentrate on the minuets of Mozart, but must lead into it by noting that they were firmly rooted in the tradition of the 18th century and that for the generation of Bach, similar criteria determined whether they belonged to a faster or slower tempo type. If we look at a minuet by Mozart, that of the G Minor Symphony K. 183, for example, knowing that there were at that time several very different types of minuets, and we dare to undertake an unprejudiced tempo determination as if we had never heard it before—then we find that a fast tempo, in 1, is appropriate for the harmonic and rhythmic structures. Only the fear "is this still a minuet" and the ever-present model of the *Don Giovanni* minuet may deter us. And does the ghost of the unmistakable *Don Giovanni* minuet tempo prevent us from so doing? A cross check: let us imagine the symphony minuet as solemn, in three. Such a rendering results in a dull stamping, making it very difficult to represent the first, third, fifth, etc. measures as having an up-beat quality. The outcome of this intellectual experiment makes no sense when we call to mind the various types and tempos of minuets and passepieds of that era. The musician of that time thus undoubtedly recognized a minuet through its harmonic and rhythmic structure.

Now to turn to the trio. The tempo established for the minuet seems much too fast, hectic, unnatural. This trio is, after all, not a second minuet, as it had been 30 years previously; it is something completely different, purely Austrian. Seen on its own terms, this trio is an intermediate form in the development of the Ländler dance—or was inspired by it. Can this actually be the case?

In the second half of the 18th century, a new source of minuet-like dances appeared on the continent: the country dances from England, where they had existed since the middle of the 17th century. They were simple, danced by everyone in public houses and quickly took the continent by storm as a basis for group dances such as quadrilles. They became a kind of lyrical anti-minuet of the common man. Shortly after 1760, the country dances overtook the minuet in terms of general popularity. Rousseau notes that they are now danced at balls instead of the minuet because they are merrier and simpler and because they are group dances in which everyone could participate. On January 15, 1787, Mozart writes from Prague of a ball that he attended: "But I watched with great pleasure how all these people jumped around with such sheer delight to the music of my *Figaro,* transformed into *contra dances* and *teutsche* . . ."

In Austria, a specifically alpine flavor is added. The Ländler—or the group of duple- and triple-time dances which went by this name—was added to the family. Typical yodeling motifs, (easily recognized in the first trio for two clarinets and two basset horns of the first minuet of the *Gran Partita* K. 361, for example) were thus added to these common dance forms.

1st clar.

These alpine dances, the triple-time forms of which soon were called waltzes because the dancers turned or revolved, were the direct successors of the jumping dances from the dance pair of the allemande: Schreit-Springtanz (stepping-jumping dance). These dances were indiscriminately called Allemandes or Deutsche, while the triple-time forms were called "Dreher," "Weller," "Spinner," "Schleifer," "Steirer" or "Ländler"; but the term Ländler was also used generically to describe all of these forms. They are the true ancestors of the waltz. Very different social classes came together musically in these late minuets as a result of the amalgamation of the stylized minuet—which was no longer closely related to the dance—with these folk dances.

After this brief historical excursion explaining how the minuet and the Ländler came to be related, we need no longer be surprised by the trio of the minuet from the G Minor Symphony. Just as the minuet embodies the *fast* passepied-like minuet, the trio is almost pure folk music, a Ländler, ennobled through Mozart's genius.

Now we only lack "permission" to play each of these two parts in the very different tempos that were customary and correct. Should Mozart not have indicated such a significant shift in tempo? Absolutely not; on the contrary, it would be ridiculous to expect him to impart such obvious instructions to musicians who had these dance forms in their blood. It only becomes a problem centuries later, for us, who are convinced that a composer should spell out exactly what we are supposed to do.

The minuet-trio pair originated in French music of the 17th century. Very often an entire chain of minuets was linked together in the manner of a rondeau, with the first minuet being repeated intermittently throughout. Since the second, third and later minuets had to form as great a contrast as possible in timbre and music with the first minuet, they were often scored for three solo wind players, e.g. for two oboes and bassoon, and thus called trio. The greatest possible contrast remained a significant feature: a simple, cheerful minuet called for a subtle, melancholy trio; every conceivable contrast in musical colors was desired, as were contrasts in style as well. These differences are especially pronounced in the minuets of Bach and Rameau. By the time of Mozart, it had become an accepted tradition to use the minuet and trio to explore a very broad range of musical possibilities.

We are therefore justified in juxtaposing the two different forms of the minuet and need not feel that we must try to force them onto the procrustean bed of an apparently correct, unified tempo. The trio should be played in a comfortable yodeler tempo, which it requires, and the minuet in a quick "one."

The minuet and trio of the great G Minor Symphony K. 550 are similarly conceived, but the direct origin of the minuet in the passepied is much more clearly recognizable here through the marked hemiolic rhythm. The same applies to the minuets of the last six quartets of Mozart, all of which are marked allegro or allegretto. (Mozart changed a few "allegro" marks in the autograph to read "allegretto" in the first printing.) The trios of K. 575, K. 421, and K. 428 must be played much more slowly than the fast, scherzo-like minuets. All these fast minuets already contain the spirit, the underlying idea of the scherzo: the tempo and the teasing element meant to irritate the listener by "false" accents, by cleverly interrupting the natural order of stress. The two extremes of the minuet are thus continued into the 19th century: the fast version is transformed directly and imperceptibly into the scherzo, the slow version into the waltz.

I would like briefly to consider the minuets of the *Gran Partita* for twelve winds and contrabass, K. 361, because this piece clearly demonstrates the contrasts between the different forms of the minuet. The first minuet is a classical, slow minuet in the style of the *Don Giovanni* minuet, although the two-measure stress here fluctuates more and is more irregular. The first trio for four clarinets is a true Ländler, which is even designed around yodeling figures. There is no real tempo contrast in the slow minuet, the difference is purely one of timbre and feeling. With its somber colors and undanceable rhythms, the second trio moves outside the sphere of the minuet. The second minuet, like that of the great G Minor Symphony and many others which are marked allegretto, should probably be played much more quickly. The rhythm and harmonic developments are much simpler; the afterbeats in the second half of the first part come from the waltz and lead back to the waltz. Now the first trio is gloomy, in the sharpest tonal and emotional contrast to the minuet. The second trio is a true Ländler-like waltz and should be played much more slowly than the minuet.

Thus we are led to recognize that all triple-time dance forms, from the gigue to the sarabande, are magically fused together with all the related folk dances in the instrumental minuet of the last decades of the 18th century. We can almost see the envious glances from courtly palaces still dancing courtly minuets, directed at the public ballrooms and inns—but we also sense the yearning that tugged in the opposite direction. In Mozart's minuets, this tension became sound.

We saw how in some of Mozart's minuets (e.g. in the G Minor Symphony K. 550) the flowing transition to the scherzo can be identified in the tempo and the irritating rhythm. Joseph Haydn, however, goes the furthest in this direction in his string quartets and symphonies. Haydn was among the first to include the minuet in the symphony, and was also in the avant garde in its transformation to the scherzo. Aside from many irregular minuets which contain a scherzo-like element not expressly stated, in his string quartets Opus 33, composed between 1778 and 1781, Haydn composed minuets with such a scherzo-like character that he expressly marked them "scherzando" or "scherzo." (The word menuetto should, however, be added as an afterthought.) Many folklike elements are found in his trios analogous to those that I have described in several of Mozart's minuets. The minuets of several of Haydn's London Symphonies have already outgrown the very broad framework of the minuet and lead directly to Beethoven's scherzos. Musicologists have occasionally held that the origin of the scherzo is unknown. The lineage of the scherzo is very clear to me: The wild dance from the Poitou becomes presentable at court as the "minuet." It is domesticated by the court and gradually evolves into the stiff ceremonial dance of the Baroque age. At the same time, fast and vital variants are preserved in the common tradition. Towards the end of its long and eventful life, the minuet proved capable of absorbing the most varied stimuli from English, German and particularly Austrian folklore. After its own demise the minuet lives on in the scherzo and waltz.

Mozart: Written and Unwritten Instructions for Interpretation

Every composer must view the writing down of his works in such a way that they can be correctly understood and rendered by the performing musicians as important. In this the performance tradition also plays a decisive role. I would like to clarify this by using one example.

(Leopold Mozart's Treatise on Violin Playing)

In the performance tradition of today, such a passage is played just "as it stands"; each note is played as written, equally long, equally loud, and with a separate stroke of the bow (for strings) or tongued (for winds). Two hundred years ago the rules were quite different; this passage is taken from the violin method of Leopold Mozart, who describes the various correct possibilities of its execution: 2 and 2 legato ♪♪♪♪ "the first of two notes played with one bow stroke is attacked somewhat more vigorously, and held somewhat longer; the second, however, [is] very quiet and slurred onto it somewhat later."

♪♪♪♪ ♪♪♪♪ or also ♪♪♪♪ ♪♪♪♪, ♪♪♪♪

as well as several other ways. He says in this regard: "But it is not enough to simply play the same figures according to the indicated bowing: they must be performed in such a way that the ear immediately perceives the difference . . ." He is concerned here not with exercises, but rather with the development of good taste! He points out again and again that the emphasis, stress, is the essential element, not the bowing. "When in a musical piece 2, 3, 4 and even more notes are linked together with a slur, . . . one must attack the first of such tied notes rather more vigorously, but slur the others very gently and ever more quietly. . . . You will see that the stress at times falls onto the first, at times onto the second or third quarter, indeed often on the second half of the first, second or third quarter. This definitely alters the entire presentation." Thus the articulation determines the rhythm and presentation of the piece.

In the 18th century, articulation on an instrument was basically the responsibility of the interpreter. The composer had to mark only those passages in which he expressly desired an execution which deviated from tradition, from the established norm. At the time of Mozart, it was not necessary to write a slur over a dissonance and its resolution, because the unity of these two notes was taken for granted; they *had* to be slurred. If this slurring, which was obligatory at that time, is performed today, the effect is a clear rhythmic and harmonic change in the customary sound pattern. We have grown accustomed to the error of omitting the slurs once taken for granted.

There are many movements in Mozart's instrumental works either containing no articulation marks or having very few marks and only at very unusual passages. By way of example, I would like to discuss the final movement of the "Haffner" Symphony. In this movement Mozart wrote only *very* few slurs, and when it is typically played today "as written," for long stretches, thus determining the character of the movement, the impression of a hailstorm of eighth notes arises. But as a matter of course, musicians of the period articulated according to recognizable patterns in the music, e.g. violas and basses in measures 9ff.

or all strings, measures 20ff.

and all similar figures in accordance with the same principles. But if we treat the slurs, as was customary at the time, not as bow strokes, but rather as emphasis signs, a pronounced rhythmical order emerges:

in the first passage: ,
in the second passage: ;

This movement thereby acquires a completely different rhythmical structure than when all of the eighth notes are played with a regular spiccato. If Mozart actually expected such an organized articulation from his interpreters (and I am firmly convinced that he did), then his work is distorted by an *unarticulated* manner of playing, so the interpretation that is true to the notes can never be true to the work. I could cite countless similar examples, but would prefer to mention a few passages where Mozart uses articulation marks, e.g. at the beginning of the same movement:

If Mozart had written no slurs, the musicians of his time would not have played legato in the first two measures, but in the third measure (as is even played today, occasionally) and in the fifth measure . He therefore had to use these slurs when he wanted this type of articulation. For the second violin, an articulation adapted to the first violin, which would otherwise be played, is expressly cancelled by the dots over each eighth note.

Dots in movements which contain few other articulation marks are also very informative, such as the final movement of the C Major Symphony, K. 338, measures 44ff:

Here, if all not expressly tied eighth notes were really to be played separately, the dots would have no meaning at all. Indeed, in the case of modern performances, everything is usually played in the same way: the eighths without dots and those with dots, all in one and the same spiccato. In fact this movement contains a whole series of passages in which the eighth notes must be tied in accordance with traditional rules for articulation: e.g. measures 26–30 always in groups of three notes, and in several other passages. If it contained no dots, the cited passage would be articulated as shown:

Mozart therefore *had to* use the dots if he wanted to have individual eighth notes bowed; only in this way could these and countless other dots have any meaning.

In the choral chaconne No. 9 in *Idomeneo,* the second violins play 16th notes from measures 117–154. In this passage, no articulation marks appear at first; only after measure 129 are there dots and slurs. These dots are usually regarded as the composer's error, and the entire passage, the part with and that without dots, is played uniformly. It makes no sense to regard this as a place in which Mozart erred. His scores are almost free of error, and in this instance there is a good and plausible explanation: Until the dots, articulation is normal, in accordance with the established rules for articulation, something like this:

But after this point, this way of playing no longer holds. For eight measures the "normal" articulation is cancelled by dots and occasional slurs, then reestablished for five bars, and finally cancelled until the end of the passage through articulation marks in Mozart's own hand.

Once we understand the principle of articulation and the use of dots to cancel the customary articulation, we see how meaningful and logical Mozart's use of these marks actually was. Without this kind of explanation, adequately documented in the tradition of the 18th century, most of Mozart's articulation marks would be illogical and incomprehensible. Moreover, it would be musically silly to believe that in the second half of the 18th century a constant rattling of eighth and sixteenth notes took the place of the Baroque "sewing machine rhythm," which we fortunately now realize to be an absurd notion because of our knowledge of the old principles of articulation. The old principles were not overthrown abruptly, as many treatises show clearly enough, but rather were gradually replaced as composers increasingly wrote out precisely what they wanted. Mozart was in this regard one of the most traditional composers. Haydn was somewhat more modern, and Beethoven and Schubert wrote out practically everything. The more autobiographically (i.e., drawing inspiration from his own life) a composer wrote, the more precisely he determined interpretation and the further he removed himself from tradition.

However, we must clearly understand that such an articulation of Mozart's works decisively changes these works, rhythmically but also harmonically, as compared with what is familiar to us today.

Even the representation of the individual tone is different today than it was at the time of Mozart. In principle, it was supposed to be dynamically animated (Leopold Mozart: "Such notes must be vigorously attacked and sustained without stress through a stillness that gradually fades away. Like the sound of a bell . . . that gradually dies away." "Every tone, even those which are attacked most vigorously, has a slight, almost imperceptible weakness preceding it . . . A similar weakness should be heard at the end of every tone."), and when, for once, it was to be sustained evenly, the composer wrote "tenuto" (sustained) above it. Today, every longer tone is played tenuto. Through the bell-like, dynamic manner of playing, the writing became transparent, because the sustained tones, in their fading away, provided room for new entries to be heard. Singers also had to shape the individual tones dynamically, giving a form to the syllables. Thus the legato—the supple linking of tones into a melody, a sweeping line—became the highest and also most difficult task confronting all singers and instrumentalists.

Tied groups of notes were treated dynamically like individual tones of the same duration. The curve under the notes is intended to give an approximate idea of the intensity of sound.

A wide range of possibilities existed for playing short, separate notes, from extremely short and bouncing to soft and singable. Basically, the rule was observed which Daniel Gottlob Türk formulates with terse precision: "Notes representing skips are articulated shorter than those progressing stepwise . . ." This was a generally recognized principle of interpretation at the time, and a composer could count on this type of execution. If he wanted a different effect, he would have to expressly call for it. It is therefore important that we realize that the composers had to write down all deviations from the norm, from the accepted rules. Since written articulation represents only a small part of the articulation expected by the composer, we must reacquire this elementary traditional knowledge.

Like his contemporaries, Mozart distinguishes between the above marks in order to suggest different intermediate stages where they are not ·evident from the context. Their meaning is by no means unambiguous, and depends on local tradition as well as on the graphic representation. Finely drawn vertical lines usually have a different meaning than powerful lines written with a splayed quill pen. The quill conveys the emotion behind the writing much more precisely than a printed edition can. Most printed editions ignore the dash or line and use dots exclusively. But where a differentiation is made, a wedge ▼ or a ♦ teardrop mark is usually used. In view of the suggestive quality all marks possess, publishers should revert to using the simple vertical line.

Accustomed as we are to ascribing a precise and immutable meaning to each mark, we find it hard to believe that similar marks can have different meanings depending on their context—and yet this seems to have been the case. Some researchers even believe that these are different ways of writing a single mark, i.e. the short vertical line or dash. In Mozart's handwriting, however, a clear dot can be easily distinguished from a clear vertical line of up to 4 mm in length. These two marks also have a different musical function. Unfortunately, there also are many passages in which the composer did not distinguish so clearly—a hastily written dot may look like a vertical line. In such places we must rely on our good musical sense.

The various treatises from the second half of the 18th century deal with this topic in very different ways. Leopold Mozart speaks only of vertical lines and dots under a slur ⌢⌢⌢, with the lines representing a hopping staccato and the dots representing a distinct bow vibrato. ♩♩♩ "This indicates . . . that the notes must be played not only with one bow stroke, but . . . somewhat separate from each other, with little emphasis. ♩♩♩♩ But if short vertical lines are used instead of dots, then the bow is lifted for each note." In 1752, Quantz writes that if vertical lines are used, one must attack sharply and the notes "must sound half as long as they are written." Notes with dots are "played with short strokes of the bow . . . and held . . ." As late as 1802 Adam writes in his clavier method for the Paris Conservatoire that ♩♩♩♩ is played in such a

way "that one takes from the note three quarters of its value"
𝄟 ⁊⁊ 𝄟 ⁊⁊ 𝄟 ⁊⁊ 𝄟 ⁊⁊

"In the second type, the tone must be detached somewhat less drily by taking only half of a note's value"; ♩♩♩♩ = 𝅘𝅥⁊𝅘𝅥⁊𝅘𝅥⁊𝅘𝅥⁊. Hiller writes that dot and vertical line call for "completely different manner of execution," but how this is to be accomplished he does not tell us. In his violin method published in 1751 in London, Francesco Geminiani demands that notes with a short vertical line over them ♩ must be played very briefly; the bow must leave the string as much as possible. Two vertical lines ♩ placed above a note mean an accent. In general, until after 1800 the treatises hold that notes with a line are to be played very short, while notes with a dot over them are to be held somewhat longer. There are also a few sources, such as the *Lexikon* by H. Christian Koch, 1802, which hold that varying the lengths of staccato tones is necessary for good playing, but ". . . regret that since one uses two kinds of marks for this, i.e. the dot and the short vertical line, no agreement has been reached as to which of these two marks is supposed to indicate a . . . sharper degree of separation." Türk writes in 1789 in his keyboard method: "Nonetheless, some indicate shorter notes with vertical lines rather than with dots."

In Mozart's case, articulation marks evidently have more to do with expression than with technical directions for playing. By their nature, they belong inseparably to the themes in which they occur, and explain the idea of the desired "pronunciation." Mozart uses the vertical line to mean two different things. As an accent mark (like a light sforzato), it is placed on long notes, for example, 𝅝 | 𝅝 | 𝅝 | 𝅝 | ("Jupiter" Symphony K. 551, Finale, measures 233ff.) or on the first note in tone repetitions ♩ or ♩♩♩♩ or when individual notes are to be brought out ♩♩♩♩ (*Gran Partita,* K. 370a, last movement, measures 18 and 22). Such accent lines are usually written in a vigorous hand that visually conveys the emphasis which the note is intended to carry in the overall sound. We should recall that in Mozart's time the accent mark > which came into widespread use at a later date was still unknown, and that other composers used marks similar to those of Mozart for accents. Thus the double vertical line of Geminiani is related to the thick vertical line of Mozart.

The second meaning of the vertical line is just the opposite: it signifies a marked shortening and greatest lightness.

Mozart uses them before and after slurs ♩♩♩♩ on notes dabbed in between rests 𝅘𝅥⁊𝅘𝅥⁊𝅘𝅥⁊𝅘𝅥⁊, and with bouncing fast notes ♩♩♩♩ (here the shortening is often linked to energy). The *dot* has a much more general meaning, or, more precisely, it can have several different meanings according to context. The most important function seems to me that it prevents an otherwise obligatory slur; for example, in a dissonance with resolution

(if no dots were used, c''-b' would *have to be* legato, e.g. over a sustained G) or, more frequently, in certain patterns.

"Haffner" Symphony, K. 385: minuet

Without dots, such a passage would have to be articulated approximately as is indicated above the notes. Mozart also uses dots when in the musical dialogue a soft or cantabile reaction follows an energetic figure, which he does not want to be slurred, but to be played staccato-cantabile (for example in the ascending and descending wind scales of the aria No. 28 in *Figaro*: "Deh vieni non tardar"

and in countless other passages).

Accompanying figures, which are intended to be played gently but not slurred, are also quite often marked in this way. Even though the dot at that time was already occasionally called "staccato dot," we must remember that "staccato" or "spiccato" only meant "separate" in contrast to "legato" (tied), but it could of course be performed cantabile. (From about 1700, there are many slow movements marked "Largo e spiccato.") Moreover, Mozart still uses the dot in connection with the slur. In tone repetitions and in piano, this sign always means what was at that time called a "tremulant," a bow vibrato performed with slightly pulsating pressure, with diminuendo and without any left-hand vibrato. Wind players executed it without tonguing, using only pulsating breathing. Mozart used this figure mostly for the chordal accompaniment of expressive melodies. If this mark is used not over tone repetitions, but on different tones, usually scales, it means the "carrying of the notes," called "portato" today. A group of tones grouped in this way is played on one bow, not completely legato, but with a slight emphasis on each note. This achieves a very penetrating cantabile. Such markings, very precise and differentiated in many places, reveal to us that Mozart must have considered the precise and correct articulation of his works of great importance. In many passages, even the individual, simultaneously-sounding voices of a score are marked differently. In each work, we must carefully probe not only the question of technical execution, but also the meaning of these markings, to be able to execute them in a convincing way.

The execution of the appoggiaturas and trills greatly affects the melodic, harmonic and rhythmic flow of a piece. The questions related to this technique are further complicated by the fact that, at the time of Mozart, some appoggiaturas were already being written as large notes, and thus could not be recognized as such. After the middle of the 18th century, an increasing number of commentators characterize the appoggiaturas in their traditional notation as old-fashioned and confusing, and urged composers to completely eliminate them and instead "write them out" in normal notation. They had been introduced in the 17th century in order to notate standard embellishments. Embellishments always had to be written as small notes and signs such as +, ꜫ, w, ᵚ, ⅋, ⸚, tr, ⸒ in order not to disturb the purity of the writing and the clarity of the notational picture. Over the course of the 18th century, this picture had lost much of its old clarity through written-out embellishments and ever more ample scoring, so the traditional rules of musical orthography, above all those that concerned the use of dissonance, were often disregarded. Thus we can well understand the reformers, led by Philipp Emanuel Bach, in their desire to eliminate the uncertainties surrounding appoggiaturas. Nonetheless, we should today clearly understand the notational practice of conservative musicians such as Mozart and Schubert, who right up to the end notated numerous appoggiaturas. We now have the "cleaned-up" editions of works by Mozart in which the appoggiaturas are written out:

 is written as

just as the reformers wanted it at the time. Perhaps this type of notation was less confusing then than it is today, because the appoggiaturas were recognized in their disguised form and played correspondingly. Today they are simply played as 16th notes when they are notated in this way, resulting in a severe impoverishment, because they are *not* sixteenths. As appoggiaturas they must have more weight, more length, more tension than the other notes.

In the G Major Symphony K. 318, Mozart writes as shown.

In the first example, the appoggiatura b' is a 4-3 suspension, a dissonance which resolves to the third. It must be played like a *long* eighth note, very intensively, within the framework of the piano dynamic, and fade away toward the main note, the resolution. This execution of the resolution of the dissonance was called *abziehen* or throwing away. If just two eighth notes were written, this expression would not be so obligatory.

In the second example, the note value of the appoggiaturas is also clear: in harmonic terms, the same thing happens as in the first example, but the figure is played twice, giving it great forcefulness and increased tension from each appoggiatura to the following measure. Ordinary 16th notes could never suggest this dramatic quality.

In the third example, a trill mark is added to a written-out appoggiatura. In the old type of notation, this passage should have been written thus:

However, it then would not have been possible to indicate the desired trill or a similar additional ornamentation. Moreover, this appoggiatura could be understood as a short unemphasized appoggiatura (because it occurs on a tone repetition). Mozart therefore had to write out this appoggiatura. Such a trill at this time was nothing other than an appoggiatura which is struck several times.

In very fast passages it can also be reduced to one simple appoggiatura. What then does this trill mean on an appoggiatura? (It was taboo, after all, to add accented appoggiaturas to written-out appoggiaturas because the effect of dissonance tension and relaxation was thereby lost.) Only an unaccented, short appoggiatura can be added to an appoggiatura *before the beat*, i.e. before the main note, whereby the actual written-out appoggiatura receives a piquant emphasis. This is the case here, and thus the entire trill (here it is probably only three notes) must be played *before* the beat.

There are many similar passages in the music of Mozart, including passages that must be played so quickly that it is impossible to correctly accommodate the trill before the beat. In such a case, the emphasis that marks the beat is achieved somewhat too late and an almost imperceptible rhythmical shift results, one of the major attractions of this ornamentation.

In the fourth example, the appoggiatura must be placed unstressed before the beat, because of the tone repetitions and because the main note has an accent stroke. Such a short appoggiatura really takes its value, its time, from the preceding note, but is so short as not to be consciously perceived by the musician or the listener.

I would now like to discuss a few appogiaturas, in which "that certain something" (das gewisse Ohngefähr) or "je ne sais quoi" determines the execution in a way similar to what happens in the previous example.

Such appogiaturas between thirds occur very frequently in Mozart. They, too, should be inserted imprecisely and unstressed between the main notes, as long as no valid reasons exist to execute them as dissonant long appogiaturas. Their execution is described as indefinable by early authors who say that only a few of the best artists could play them with appropriate subtlety. Here, too, we must understand that the rhythm-determining pattern of accents is established not primarily by time, but rather by emphasis. This means that the beat is where the emphasis is. To put it another way, an unstressed, short appoggiatura can never be played on the beat; the beat moves of its own accord to the emphasis.

In the symphonic works of Mozart, the chords of the strings also are part of these rhythmical subtleties that produce their effect only through illusion. On a string instrument, only two strings can be played *simultaneously*, without forcing. Three and four-part chords today are usually played *divisi:* each violinist plays only one or two tones of the chord, so that all tones can be produced at the same time. But this was by no means Mozart's intention. As a brilliant orchestrator who himself played the violin quite well, he expressly demanded that *every* musician play the entire chord, arpeggiating it. The resulting slight imprecisions in the attack, the very fast sequence of the chord tones, causes a powerful rolling attack, which has a much more dynamic effect than divided chords which are played as precisely and cleanly as possible.

In conclusion I would like to mention the short, accented appogiaturas. The treatises say these should be used where a fresh or arrogant effect would make a long appoggiatura appear too "drowsy." Mozart evidently was well aware of how difficult it is to recognize the passages in which these short appogiaturas have to be inserted and so always wrote them out in large notes.

I know of no passage in Mozart's works where short appogiaturas are required but not written out. In the case of Mozart, therefore, it is unnecessary and incorrect to play short, accented appogiaturas where they are not indicated. This is one of the most frequent and grievous mistakes, and has given to many works of Mozart a strangely motoric, aggressive effect, as if they were Hungarian music in which the first syllable must always be emphasized.

In summary, I would like to reiterate that all marks used by Mozart, his articulation marks, appogiaturas, trills, etc., can be understood only on the basis of the knowledge expected of every musician of his time. They are not yet playing directions—for he depended upon the generally accepted conventions of his time. They simply supplement these conventions in passages where the composer intends an unusual or very specific effect.

Claudio Monteverdi
Discussions of His Works

L'Orfeo
Text and Music; Tempos

At a very early stage in the cultural development of the Western world, the many and varied artistic possibilities offered by an alliance between poetry and music were recognized. Every poetic statement, no matter how clearly formulated it might be, contains different nuances and emphases, so that several different interpretations are often possible. In music, no concrete statement exists, yet in its earliest stages it was able to move human beings—touching, cheering and arousing them. Since the effects of music have always been felt to be magical, music is a fundamental component of the cult aspect of all religions. So we can understand why it was that even in antiquity, poets adapted the possibilities of music to their own purposes and performed their works in song. In some cultures, 'singer' and 'poet' have the same connotation. When we think of the Greek epics and possibly even the drama, we must imagine them being sung before an audience.

In the Christian, Western culture of the Middle Ages and the centuries that followed, poetry and art music were intimately related. In the extremely complicated polyphonic ballads, virelais and motets of the 13th, 14th and 15th centuries, music is in the foreground; the text is often almost impossible to understand. Later, during the High Renaissance, interest in the Greek poetry of antiquity was renewed and every effort was made to reintroduce the old form of recitation—even though the people of the time had only a vague notion of how this was to be done. Around 1600, a completely new musical style emerged: recitative, monody, the vocal concerto.

In the first decades of the 17th century, Claudio Monteverdi developed the language of his music dramas by integrating this new interest in speech-song with his solid professional training as a composer and writer of counterpoint. His first opera, *L'Orfeo,* was the first work in this new genre as well as its first major achievement. With *L'Orfeo,* the speech-song or recitative, which had been created by the "Florentines" was given musical depth. The word became the master, the element which the music was intended to serve. An interpretation stressing rhythmic and harmonic aspects, and the melodic line was accorded an independent value. This resulted in a text interpretation based on music qualities, and on a completely new tonal language, never heard before.

Monteverdi wrote his *L'Orfeo* just a few years after the first experiments had been made with the new recitative dramatic style. The librettist Alessandro Striggio, an official at the court of the Duke of Mantua, was a friend of the composer. *L'Orfeo* was thus developed in close collaboration between poet and composer. The choice of the Orpheus legend for Monteverdi's first dramatic work is characteristic: as "Greek drama," the theme was suitable for the new pseudo-antique fashion while the new dramatic recitative style was enhanced by the irresistible power of music.

L'Orfeo is the first opera in which poetry took precedence over music, in keeping with these new ideas, yet by fusing the new declamation with traditional musical practice it anticipates many of the forms and techniques which would appear in the operas of the following centuries: the aria (even with da capo), the strophic song, various "leading motives," dramatically motivated instrumentation and, of course, the recitative. Although Monteverdi did not create all of these forms, he integrated the new and older musical techniques into a completely new whole.

In addition to the newly-invented dramatic speech-song, Monteverdi's first opera, indeed the first real opera in music history, contains many traditional elements of Renaissance music, especially madrigals and dances. Here, on the threshold to the musical Baroque, the old and new styles blend together ("Prima prattica" and "Seconda prattica"). The madrigal composers of the 17th century had invented their own musical idiom, their own world of sound, for pastoral poetry: simple, dance-like pieces associated with frolicking shepherds and nymphs. Monteverdi incorporated such pastoral madrigals into the appropriate scenes of his *L'Orfeo,* thus flouting the stylistic purism and musical uniformity of the dogmatic "Florentines." (The operas composed by them were pure recitatives.)

The newly-invented monody (the recitative) was brought by Monteverdi to the utmost intensity of expression. In so doing, he recklessly broke some of the taboos of the theory of harmony—"for the sake of truth" as he emphasized in a debate. This opera, which so brilliantly ushered in the age of Baroque music, is also the last great work to display the wealth of forms and the luxurious and colorful sound palette of Renaissance music. The orchestra required for *L'Orfeo* corresponds in detail to the orchestra of the Intermedii, which had been played decades earlier as musical interludes performed between the acts of theatrical performances.

Monteverdi was a hands-on musician. At the age of 23, he joined the orchestra of the Duke of Mantua as a violinist. Here he found rich stimulation, since several of his colleagues, Giacches de Wert, Giovanni Gastoldi, and Benedetto Pallavicino, were widely acclaimed composers. He took several trips—in 1595 to Hungary, in 1599 to Flanders— which provided him with opportunities to hear other leading European orchestras and to become acquainted with other composers. The musical inspiration gained from these trips was reflected in the madrigals Monteverdi wrote during these years, and also very clearly in the shepherd scenes of *L'Orfeo*.

In 1601, Monteverdi became *Maestro della Musica,* director of court music for the Duke of Mantua. His *Favola in musica L'Orfeo* was written for a performance at the Academia degl'Invaghiti on February 22, 1607. Subsequently, it was repeated at the court theater and in other cities, including Cremona and Turin. The performance halls were tiny by today's standards; the audience was hardly larger than the group of performers. The two printed editions of 1609 and 1615, both dedicated to the Gonzaga prince Francesco, are an indication of the unusual success the work enjoyed.

Monteverdi's *L'Orfeo* is the first work ever designed to fill an entire evening, which was an absolutely sensational idea. Until that time, only lyric poetry had been set to music. The madrigals created in this way lasted two to four minutes at the most. At this juncture, Monteverdi composed a shepherd poem—a fable (he himself called it "favola in musica")—a drama that lasted about ¾ hour when spoken, 1½ hours when sung. He was thus confronted with the self-imposed task of finding a convincing way of integrating the individual elements into a whole new form. His basic materials consisted of the madrigal, the newly-invented speech-song, and his fertile, unique imagination. However, a structurally unifying framework still was needed to fuse the many individual parts into a whole. Interrelationships had to be established in musical and dramatic terms as well as through tempo relationships. The entire opera is constructed on a basic tempo from which the different tempos of the individual short pieces are derived. The relations are so natural that the listener has the impression of a complete, organic work. These relations are based on the traditional tempo proportions originated during the Middle Ages, though Monteverdi uses only the simplest of them and invents some new ones, which are equally simple. It is important that the interpreter know and recognize these relations. The approach of determining tempo purely on the basis of intuition and feeling customary today can result in a chaotic presentation, since the tempo proportions provide the essential structural framework which ensures the unity of the work.

The opera opens in an atmosphere of the greatest joy with the pastoral world sharing Orfeo's happiness that Euridice has finally accepted his protestations of love. Orfeo's surroundings mirror his joy. The happy music expressing this idyll is overshadowed by the memory of past suffering and longing. Serenity in music possesses inner truth only when it is imbued with the memory of past longing, past suffering, just as beauty can only fully reveal itself against a backdrop of ugliness. The new music is based on contrasts such as these, the Baroque principle of chiaro-oscuro. Monteverdi has Orfeo express his joy in a song of praise for nature, a technique frequently repeated in the following centuries: his soul's rapture opens man's eyes to the beauty of nature. Orfeo's song of praise glorifies the sun. In a similar way, when Penelope finally recognizes her husband who has returned home (*Ulisse*), she expresses her joy in a moving description of nature. Later still, in Mozart's *Lucio Silla,* Celia expresses her happiness by singing the praises of the rain which revivifies nature. This is a very perceptive psychological observation: the eyes of the suffering are closed to the beauty of their surroundings—only a happy man can see.

Orfeo's "song to the sun" begins as a recitative, i.e. freely declaimed. Later it turns into an arioso with sweeping melody and rhythmical structure. This difference can be clearly recognized in the score: sustained notes in the bass give to the singing voice the freedom of declamation, which is limited where the bass is clearly rhythmical, where it becomes a counter-melody. (The same principle came to govern the instrumental music of the 17th and 18th centuries as well. Thus we frequently encounter sonata passages in which the accompaniment rhythmically stiffens: here the soloist is "set free," as it were—only when the accompaniment once again becomes rhythmically structured does the piece again assume a specific form.)

Monteverdi uses rondo-like forms and tempo interrelationships to combine several sections into a unit. In the second act, for example, he forms a kind of cohesive madrigal from a ritornello and alternating combinations of three shepherds and a nymph; the second shepherd, a tenor, ranks next in importance to Orfeo; the first shepherd is a male alto singing falsetto; the third is a baritone or low tenor; the nymph a soprano. The second shepherd introduces the rondo-like form with his proposal that all proceed to the temple and sacrifice to Imeneo, the god of marriage: the marriage should be consecrated. The ritornello is next, followed by a duet of the second and third shepherds, sung by the tenor and baritone or high and low tenors. Following a repetition of the ritornello, we hear a vocal trio of nymph and first and third shepherd. The ritornello is then repeated a third time. Thereupon we hear a duet between the alto and tenor. Surprisingly enough, instead of the ritornello we would now expect, a chorus of all the shepherds and nymphs now follows, ending the scene.

At the appearance of the Messaggiera, the bearer of bad tidings who announces the death of Euridice, the mood of the scene is transformed from the greatest joy to the deepest anguish, overcoming Orfeo and his pastoral companions. The piece turns tragic at this point, and the tempo suddenly becomes twice as slow. The work takes on a dark, sombre character that is relieved in only two passages: when Orfeo believes he will be able to lead Euridice back to the world of the living, and when the shepherds' ritornello at the beginning of Act Five again portrays the serene Thracian landscape.

Monteverdi carefully distinguishes between the two regions—the sunlit happiness of the pastoral world and the tormented shadows of the underworld—in both sound and tempo. For this reason it is not proper to seek a tempo for each individual piece, independently of the overall context. If one and the same piece—for example the ritornello of the shepherds—is played in a different tempo, in keeping with the given situation, which is often done, the piece is musically reinterpreted. We can hardly recognize it, since it forfeits its function as a signal for a specific situation.

To summarize my thoughts on the question of tempo in *L'Orfeo: one basic tempo runs through the entire piece and forms the basis for simple tempo relationships relating to the different situations and emotions appearing in the work. The tempo of the entire work is determined basically by the tempo of the first piece.* Although these relationships are hardly perceptible when we hear the music, we feel a natural interrelationship which provides the work with its compelling unity.

Instrumentation and Arrangement of L'Orfeo

L'Orfeo has come down to us in a score printed under Monteverdi's supervision. As was customary later as well, the recitatives are notated on two lines, the madrigal choral parts in a five- or six-part choral score, and the short instrumental interludes also in a five- or six-line score. At the beginning of the score, Monteverdi provides a list of 37 instruments, but only in a few instances in the score does he indicate which instrument is to be used where. In the opening instrumental ritornello and in the prologue there are no instructions specifying which instruments are to be played. In Act One, "Tutti stromenti" is written at the first chorus—but at the beginning of Act Three we read, "Here *begin* the trombones, cornettos and the regal," which leads us to believe that these instruments were not included among the "Tutti stromenti" of the first act. (It makes quite a difference whether the trombones and cornettos play along with a chorus of shepherds or not.) Very few movements in L'Orfeo bear precise instructions as to how they are to be performed— everything else is left open. Several instruments contained in the list never again appear in the score by name, while other instruments are mentioned in the score yet not listed at the beginning.

In Monteverdi's *Marian Vespers* of 1610, the performer is confronted with similar problems. A large number of instruments are listed in the course of the work, but no precise instructions are given as to where and how they are to be played. This is also true of several of the madrigals: two violin parts may be written out, but in the title or the preface the following note is written: "This madrigal must be played with six instruments." There are also instructions for tutti with no solo part marked. This seeming inconsistency points to the fact that interpretation can be quite individual, even when we take into consideration all the instructions provided by the composer. I believe that many interpretive possibilites exist which are stylistically correct and do not contradict what Monteverdi intended, even in the case of works which could be described as simple from the viewpoint of the arranger.

Monteverdi's instrumentation seems rather spartan when compared with the orchestras of the late Romantic period. Nonetheless, a very meaningful and dramatically effective plan can be discerned from the sparse instructions, a plan which can be explained on the basis of the tonal symbolism that characterized the period around 1600. The five acts of L'Orfeo take place in two settings: the first, second and fifth acts are set in the pastoral landscape of Thrace, while the third and fourth unfold against the backdrop of the underworld. Monteverdi assigns two fundamentally different instrumental groups to these two realms: the strings and flutes, lutes, harpsichords and the organ belong to the world of the shepherds, while the cornettos, trombones and regal symbolize and depict the underworld.

Trumpets occur only in the introductory toccata, since at that time they were always associated with royalty and gods so could not simply be used for tonal color in the orchestra. (Trumpeters were associated with army officers, not musicians.) Monteverdi writes: "This toccata should be played with all instruments three times before the curtain is raised. If mutes are to be used with the trumpets, the music should be played one tone higher." The reason for this instruction has to do with the fact that the trumpet mutes used at the time transposed the instrument one tone upward. It is very probable that Monteverdi preferred the D major version (with mutes) because of the link to the first ritornello which begins in D minor, to the C major version. Muted natural trumpets sound much softer than open instruments; the four court trumpeters probably stood before the closed curtain, with the orchestra sitting behind it. The trumpets were to be muted for the sake of tonal balance and probably also to avoid startling the members of the audience who were sitting directly in front of the trumpet players in the small room. All three repetitions must of course be played either with or without mutes; a contrast in the repetition would be stylistically wrong and not possible with original trumpets because of the transposition resulting from the use of mutes.

Although this toccata is usually described as the first operatic overture, it has *nothing* to do with the actual opera: it is a true fanfare, the "Gonzaga fanfare." Like all princely families of the time, the dukes of Mantua had the right to maintain trumpeters and, like other nobility, they also had a musical coat-of-arms, a characteristic melody which was played at the beginning of a concert, as the audience was assembling in the hall. Incidentally, in 1610 Monteverdi included this very fanfare in the introductory movement to his *Marian Vespers*, dedicated to the pope, probably to indicate that this work had originated at the court of the Gonzagas in Mantua. This fanfare was misconstrued by various arrangers as an overture, which led to erroneous musical realizations.

For example, the trumpet toccata was interwoven with the true introductory ritornello into a larger overture. (At the same time, numerous parts were added to the simple trumpet parts.) Such an interweaving, no matter how effective, is wrong in several respects, for the ritornello, here used as the B part of the overture, also had a specific function in Monteverdi's musical and dramatic plan. It was intended to symbolize the world of the living, the pastoral sphere: a musical stage setting, as it were. This ritornello is played at the beginning and end of the pastoral scenes in the first and second acts, and at the beginning of the pastoral scene in the final act. Because it represents the landscape, it must not be linked emotionally with the action, i.e. it must sound exactly the same in the last grief-filled act as in the first happy act. The landscape remains the same, only the fates of the humans change; the music can change only in relation to the human fates.

The successive appearances of the pastoral world and underworld at the end of the second and the beginning of the third acts is underscored by an abrupt change in instrumentation. The meaning of "stage design in sound" is clearly evident here.

Monteverdi makes greater use of the chorus in *L'Orfeo* than in his late operas, both in the shepherds' scenes, where dancing shepherds and nymphs sing, as well as in the underworld, where a sexless chorus of spirits comments on the action. Here, too, the composer has realized in sound and with great consistency the fundamental differences characterizing the two spheres. The five-part shepherd choruses are to be sung by men and women: two female soprano voices and alto, tenor and bass male voices. However, the choruses of spirits in Acts Three and Four, also in five parts, are written only for male voices: two altos, tenor and two basses. (During Monteverdi's time, the alto was still a high male voice.) Thus the two spheres are clearly delineated not only in terms of the instruments used, but also in terms of their vocal sound. The choruses of the underworld must of course be accompanied by instruments associated with underworld scenes, the cornetts and trombones, not by the strings and flutes of the shepherd scenes. Unfortunately, these subtle points are ignored by most arrangers and not replaced by other modes of differentiation.

The string ensemble in *L'Orfeo* is the most elaborate in all of Monteverdi's works; violini piccoli (tuned a third or fourth higher than normal violins and sounding an octave higher than notated), ordinary violins, violas, celli (Monteverdi calls the cello "viola da brazzo" in order to emphasize its relation to the violin family rather than the gambas), gambas and violones. To be sure, the gambas of Monteverdi's age bear little resemblance to the familiar gambas of the late Baroque period. The few remaining instruments pre-dating 1600 are unusually large with ribs twice as broad as those of the later instruments; their sound is very deep, incredibly dark—it seems to sound one octave lower—and powerful. (In short, in absolute contrast to the delicate, nasal sound of the gambas built 100 years later.) They sound very good when used with trombones. Monteverdi expressly calls for them in the choruses in the underworld.

Practical involvement with music on many different levels has convinced me that the entire instrumentarium of an epoch forms a unity despite its colorfulness and multiplicity, and that it is impossible to admix instruments of other epochs or of differing musical designs. For example, the modern harp, no matter how sensitively played, has no place in the context of these early Baroque sounds: its resonance is too long, its sound too dark and clouded. By contrast, the Baroque harp has a bright, airy sound due to a small resonator and because it is not burdened by any kind of mechanism, which distinguishes it, clearly but not in an extreme way, from the other plucked instruments, lutes and harpsichords.

Monteverdi calls in L'Orfeo, for an "arpa doppia," a double harp. But the score does not call for one single harp tone in the first or second act. Yet before the third act, the instruction appears: "Now the harp falls silent." This instruction indicates that it must have played prior to this point. Harpists of Monteverdi's day evidently knew even without notes what they were supposed to play. Act Three contains a harp solo of a type that cannot be played on a modern harp because of the tones that it encompasses! A chromatic harp with a very complicated type of cross-stringing must thus have been intended.

Like the colors of a painter's palette, the range of continuo instruments with plucked strings extends from the large Italian harpsichord with its sharp, brilliant sound; across the distinctive virginal (a small, cross-stringed small harpsichord with only one 8' register); the chitarrone with metal strings, according to Praetorius (the chitarrone was the preferred instrument for accompanying singers in the new style of monody); the gentle and sensitive-sounding lute (with gut strings); on to the harp, thus from the sharpest to the softest sounds. In addition to these, Monteverdi calls for an "organo di legno," a delicate-sounding organ using wooden pipes exclusively. Its sounds often provided the background for the harp, lute or chitarrone. They unite the overall sound of the tutti, without themselves appearing in the foreground.

The raspy regal, called for in the two acts which take place in the underworld, provides the sharpest musical contrast between these scenes and the shepherd scenes. In 1619, Praetorius writes that it is one of the most appropriate instruments for the various types of continuo, as well as *the* continuo instrument for brass players. This keyboard instrument surely demonstrates that "beauty" of tones practically defies analysis. The best regals have a wonderfully aggressive "ugliness"—but we perceive this sound as beautiful because it uncompromisingly serves true expression. Such artistic truth embodied Monteverdi's professed credo.

With very few exceptions, the composer allows the interpreter to assign the "fundament" instruments, which were to be used to execute and harmonize the bass part, for the accompaniment of the different characters. Not even Monteverdi provides an unambiguous answer to the important question of which chords should be played above the bass. For example, the harmonies in the solo version of the "Lamento d'Ariana" and in the later five-part version are completely different. If we compare the ritornellos of "Poppea" in the Venetian and Neapolitan manuscripts, we find that *the same bass* was harmonized differently in each instance. Thus they represent different correct versions of the same pieces; Monteverdi probably wrote only the bass. From several such examples we can surmise that there is not *one* correct interpretation for the continuo, but several. Of course, there are many rules, such as the one dictating that a major chord must be played at the end of a piece; that every chromatically raised bass tone requires a sixth chord, etc. But we often see that Monteverdi calls for different harmonic solutions for exactly the same bass progressions, even when the same outer voices are supplied.

Let us look at several examples that demonstrate the different results that the same source, Monteverdi's first printing of 1609, can lead to in modern editions. Monteverdi writes of the first chorus and dance of shepherds: "This ballet should be sung to the sound of five violins, three chitarrones, two harpsichords, a harp, a contrabass and a piccolo recorder." His instructions are ignored in several editions: there is a version with plucking string orchestra and (not overblown) large flutes, which pause during the instrumental dance. Another version uses strings and oboes; additional voices were also composed and added here by the arranger.

One of the first high points of the work is the jubilant song of praise to the sun, sung by the joyful Orfeo. Monteverdi provides no instruction for the accompaniment, but Orfeo was probably to accompany himself on the "lyre," using either a harp or a lute which make a flexible accompaniment possible, because the singer, in keeping with the old traditions, could sing freely in the rhythm of speech, without adhering to a strict beat. *One* accompanying instrument might be able to follow such a free speech-song, but not an entire orchestra. When the recitative is orchestrated, contrary to the wishes of the composer, not only is the overall sound changed, but the artistic substance of the composition itself is transformed through the necessary addition of rhythm. It is not for nothing that several authors of Monteverdi's time warn that all speech-songs should be sung in a free tempo in keeping with natural speech.

Orfeo's jubilant song is answered simply, chastely and with moving simplicity by the young Euridice. With a complete absence of pathos, she describes how happy she is, how much she loves her Orfeo. Here, too, Monteverdi leaves the accompanying instrument open. However, he can only have meant an easy-sounding continuo instrument. At times, an orchestral version is used here as well. High-pitched strings and flutes are frequently designated to create a bright, youthful atmosphere. Again, the question: is such an instrumentation necessary, does it help us to convey the mood, the characterization desired by the composer? If yes, we must agree to it; if no, we should follow the original version.

Blatant examples of the extent to which modern or, better put, late Romantic interpretations deviate from the original can be found in Orfeo's famous lament at the death of Euridice. Here Monteverdi allows the poetry to hold sway: the singing follows the grief-filled melody of language, which rather naturally expresses this moving song of lamentation. Nonetheless, some arrangers have felt it necessary to add a full orchestration. In my view, this addition dilutes the point, the meaning of the words. The deep effect of language can hardly be intensified through superficial musical effects. The composer recommends using only a minimal continuo: he calls for "un organo di legno et un chitarrone" as accompaniment.

Another question relates to the *size* of the chorus. Monteverdi wrote his *L'Orfeo* choruses for a very small madrigal ensemble, at the most three singers per voice. A larger ensemble would not have fit in the small hall in Mantua in which the first performance took place. Moreover, these choruses are true madrigals in style, and so the smallest ensemble is called for in terms of traditional usage as well. Of course, today the size of the ensemble must be adapted to the size of the hall and what is adequate in a smaller space can be meaningless—no matter how authentic it might be—in a larger hall.

Aside from the choruses, Monteverdi also described precisely which parts were to be sung by men and which by women. Even on this most important matter, modern arrangers think they should or can improve upon the composer. I turn to the concluding duet, in which Orfeo is taken into heaven by his father Apollo, as a particularly striking example. In the original, Apollo is a tenor, like Orfeo; a kind of divine super-Orfeo. This amalgamation of the two characters is central to the final apotheosis of the singer. If a woman or a countertenor sings the role of Orfeo one octave higher, *this meaning* of the scene is lost. Furthermore, is it believable that Orfeo's father Apollo, of all people, is sung by a soprano? Above all, a crossing of parts is often used which is not justified musically, when for example a lower third becomes an upper sixth through octave transposition.

One of the few passages in which Monteverdi calls for a very specific tonal color is the accompaniment of Charon, the icy watchman of the underworld. He is "to sing to the sound of a regal." Modern arrangers have naturally not failed to take advantage of this passage. They have *had* to make more of it with trombones and tubas which bestow on the servile Charon the majesty of a prince of the underworld. In contrast, how concretely and simply the blaring regal underscores both character and situation!

This opera contains a great, almost aria-like song for Orfeo, when he undertakes to beguile the gods of the underworld, with every means at his disposal, to release Euridice to him. Here Monteverdi calls for the most important instruments, as emblems of music itself, to appear in obbligato, solo passages, representing the three possibilities of creating musical sounds: bowed strings (violin), winds (cornett), plucking (harp). Even this critically important turning point in the opera has not been spared major retouching in many arrangements; the solos for cornetts, violins and harp prescribed by the composer, but left completely free, have been assigned to other instruments with a lush bed of orchestral sounds laid beneath them.

It is, I think, interesting that virtually none of the arrangers project the work into the present time by radically modernizing it, but rather offer it in a "new" packaging at least 100 years old, i.e. in the style and sound of the last century, the age of Wagner. I cannot, as the reader has learned, be objective about such juxtapositions. Whoever will concern himself with the music of Monteverdi and his age must necessarily take a stand and become a believer. The listener must also be called upon to listen critically and not just for enjoyment, and then choose the approach he finds more convincing. He should take a position, he should justify to himself why he accepts one approach and rejects the others.

Il Ritorno d'Ulisse in Patria

Three of Monteverdi's operas have survived into our own time: *L'Orfeo, Il Ritorno d'Ulisse in Patria* and *L'Incoronazione di Poppea*. He wrote the first of these works in Mantua in 1607 and the latter two in Venice after 1640. During the intervening 33 years, an historical and musical transition from the Renaissance to the Baroque occurred. So it is little wonder that the differences between the first and last two operas are so very great. The differences are actually much greater than one would expect in works of the same genre by the same composer.

It is unfortunate that the dramatic works Monteverdi wrote between *L'Orfeo* and *Il Ritorno d'Ulisse* have not been preserved. Only the *Lamento d'Ariana* (a short opera scene which Monteverdi published in two different madrigal versions) and the short *Combattimento di Tancredi e Clorinda* give us clues to the development of Monteverdi's dramatic style during this interval. In *Ulisse* and *Poppea,* the musical focal points which in *L'Orfeo* still lay in the madrigals are definitively lifted or, to put it better, shifted. Monteverdi's primary concern in *L'Orfeo* is the optimal expression of the text; the music is never allowed to distract from the words, never to be an end in itself. In clarifying and carrying the words, the music must underscore and support their meaning so that, without really being aware of it, the listener is reached via two antennae at the same time. An opera conceived in these terms can contain no arias, no closed pieces of music, since such a way of composing would interfere with the primary objective of the new speech-song convention: to opitimize and enhance the poetry.

Il Ritorno d'Ulisse is very different from the musically rich madrigal opera *L'Orfeo*. The original subtitles of both works precisely sum up the essential difference: *L'Orfeo* is described as "favola in musica," while *Ulisse* is called a "dramma in musica." Modern music drama resembles *L'Orfeo* no more than it does the actual Baroque aria opera which came into fashion shortly afterwards. Here the singer was the main attraction and major focus; the word, the dramatic action, became less and less important. Just a few decades later, Baroque opera with its closed musical numbers and arias had become a musical revue badly in need of reform.

Il Ritorno d'Ulisse is thus neither in formal terms nor as a music drama that which we understand today by the term Baroque opera. It contains no arias, no closed numbers; recitative-like and arioso-like elements blend smoothly with each other. The word, the text, still determines the musical progress of the piece as well. The 13th to 23rd songs of the *Odyssey* form the basis of the action, not a classical hero drama or ancient Roman theme, such as were popular during the high Baroque in which poets and composers followed the original poetry of Homer with pains-taking pedantry. Monteverdi's characterization of the suitors as well as of all minor roles was carried out with scrupulous care. Since the educated public of the time was thoroughly familiar with the smallest details of this major work of Greek poetry, Giacomo Badoaro and Monteverdi could dispense with the dramatic development of tension and relaxation. They illustrated the generally known action as a sequence of epic scenes. Thus not every figure had to be drawn in accordance with the rules of drama. It was enough in some cases to simply allow minor figures to briefly wander by, because they were all very well known to the audience.

Following the general custom of the time, the work was preceded by a prologue constructed around a group of symbols: man is a fragile toy in the hands of the three Fates, Time, Chance and Love. Even the gods are subject to these powers. The actual drama depicts a human being at the mercy of the arbitrariness of the gods, although the gods themselves are nothing other than immortal supermen subject to the whim of the Fates.

The action takes place on three levels: (1) the Fates in the Prologue; (2) the gods in the gods' scenes of the first and last acts in which the plot is worked out (in the first act, Neptune wants to prevent Ulisse from returning home in order to punish him for the blinding of his son Polyphemus; in the last act, Neptune is pacified by the other gods, Ulisse can finally find rest and Penelope is allowed to recognize him); (3) the actual plot.

In addition to the clearly delineated scenes of each of the three levels, there are four other places in which the worlds of gods and men touch: when Minverva consoles Ulisse and gives him advice; when she con-veys Telemaco in her cloud chariot from Sparta; when she encourages Ulisse in his return home; and when she finally stands by him in his fight with the suitors.

The manuscript of Monteverdi's *Il Ritorno d'Ulisse,* now housed in the National Library in Vienna, was part of the holdings belonging to the Emperor. How it came to Vienna has never been ascertained, but the close relationship that Monteverdi had to the Hapsburgs is well known. The Hapsburgs were variously related by marriage to the princely Gonzaga family, and Monteverdi cultivated these old relationships even after his departure from Mantua. It is possible that the *Ulisse* manuscript originated in Venice during Monteverdi's lifetime and somehow reached Vienna. In the early years of the development of opera, a lively demand for repertoire was naturally felt at the centers where this genre was cultivated, especially in Vienna. The masterpieces of the famous Claudio Monteverdi were therefore objects of great attention. The manuscript of *Ulisse* is written in a way that reveals the hand of an authoritative expert. Some passages are erased, not in order to correct mistakes, but to modify and improve. There has been much debate about Monteverdi's authorship of this opera, and doubt has been expressed as to whether the Viennese manuscript is in Monteverdi's own hand. The first point is generally regarded as having been settled in the affirmative, but by reason of its appearance the manuscript is usually ascribed to a contemporary copyist. This view is based exclusively on a comparison of writing samples. For musical reasons—i.e. because of these improvements—I tend to believe that it was written by a competent colleague of Monteverdi. The handwriting is almost perfect and practically free of errors.

As was customary at the time, the original score represents more a "director's part" than a typical score; only the bass and the vocal parts are written down, together with the instrumental overtures and the interludes. Of the latter, several are completely composed, with middle voices. In some, only the bass exists, while both the bass and the upper voices are provided for others. Clearly, quite a bit has to be added. The extent of such additions is controversial and will never be established with certainty. Some editing is therefore indispensable and must concentrate on three points: (1) the distribution of the basso continuo among different instruments, in order to bring out the character of the music and of the dramatic persona; (2) the execution of additional instrumental parts, where they were most likely expected; (3) instrumentation. While the first point is not problematical, if instruments are used that Monteverdi himself occasionally prescribes in his works (harpsichord, virginal, organ, regal, harp, chitarrone), objections can arise about the added instrumental voices. The requirement for such voices clearly appears in the manuscript, in those passages where an aria-like piece ends with a few measures without singing, with "ritornello" written above the bass voice. However, it would be impossible for the instruments to begin playing only in these last measures, which means that they must already have been present. Also, where only the upper voice and the bass are written in a ritornello, the middle voices must certainly be added.

Monteverdi himself can and should provide some assistance to us here, since he left behind extensive directions and models for us, for example in his L'Orfeo and in the very operatic Marian Vespers. In addition to these express instructions, very clear formal clues are contained in the works themselves: the constant alternation between recitative and arioso writing demands a tonal differentiation. These two styles are, after all, very distinct from each other: in addition to individual remarks in the manuscript, and through lines that are left blank in other opera scores which follow the same principles, they provide the schematic form in accordance with which the instrumentation must be inserted. A particularly beautiful example of this alternation between arioso and recitative parts is found in Il Ritorno d'Ulisse, in Penelope's first monologue: here the thrice-repeated "torna, torna, deh torna Ulisse" and "torna il tranquillo al mare" distinguishes itself by an arioso style from the long recitative part. This differentiation evidently intended by the composer between a continuous recitative and the ariosos must somehow be made audible. It is not audible when the opera is continuously accompanied by a harpsichord—nor is it audible when we use string sound throughout for the accompaniment. But it becomes very audible if we accompany the recitative with the harpsichord and employ a richer instrumentation for the ariosos. This possibility was used by many composers of the time. Monteverdi's student Pier Francesco Cavalli, for example, placed empty lines between the vocal part and the bass at arioso passages in several operas, or he would write out two or three bars of an instrumental part which the performing musician then completed.

We are aware that it is possible to go even further in the performance of these middle voices without violating the style, but dispensing with them entirely cannot be justified. In contrast to the all-too-liberal arrangers, there are those representing the opposite extreme: super purists who only want to realize the handed-down, skeletal score and reject any additions. This sort of loyalty to the work does not serve the intention of the composer, since it negates the presuppositions on which he has based his work. It is just as incorrect to reveal only the "skeleton" which was written down by Monteverdi as to cover it with the inappropriate "flesh" of a much later age—as frequently happens.

As to the third point, the instrumentation, very little need be said. In the manuscript, "violini" and "viole" are mentioned only once, as if by accident, and "con tutti gli stromenti." The instrumentation is based in my arrangement on a string group of violins, violas, gambas and violones, which are occasionally strengthened and enriched by various wind instruments. At the appropriate places, improvised embellishments are added by individual instruments. In addition to the string instruments, there are recorders (Renaissance recorders with a wide bore, made from one piece of wood) for charming and brilliant scenes; piffari (discant shawms on which only a limited scale can be played) and dulcians (precursors of the bassoon), for pastoral and comic scenes. For the accompaniment of Neptune's passages, and in places where gravity is demanded, trombones are used, with trumpets—obligatory in those days—for the appearances of the gods. In addition to these melody instruments, which were also used soloistically in places, there is a wide range of continuo instruments: a large Italian harpsichord as the main instrument, a small virginal to accompany recitatives of Melanto, Eurimaco and Pisandro. Lutes and chitarrone for the continuo of the songs of Melanto, Eurimaco and Anfinomo, and in combination with the organ and harpsichord for recitative accompaniment of Ulisse, Telemaco and Ericlea; a harp, above all to accompany Penelope, but occasionally also for Ulisse; an organ for the scenes with the gods, a regal for Neptune, Antinoo and the comic scenes with Iro. Such an instrumentation should not be considered definitive; rather, as in every realization of this type of work, it should represent one of many possibilities, although great stress is placed on the fact that in both technical and stylistic terms it involves possibilities that existed at the time of Monteverdi. Restricting myself to resources that existed at the time the work was written is done not for reasons of historical verisimilitude, but because I believe this type of realization to be the best one for today as well.

Monteverdi's music does not need the benefit of a later instrumentation and harmonization to be effective. The music is so one with the text, so truly theatrical and dramatic, that it must ultimately speak best to the present-day listener when it is clothed in its original garment of sound.

Early opera is theater, first and foremost. The music is intended only to underscore the accent of the words, to enhance expression, to enable the public to follow the drama with every fiber of their beings. This is very difficult for the German-speaking listener, as for any non-Italian, since the major component, the language, is incomprehensible. Yet these works do not lend themselves to translation because of the intimate way in which words and music are interrelated.

L'Incoronazione di Poppea

As we have already noted, opera was "invented" as an art form in Florence around 1600; it was adopted, enriched and enhanced by the courts in Mantua and Parma, which zealously cultivated the arts. *L'Orfeo* was written in 1607, *Ariana* in 1609, *La favola di Peleo e di Tetide* in 1617, *La finta pazza Licori* in 1627, to mention just a few of the works of Monteverdi. Monteverdi, who was well known to the Florentine opera pioneers Caccini, Peri and Gagliano, imbued their rather dogmatic ideas with artistic vitality. Even as maestro at St. Mark's Cathedral in Venice, after 1613, he provided several courts and Venetian nobility with music dramas.

Nonetheless, as late as 1620 he claimed that his interest in operatic works was only peripheral, compared to his duties as a church musician. The operatic wave swept over Rome around this time, and Cardinal Rospigliosi, the future Pope Clement IX, practically formed a "school" of opera in the Eternal City. Opera finally returned again to northern Italy in 1637, this time in a new guise. In Venice, the world's first opera house was opened: any ordinary citizen could attend a performance for the price of a ticket. At its opening, a *Roman* ensemble played *Andromeda*, an opera by Monteverdi's pupil Francesco Manelli. In the years that followed, many theaters were opened in Venice. Run as independent economic enterprises and financed by admission fees, these theaters were dependent on popular success for their economic survival.

Now Claudio Monteverdi once again turned to opera. Having performed *Ariana* again after more than 30 years (probably in a new version at the Teatro S. Moisé), in 1641 he composed *Il Ritorno d'Ulisse* (S. Cassiano) and in 1642 *L'Incoronazione di Poppea* (SS. Giovanni e Paolo). In these works he makes use of all the innovations developed by his young competitors, who had also been his pupils, and takes the genre, which more than 30 years previously he had brought to its great success, to new heights. This detour via Rome explains the remarkable stylistic differences that distinguish *L'Orfeo* from the two late operas. What is truly astonishing, however, is the intellectual freshness with which Monteverdi, at 74 years of age and just two years before his death, was able to surpass his students in the most modern style, setting standards which would remain the touchstone of the musical theater for centuries to come. We strongly believe that *L'Incoronazione di Poppea* is one of the most important works in all of operatic literature, a work that can only be compared with the masterpieces of Mozart and Verdi.

After a lifetime of experimentation, Monteverdi found his way in his late works to a completely new style of music drama, which interprets and dramatizes the text while remaining subordinate to it. He had always been interested in the "optimal imitation of nature," and in *Poppea* he finally discovered the tonal language which encompasses all of human nature, character traits, expression, and dramatic body language. Monteverdi selected his librettos with great care, with an eye to the beauty of the poetic language as well as the very specific emotions and contrasts he wished to express through his music. Thus he wrote in the preface to his *Combattimento* (1624) that he had selected Tasso's text because it "expresses with naturalness . . . the desired emotion . . ." and because he found in it "the opposing forces that appear to me suitable for transposition into music, . . . namely, the moods of war, prayer and death." Giving precise reasons, he rejected librettos that appeared unsuitable to him. In 1616 he wrote to Alessandro Striggio, who had sent him a text: "I cannot imitate the language of the winds because they do not speak; how can I possibly arouse empathy here? Ariana moved the listeners because she was a woman; by the same token, Orfeo stirred the audience because he was a human being, not a wind . . ." His interpretation of a text was derived from penetrating dramaturgical analysis, as we learn from his correspondence of 1627, concerning *La finta pazza Licori.* We therefore can be assured that Monteverdi selected the *historical* libretto of *Poppea* with great care (operas were ordinarily supposed to deal with mythological themes) and that it met his requirements exactly.

Neither Monteverdi nor Mozart take positions with regard to the moral questions raised in their operas. As I see it, the conclusion of *Poppea*, just as in the Da Ponte operas of Mozart, is *desperate*, not happy. This is also true for the second, quite comparable opera of Monteverdi, *Ulisse*. Both operas officially end with a "happy" final duet. The true conclusion of *Ulisse*, which underlies the apparently happy ending (lieto fine), is desperate: two people who have been separated from each other for 20 years have become estranged. They cannot take up at the point where they were when they were torn from each other; they can never again find their way back to each other. During their separation, each so changed that neither can recognize in the other the former lover. In view of this total inability of Penelope and Ulisse to find each other, Monteverdi takes what was at the time the only possible way to achieve a happy ending after all, by having Jupiter appear in a cloud and allow Penelope to recognize her husband. This is basically not a happy ending. Monteverdi has Penelope sing a rather simplistic melody: "si si, si si, ti riconosco" (yes, yes, I recognize you again), presumably because he wanted to express the unreal aspect of this passage through a primitive formulation. Anyone seeing this conclusion will feel that it is actually sad. We know, after all, that Jupiter, who appears and makes everything good with a wave of his hand, does not really exist.

I hear a very similar sadness in the conclusion of *Poppea*. Naturally, one could play the devil's advocate and say: 'It's great, how Amor confuses everything, how he tears the masks from the faces of people.' Yet it is ultimately no *lieto fine* when Amor's power is so ineluctable that it is capable of destroying everything, in its path. So when Poppea and Nero sing an apparently happy final duet, the listener is left with the distinct impression that the price for this supposed happiness was too high. We do not know what may have moved Monteverdi to compose such an amoral book as *Poppea,* an opera in which indeed all morality has been abandoned—, but we must recall that he did not elaborate this theme for us but for an audience whose social and moral habits were completely different from those cultivated today.

The basic theme of *Poppea* is the destructive power of Amor, a power capable of destroying society as well. Amor shows how the entire world can be changed at his slightest whim, how this whim suffices to unmask all people. The emperor of the Roman Empire becomes the puppet, the plaything, of an ordinary street walker who not only seeks to possess and dominate the emperor himself, but who also forces the total reversal of the empire's moral foundations, until finally even the Roman Senate, the most powerful body in the known world, is reduced to a ridiculous assemblage of obedient marionettes. The senators crown the prostitute as Empress. They lay all the provinces at her feet and praise her as the most virtuous of women. However, I do not find a rejection or a denial of moral values in this piece. It is much more a portrayal of Amor's power to break down all moral barriers.

Monteverdi shows what happens when Amor's sway is unconstrained, but he by no means says that the resulting condition of moral anarchy is desirable. He was certainly not moved by cynicism when he composed such an amoral book; perhaps the complex characters, the constantly changing psychological dilemmas and situations fascinated him. But most liklely he wanted to shock his audience by depicting the total victory of ruthlessness and amorality. He wanted to shake the ground beneath the viewer's feet and, *without showing him directly,* to let him see for himself where the absence of genuine love, empathy and order can lead. The title actually says a good deal: the courtesan is crowned as Empress, an insult to the legitimacy and dignity of the Senate and the Roman people: the impossible is made possible simply through a whim of Amor (Prologue).

Because of the way in which he planned his composition to illuminate character, Monteverdi strengthened the negative aspects of all of his major characters. It is noteworthy and shocking that not a single figure of so serious a drama is portrayed sympathetically, in a positive light. Ottavia, who is usually portrayed today as a tragic heroine, appears a cold, unemotional person as characterized by Nero, Seneca and her nurse. She reveals her true character as a disreputable blackmailer in the scene with Ottone; not only does she want to force him to murder his beloved Poppea, but she threatens him with defamation, torture and death if he fails to obey. Here we also see how Monteverdi works with a dramatic text by word repetitions, reversals and realistic musical-gestic diction: the word repetitions ("dammi aita [help me] / col sangue [with (Poppea's) blood] / vuo che l'uccida [I want you to kill her]) are never musically based, but always arise out of the immediate psychological situation. First the ever more desperate pleading for help, then the hesitation, and at the same time the growing sense of outrage at the terrible utterance ("voglio . . ."). Rests are every bit as important as the notes, e.g. the stunned reaction of Ottone. Every lightning change of thought and emotion is reflected in diction and music. If we compare the form of Busenello's dramatic poem with Monteverdi's realization, we see how close he came to his goal of imitating nature. Monteverdi has Ottavia hurl her furious "precipita gli indugi" into the middle of Ottone's verses after "Dammi tempo," [Give me time] preparing the way for her threat. This kind of realistic interruption can be found in many other passages as well.

Monteverdi treats Seneca, the second "honorable person" of the opera, even more brusquely. He is portrayed from the outset in the judgment of the people (soldiers, Valetto) as thoroughly unpopular and unlikeable. Monteverdi points up his vain and pompous pontificating ("la cote non percossa non puo mandar faville" [stee which is not tempered does not glisten]) in ordinary sequences, and occasionally with empty coloraturas in which none of the words are emphasized. The sententiousness of his answers and statements is accentuated by their stiff musical form.

Monteverdi uses every means at his disposal for the careful psychological portrayal of Nero and Poppea. Nero's split personality and Poppea's instability and calculating slyness offer every possibility for the most rapid shifts of emotions. Nero is both the Imperator, which is expressed in every imperious phrase, as well as a spoiled, stupid and immature playboy whose every wish is instantly gratified. In the scene with Seneca, he rebels for the first time against his mentor, the *éminence grise* at the court. Here Monteverdi uses the "concitato genere" which he invented for expressing the emotion of anger: fast sixteenth notes sung on one tone (Monteverdi describes the execution and effect of this technique in the preface to his eighth book of madrigals). After the death of Seneca, Nero, who regards himself a poet and musician, praises Poppea's charms in song with his poet friend Lucano, whereby he becomes so carried away that Lucano worries he may be losing his mind.

The various aspects of Poppea's character are revealed in the very first farewell scene: the wily, sensuous power with which she ensnares Nero, with which she forces him to return ("Tornerai?") is played in true courtesan fashion. Nero has hardly exited (Scene Four) when she rejoices ("Speranza . . ."): she will achieve her absurd goal of being officially crowned Empress of Rome. Poppea constantly vacillates between all too "genuine" feelings and calculated coldness: we need only look at the very erotic tenth scene of Act One, in which Poppea suddenly takes advantage of Nero's infatuation and denounces Seneca in the sweetest tones. These extraordinary musical characterizations probably underlay Monteverdi's enthusiasm for the opera; here he had fully unfolded his unique talent for music drama.

This variety of colorful characters, each displaying a wide range of emotions, is juxtaposed to a group of comic figures who comment on the main plot, which is both abstract and artificial as well as oppressively naturalistic. The figures of the vulgar sphere alone awaken our sympathy and understanding; they are rooted in the real world. They are not entirely likable, but we know that they have feelings, that they are authentic: the soldiers, Arnalta, the Nurse, Valletto and Damigella, as well as the three friends of Seneca (following Tacitus, Monteverdi writes for three persons, not for a chorus), who want to keep Seneca from death by means of a more comic than happy affirmation of life, and the consuls and tribunes, who in a stiff and ridiculous scene, undertake the formal, official coronation of the courtesan, revealing themselves as creatures of the Emperor. Monteverdi finds a very charming, madrigal-like, folkloristic tonal language for the comic figures and scenes which relates to the pathos of the serious figures only in a parodistic way.

The Libretto

In many passages, Monteverdi intervened in a dramaturgical sense in the libretto, as a comparison between the libretto and the musical score of the opera shows. The opera contains passages not found in the libretto, as well as cuts and reversals that clearly demonstrate Monteverdi's concern for the text. Neither Monteverdi nor Mozart (after *Idomeneo*) ever set a text to music for which they did not bear a significant amount of responsibility, which is attested to by the letters of both composers.

Busenello, Monteverdi's librettist, took the historical outline of his great libretto from the 14th book of the *Annals* of Tacitus. Monteverdi's work represents a carefully conceived interpretation of this libretto. Several scenes and figures are eliminated, including the fourth scene of Act Two which depicts the apotheosis of Seneca. He reduces the sixth scene of the second act to a duet between Nero and Lucano, and eliminates the courtiers Petronius and Tigellinus. The next (seventh) scene between Nero and Poppea is also eliminated. In the last scene, the dialogue between Amor and Venus (in the Venetian manuscript) and the chorus of amorettes (in the Neapolitan manuscript) are eliminated. In my view, this change reflects a very meaningful concentration undertaken by the composer himself. After Amor has intervened in the murder scene, there is no longer any need for the deus ex machina. Fate is fulfilled on a purely human level, and would only be called into question again by such an intervention. Amor has fulfilled his prophecy announced in the Prologue, and the action moves to the earthly, erotic final duet.

Many other smaller cuts and modifications in the Busenello text point to interventions by Monteverdi. For example: the first and second scenes are combined naturalistically, because Monteverdi has the first soldier begin before the last line of Ottone, while the second soldier, heavy with sleep, repeats the words of the first, "chi parla," in the middle of Ottone's last line. After that, too, they sing the two first stanzas in a dialogue-like fashion and simultaneously. In the third scene, Nero sings his first line directly after Poppea's fifth line; she then resumes from the beginning and continues at the sixth line; in this way the dialogue is enlivened. Nero's statement about Ottavia leads to two excited repetitions by Poppea. Poppea sings her "Tornerai?" three times during Nero's last stanza. In the fourth scene, Poppea repeats again and again the last two lines of the first stanza between the stanzas of Arnalta. In the tenth scene, Poppea goadingly repeats several times her and Nero's words about Seneca, thereby achieving an instantaneous death sentence. Scene Nine of Act Two has already been discussed (the extortion scene between Ottavia and Ottone).

The Edition
The situation confronting a musician who performs an opera by Monteverdi has already been discussed at length. In the case of *Poppea,* my setting is based on the two manuscripts of the opera preserved in Venice and Naples, as well as on the printed libretto. The two manuscripts are copies, prepared by unknown copyists during Monteverdi's lifetime, in which only the vocal parts and the accompanying bass are written out, almost without figures, as well as several short instrumental pieces. There is almost no information as to instrumentation, harmonies, tempos etc. It has not yet been possible to establish the relationship these two versions have to the missing autograph. It seems that the Neapolitan manuscript goes back to an earlier version of the work than does the Venetian manuscript. Several corrections in the latter appear to come from Monteverdi's pupil and competitor Cavalli. The "workshop" custom was evidently still so strong at the time that Monteverdi seems to have written several of his works with a group of collaborators. (Monteverdi had worked together with other composers: on *Ariana* possibly with Jacopo Peri; *Maddalena* with Salomone Rossi and Muzio Effrem; and *Adone* with Francesco Manelli.)

The Vocal Roles
All roles were cast in the original vocal register for our interpretation of "Poppea." Ottone accordingly is an altus, his weak character well portrayed by the vocal register, in contrast to the other figures. Nero is a

soprano part written for a castrato. He thus initiates a development which would become obligatory for later Baroque operas: the "main hero," the "primo uomo"—as unmasculine as he may be in this case—always occupies the highest register. Because of the great musical importance of the register, particularly of this role (the duets with Poppea, in which the voices are interwoven, the dialogue with Seneca, the duet with Lucano) and of the psychological extremes of this figure, this musically optimal solution also seems dramatically justifiable, especially since other transvestite roles and scenes appear in this work. Valletto is a true "trouser role," Arnalta, the "comical old woman," a true male role—it was customary in Venice for such roles to be sung by a tenor. In the scenic realization, however, I decided in favor of a transposition of the part of Nero to the tenor register, for reasons of dramaturgical credibility.

In this work, such a change is also musically justifiable, because the instrumental parts first had to be added; the orginal "score" contains only vocal parts and bass. In a Mozart opera, on the other hand, it would require a major modification of the score to rewrite a high voice part for tenor. A convincing proof of this is Mozart's approach in the Viennese concert version of *Idomeneo*. The modifications and interventions which the composer here had to undertake go far beyond a simple transposition of the vocal register.

The *Marian Vespers*
(Vespro della Beata Vergine)

Works of Art in Honor of the Virgin Mary

Works of art honoring the Mother of God have always held a special position in Western civilization. In religious painting, musical instruments played by angels were commonly depicted, especially in paintings of the Madonna, at a time when instruments were not yet officially permitted in the church. Many of these paintings, however, do not portray a realistic "church concert," but are intended allegorically, for usually the most common instrumental combinations of secular music are painted.

A true parallel to the painted Marys is "Marian music": compositions in honor of the Madonna. The setting to music of texts of the Song of Solomon and similar works had been since antiquity "more secular," more passionate and in any given age "more modern" than other church music, which was almost always conservative. Thus even Palestrina, who a generation before Monteverdi had set the standards for the stylistically strict and appropriate church music, writes in the preface to a collection of motets: "I have directed my muse here to poetry dedicated to the praise of the Holy Virgin, the Song of Solomon. I employed a more passionate style than in my other pieces of sacred music—this poetry seemed to require such a treatment . . ."

So it is certainly no coincidence that it was a Marian vesper in which for the first time in music history the traditional stylistic and musical framework was broken in every conceivable direction. In this revolutionary work, the innovations of modern Venetian instrumental music and of operatic style, then only a few years old and in which Monteverdi himself had played a decisive role, were applied for the first time to a major sacred vocal work.

The Vespers of Monteverdi

Monteverdi was of course familiar with all the innovations his colleagues in nearby Venice had made in the area of sacred music. Since 1591, he had held a position of "Suonatore di Vivuola" with Vincenzo I Gonzaga in Mantua, and had participated in numerous trips with the princely orchestra. Thus he had an opportunity to compare how music was made in different places and to draw inspiration from this experience. His *Scherzi musicali* of 1607 were inspired by the French style. Here he combines three instruments, two violins and a chordal instrument, with the three singing voices; the instruments must play not only the ritornellos between the stanzas, but also obbligato insertions during the singing. In *L'Orfeo,* his first opera written in 1607, he uses the shimmering palette of the Venetian canzone orchestra: violins, violas, cornettos and trombones are added to the continuo group of organo di legno, harpsichord, regal, lute (chitarrone), harp and low string instruments. In this context, it is interesting that Monteverdi, perhaps because he himself played the violin, was the first composer to dispense with the preponderance of wind instruments in this early Baroque orchestra in favor of the strings.

Monteverdi uses this very orchestra for his *Marian Vespers* as well. He even has the instruments play the almost identical independent sonata, or, as it is called there, toccata, at the opening chorus "Domine ad adjuvandum me festina," as at the beginning of *L'Orfeo.* This parallel between the opera and the sacred music goes beyond the elements of style and sound. In his *Vespers,* Monteverdi for the first time brings not only the operatic *style* into church, but also displays the operatic *orchestra* here in all its grandeur—in the very first piece with this literal quotation from *L'Orfeo!* In keeping with the custom of the time, the composer did not provide the interpreter with a performance-ready score. He neither wanted nor intended to do this, since such an approach would reduce the multitude of possible interpretations. Because of this, it is likely that, in those days, every performance of a major work was unique and characteristic.

Sound and Instrumentation
The sound aspects of Monteverdi's *Marian Vespers* and the tasks involved in their realization can be understood and solved only in terms of the historical context of this work. Our point of departure must be the instructions provided by Monteverdi in the entrance chorus, in the "Sonata sopra Sancta Maria ora pro nobis," and in the Magnificat, as well as the division into two spatially separated choruses, which appears to be mandatory for several sections of the work. Descriptions given by his contemporaries also provide us with precise information as to the ways in which separate works were set and performed at the time. Great attention was also paid to spatial location, particularly in this "theatrical" sacred music.

In the three parts of the *Vespers* mentioned, the following instruments are specifically called for: two violini da brazzo (violins), four viuole da brazzo (a generic term for various string instruments ranging in size from a present-day viola to a cello-like instrument), contrabasso da gamba (violone), three cornetti (cornetts), two flauti (recorders), two piffari (discant shawms), three trombones and organ. It is likely that several continuo instruments, such as the harpsichord, virginal, lute and dulcian, were also added to this instrumentarium. They are not expressly mentioned in the original printed score, but we know that in such large works, especially those designed for several choruses, the most varied continuo instruments had to be used, both in order to be able to assign a fundamental instrument to each chorus and to achieve the necessary tonal contrast.

The many monody-like solos call for a corresponding accompaniment; the lute emerges here as the instrument which soloists of the period used to accompany themselves, an approach necessitated by the rubato style of the monodies. The fact that in larger ensembles with wind players, appropriate wind instruments also had to play the bass with the organ and the harpsichord, even if they were not expressly demanded by the composer, is confirmed by Michael Praetorius in his *Syntagma Musicum* of 1619, which is devoted almost exclusively to the performance practice of contemporary Italian music: "It should also be especially noted . . . that it is very good, indeed, almost necessary, to have the general bass played with a bass instrument such as the bassoon, dulcian or trombone, or, best of all, with a bass violin which excellently helps adorn and strengthen the fundament."

No original score exists for Monteverdi's *Marian Vespers*. The work has been handed down in an edition of printed parts, supervised by the composer himself. Since the instrumental parts were printed separately in the vocal part books wherever they deviate from the voice parts, we can assume that the same musicians also played along with doubling the vocal part when it was deemed necessary by the maestro in a given performance. This is proved by various passages, such as the instruments which are suddenly left over in the ritornellos of "Dixit Dominus."

Most of the choruses of the *Vespers* are designed for two choirs; this means that the orchestra must be placed to support the double choir effect, without the musicians having to change their seats. Praetorius precisely describes the then current approach to the set-up and execution of these works written for multiple choirs: "When in a concert the one chorus [is played with] cornettos, another with violins, a third with trombones, flutes and such instruments," it is necessary to "use viols for one versiculo; trombones for the other; for the third flutes and bassoons." Regarding the placement of musicians, he says that he "has *ex observatione* also found it better if the same capella or chorus fidicinium (string group) be placed somewhat to the side of the organ, and place the concerted voices separately, seeing to it that the vocalists are not drowned out or muffled by the instruments, but rather that each can be heard and perceived distinctly from the rest. Attention should be paid to separating the boys and other concentores (who lead the concertato and other voice parts), as they are divided in the choruses, and where possible a fundament instrument should be assigned to each boy or each choro . . . The capella fidicina, however, must be placed on the side in such a way that it can come to the aid of all the boys and choruses." In this book, Praetorius provides not only the most precise description that we have of music-making at the time; he even refers in his instrumentation instructions specifically to Monteverdi's *Vespers!*

In the festive homophonic sections, such as the "et spiritui sancto" in "Laetatus sum" or in the magnificent concluding sections of the "Dixit Dominus," "Laetatus sum" and the Magnificat, the sound of the full string and wind orchestra must imbue the entire piece with magnificence and radiance. Praetorius compares this full sound of the entire chorus and orchestra to the full organ: "If the entire capella . . . makes music and, just as on an organ, joins in with the full instrument. This will result in music with glorious ornamentation, magnificence and splendor. . . . Such harmony will be even fuller and display even greater magnificence if one uses a large bass pommer, double bassoon or large bass viol (in Italian, Violone), and other instruments as well when they are available for the middle and upper voices." Joy in ostentation began to be a decisive factor during this time of the emerging Baroque style. Sound combinations of solo instruments with singing voices or different instruments, also in octaves, are described as promising special effects. The realm of sound, of timbre, had been discovered as a mode of expression, although it was not utilized primarily by the composer, but rather by the performer.

Such combinations should also be selected for various solos and solo passages in the *Vespers,* where strings or flutes or both together are played along with the soloists, for example in "Virgam virtutis" or "juravit Dominus" in the second chorus, or in "plena est omnis terra" in "Duo seraphim." The meaning of instrumentation in the manner of registers is especially clear in "Laetatus sum." In this piece, an eight-bar figure in quarter notes, "custom-designed" for the dulcian, recurs five times, expressing the perseverance of the journey to Jerusalem. Such figures were later called andante basses.

The double-choir movements are simpler in their instrumentation. One example is the ten-part "Nisi Dominus." Here the assignment of the dark strings to the first chorus and the bright flutes, trombones and dulcian to the second chorus creates clarity in the passages where the two choruses sing together, rhythmically interacting with each other. Another example is the eight-part "Ave Maris stella," in which the strings accompany the first chorus, piffaro, recorder and three trombones the second chorus. This principle should also be followed for the ritornelli; i.e. the first, as belonging to the first chorus, played with strings; the second, belonging to the second chorus, played by a recorder quartet with dulcian bass. Praetorius writes of this combination: "If one wants to use a flute chorus below and beside choruses of other instruments, I consider it better that a *QuartPosaun* [Bass trombone in F, a fourth below the normal tenor trombone] be added or, which is easier, a bassoon (dulcian)." The third repetition of the ritornello belongs to the first chorus, i.e. strings again, possibly with ornamentation.

As far as instrumentation is concerned, a very special place within the work is held by the "Sonata sopra Sancta Maria ora pro nobis" and the solo parts of the Magnificat. Here the instrumental part is given so much importance, even in terms of the composition, and is so polished that these pieces were instrumented by Monteverdi himself. This was done so precisely that it is not necessary to add anything other than the wind instrument which carries the cantus firmus. It is clear that these pieces involve solos which could not be doubled—although this often happens today, unfortunately. The meaninglessness of a doubling of the violin parts in the sonata, for example, is obvious if we consider that the two violin parts and the two cornett parts correspond to each other and alternate in pairs, even in the long solo sections. Doubling the violins would interfere with this polarity. Although we are accustomed today to hearing soloistic winds pitted against a powerful choir of strings in the modern orchestra, this relation was completely unknown at the time of Monteverdi. It is also unnatural, since solos can correspond only to solos, unless a true soli-tutti effect is desired, which is not the case here.

It is interesting that a high degree of virtuosity is demanded of instruments such as trombones, which today are rather inflexible. The sonata is a true instrumental dance (intrada and galliarda) for soloistic violins, cornettos, trombones and bass, to which the cantus firmus "Sancta Maria ora pro nobis" is sung independently. In other words, even without it the sonata would be a complete musical piece. In the solo sections of the Magnificat, a trombone or other wind instrument must play the choral cantus firmus together with the choral singers, as is the case in all choruses built above one or more cantus firmi, while the vocal and instrumental soloists sing or play their virtuosic passages. Predominantly instrumental and vocal pieces alternate regularly. Tutti and solo parts can be clearly differentiated in both the vocal and instrumental parts.

The succession of these parts follows a grand plan in which text interpretation and dramatic tonal contrasts are the critical elements. This work is highly theatrical because it employs a sophisticated disposition of timbres, as well as stage effects, such as the echos in "Audi coelum," which are fully exploited both musically and linguistically (gaudio—audio; benedicam—dicam; vita—ita).

The Instrumentarium

Because instruments of the period are not commonly used today, we should perhaps briefly discuss each of them, and also learn the opinion of a contemporary expert, Praetorius, who regarded Monteverdi's *Vespers* as an exemplary work.

The **violin**, which Monteverdi calls violino da brazzo, developed over the course of the 16th century, having demonstrated its usefulness in folk music. At that time it began its grand career as the leading solo instrument of the Baroque period and as the basis of the string orchestra.

Outwardly, it was already quite similar to the violin of today. Violins of this period are still played in concerts today, but their completely different internal construction, bass bars, neck position, bridge, stringing and bow all result in a fundamentally different sound. "The discant violin, the Italian violino, calls for beautiful passages, varied and long scherzi, *ripostine*, fine fugues, which are repeated and recapitulated in different places, graceful accents, quiet long strokes, groppo, trills, etc."* All of these features are found in abundance in Monteverdi's *Vespers.*

In the 17th century, **viola** was a generic term for a large number of instruments ranging from the viola to the cello; "viuola da brazzo" is used by Monteverdi to describe this group. The same is true of the design of these instruments as was said of the violin. Since only the viola (called "Bratsche" in German) is left of this group today, I would like to point out that at the time of Monteverdi there were several different kinds of violas, each of which was tuned differently. The largest was much larger than the largest violas in use today; the instrument could only be held and played by being supported on the *right* shoulder, and held across the chest to the left-hand side. Larger instruments could no longer be held "da brazzo" (on the arm), but had to be grasped between the knees, like the cello. Because such instruments were built in many sizes, the string orchestra displayed great variety and a great wealth of colors, particularly in the middle voices. The **cello,** which was the generally preferred bass instrument, was also called "viola da brazzo." This somewhat confusing name was intended to distinguish it from the "viola da gamba" and to document its relationship to the family of the violins and violas.

Even at that time, the **violone,** our present-day contrabass, was usually tuned in fourths. In order to produce complicated passages with great clarity, it was furnished with frets, like the viola da gamba. "The large bass viol, the foreign violone, goes very gravely and is appropriate for the low voices; with its sweet resonance it supports the harmony of the other voices . . ."

The **cornett** (Zink in German, cornetto in Italian) is a woodwind fingered like a recorder and blown like a trumpet, but its mouthpiece is much smaller. It is one of the most commonly used wind instruments of the 16th and 17th centuries: ". . . especially the zink (cornett) should not be mixed in and used in a quiet, good and sweet piece, but only in large-sounding music." In the *Vespers,* cornetts are called for both in the thundering tutti and in delicate solos, so we must assume that Monteverdi wrote these parts for very skilled soloists. Praetorius stresses that very difficult tasks can be assigned to these instruments: "Whoever can properly handle his Zink and similar instruments and control them is a master of his instrument. . . ."

* [Ed. footnote: Concerning groppo, trillo and other Baroque ornaments, see, for instance, the article "Ornamentation" in *The New Harvard Dictionary of Music.*]

The **trombone** of the period differs greatly from its modern relative: it had a much narrower bore and the bell joint was much smaller. The tone was thus slimmer and mixed wonderfully with string instruments, which were quite delicate at the time. However, it was also so flexible that complicated coloraturas could be produced on it. "Some (including Phileno, the famous Munich master) through intensive practice on this instrument have learned to reach the low D, and in the discant to play up to the c" d" e" without special effort and commotion. I have also heard a musician in Dresden, Erhardus Borussus, who is supposed to be in Poland at the present time; he had forced his instrument in such a way that on it he reached almost the height of a zink, namely the uppermost g" sol re ut; also the low range of a bass trombone, namely *A*, with so rapid coloraturas and skips, just as on the viol de bastarda or on a cornett." It is very likely that Monteverdi wrote his sonata with musicians like this in mind.

The **recorder** of the 17th century was made from a single piece of wood; its bore was more than twice as wide as that of the modern Baroque recorder. The sound of this instrument is full and velvety, sweet in the low tones, but very powerful in the high range.

The **dulcian** is the direct precursor of the bassoon. Its sound is soft and capable of modulation: "The dolcians, like the bassoons, (are) quieter and softer in their resonance . . .: for that reason they perhaps were called dolcianen quasi dulcisonantes because of their sweetness."

The discant shawm is called a **piffaro** and is a forerunner of the oboe. Only one functional scale can be played on this instrument, i.e. some half tones cannot be played. According to Praetorius, the sound of this instrument called to mind the "cackling of a goose."

It would seem proper that only instruments of an Italian design, and therefore having an Italian timbre, should be used as continuo instruments or "fundament" instruments, as they were called at the time. Praetorius writes of the style of playing the continuo: "Out of this general bass (part) or score he should play simply and straightforwardly, but as purely and precisely as possible, as the notes follow each other. Nor should he make many runs or coloraturas especially with the left hand which plays the fundament. But if he wants to introduce some speed or movement with the right hand, for instance in a sweet cadenza or other insertion, it must be done with great care and modesty, so that the concentores [singers] are not impeded and confounded in their intent, nor their voices thereby suppressed and obfuscated."

In addition to the keyboard instruments, the **lute** is very important as a continuo instrument for this type of music. "It is intended solely for use with a discant or tenor viva voce, like the viol de bastarda. (Because of its size and wide fingering, no coloraturas or diminutions can be played on it, but must be fingered as best one may.) At the same time it can also be used, and sounds very sweetly, with other instruments in an entire concert or otherwise along with the bass or instead of the bass."

These various instruments, the specialized knowledge of the musicians who play them, scrupulous precision in stylistic matters: all are for naught if such matters are regarded as ends in themselves and not as a means—although incomparably valuable—for allowing this music to come alive again in all of its vitality and brilliance. This and nothing else must be the ultimate objective and the final meaning of all our efforts, if we wish to render in sound the works of one of the greatest geniuses of the past centuries in a manner that communicates something of the spirit of his age.

Johann Sebastian Bach:
Discussions of Works

The Brandenburg Concertos

The Brandenburg Concertos have less in common with each other than the individual parts of any other collection of instrumental works with which I am acquainted. As strange as it may seem, their diversity is the very quality that fuses them into a whole. Each concerto is written for a distinctly different ensemble, and their diversity in formal terms is as extreme as in instrumental and stylistic aspects. In this work, the concertizing of a soloist or of a group of soloists, engaged in dialogue or "contest" with a ripieno group, perhaps a small string orchestra, is occasionally reduced to a purely formal idea that can be discerned only musically, as in the slow movement of the Fifth, in the entire Third and in the Sixth.

In the copy he dedicated to the Margrave of Brandenburg, Bach seems to have offered a catalogue demonstrating his breadth as an instrumental composer, with the objective of presenting the greatest possible diversity. This explains the remarkable fact that the only unifying elements in these concertos are the names of the composer and of the nobleman to whom they are dedicated.

In every regard, therefore, these six concertos represent the utmost in diversity, in variation. Variety appears to be the unifying element—it is much more important than unity.

The *First Brandenburg Concerto* is one of the earliest works in music history to exploit the possibilities of the natural horn as a solo instrument. The entrance of this instrument into the intimate sphere of art music must have caused a sensation. The hunting horn, corno di caccia, was chiefly used for the actual purposes of the hunt, signaling what was happening to the far-flung groups of hunters. This true "open-air" instrument was primarily played by hunters and their assistants. Travelling hunter-virtuosos were probably the first to play Bach's concerto, which is made quite clear by their entry in the first tutti, a genuine hunting fanfare, in which the eighth notes are adapted to the triplet hunting rhythm. The rest of the orchestra plays a quite "normal" Bach orchestral tutti, apparently unaffected by the horn signals so alien in rhythm and musical figures. The concertizing dialogue takes place in the alternation between the oboe and string groups (measures 6–7); after measure 9, the horns are used as equal concert partners: from the beginning Bach calls for the—in terms of intonation—extreme natural tones f, f-sharp and a (the 11th and 13th partials). Since the musical groups of tones or "figures" in this movement correspond to generally known patterns, Bach could allow the musicians to determine the necessary articulation, and so wrote no articulation slurs.

In the first movement, the concertizing takes place between true tutti blocks, like a confrontation, an animated dialogue of the three groups:

horns, woodwinds, strings.

In the second movement, the solo oboe, the violino piccolo (a small violin with a sharp, strange sound, which is tuned a minor third higher) and the bass group imitate each other on a subtly impressionistic tonal basis. Here the very unusual articulation is written out by the composer. The first four measures belong to the solo oboe, the harmony tones of which are harmonically reinforced by the second and third oboes and by the basses. The strings play along, with the bow vibrato that was so popular at the time for delicate passages. These four measures are repeated at the upper fifth by the violino piccolo, with the roles of the wind and string choirs now exchanged (the bow vibrato is now a "frémissement" of the winds). This passage exposes the material which will be developed. Now in a three-part sequence the theme is first taken up by the bass, with the chorus of strings and winds bringing a kind of accompanying theme in stretto. Then the solo oboe and the violino piccolo take up the theme in stretto, whereupon a three-bar transition follows. This sequence is repeated two more times—one has the impression that it could be repeated indefinitely—only to break off abruptly after the bass theme in the second repetition. The beginning of the expected stretto becomes an oboe cadenza, and in the unexpected close the three-chorus effect (bass, oboes, strings) is once again emphasized through alternating chords.

The third movement is a true concerto movement with six rondeau-like tutti blocks. The violino piccolo is the main soloist, seconded by the first horn and the first oboe. The second tutti, pianissimo, is a sound sensation (in movements of this type we expect each tutti entrance to be forte) marked by unusual oboe and violin solos. The fourth solo (violino piccolo and first ripieno violin) collapses in an adagio chord; it is brought to life again by a "false" attack of the rondo theme, with the actual tutti entry following four measures later. Although this movement has the character of a finale, it is followed by a minuet with the most varied kinds of trio combinations. It was quite customary at the beginning of the 18th century, for example in Handel's *Concerti Grossi,* to conclude very stirring concertos with a soothing minuet, probably to send the members of the audience on their way in a state of relaxation.

With its very rich rhetorical design, the *Second Brandenburg Concerto* is a complicated musical dialogue employing inversions and other artistic devices. Again and again there is an exchange of parts of the outer voices. The idiomatic quality of the instruments (the instrumentation of the solo quartet, all four of equal value, is extreme: a high natural trumpet, a recorder, an oboe, a violin—all of which represent the range of the possible ways of tone production) gives the impression of imitation because of the transfer of specific instrumental figures to the other instruments.

The first movement contains a number of pure tutti themes and several others which are used only by the solos. This alone is enough to create a dialogue. Bach provided no dynamics, which indicates that he expected the usual dynamic relations of his day to be employed (which differ from those of our own time): the solos were played piano, the tutti normally forte. The soloist did not need to struggle against the tutti, because he was not accompanied by the full orchestra, but was rather engaged in a dialogue with it. In response to the challenging first statement of the tutti there followed the reactions or "objections" of the individual solo instruments and thereupon the reaction of the tutti. In these different statements it is important that articulation is handled differently in the different voices at the same time. Bach sometimes writes this out explicitly in the notes. Through a different articulation in the different voices, the uniqueness of the individual instruments becomes clearer, the overall sound more diversified. Bach evidently also expects the articulation to change when a figure appears several times, because it always has a different meaning within the rhetorical context. Analogy as it is normally understood today, i.e. that a similar passage is to be performed the same at every recurrence, is not customary in Baroque music. Here, because of the relationship to speech, the manifold possibilities of execution are actually sought out and employed.

The second movement has a double affect: one comes from the bass, the other from the solo instruments. The designation "andante" refers here primarily to the bass, which moves in continuing eighth notes which must be played evenly. Bach uses this ostinato evenness as a counterweight to the strong expressiveness of the three upper voices.

The third movement begins with a trumpet solo which diverges from the tradition of the Baroque concerto movement and of Baroque rhetoric, for the statement which begins such a movement is normally performed by the tutti and called into question by the solo. Here the previous movement leads directly to this solo, which thus is an answer to the last figure of the second movement. These two movements should therefore not be separated by a pause. The tutti in the third movement functions only as a continuo accompaniment, the thematic material is exclusively developed by the soloists and the bass. In terms of the dramatic structure of the piece, this means that the entire final movement represents an agreement to the challenge of the first movement.

While the most varied combinations of brass and woodwinds, strings and harpsichord are used in the first, second, fourth and fifth concertos in a variety that is entirely unique and fantastic for the period, the third and sixth concertos are written exclusively for string instruments. In the *Third Brandenburg Concerto* the entire violin family is presented. I know no other work in musical history in which this principle of representing an instrument type is carried out as rigorously as here: three violins, three violas and three cellos—a combination which can be understood only out of a fanatical obsession with numbers (the tutti sections are consistently in three parts, and each part is again subdivided into three parts)—concertize to an accompanying basso continuo of violone (contrabass) and harpsichord.

In this concerto, all conceivable possibilities of the "solo" and "tutti" principle are utilized and represented: from the true solo of a single instrument to the accompanied solo, to the concertizing dialogue of different instrumental groups to the three-part tutti, in which the three instruments of each of the three groups play their part at the same time, orchestrally, in unison. In the first tutti (to measure 8), each group begins with a different theme. Together with a later newly-introduced theme (first violin, measures 78–79), these three themes form the material which gives to this movement its great harmonic and rhetorical richness employing exchange of parts, all kinds of divided parts, and variation. Each of these themes has numerous subdivisions, just as in speech, primary and secondary clauses are separated through punctuation marks. Such separations are found, for example, in the middle of the second measure, at the beginning of the fourth measure, and so on. Thus, already in the first eight measures we observe repeated alternation of staccato and legato, because the statements of the corresponding clauses demand different degrees of hardness and softness. This demand of the treatises of the 18th century is confirmed again and again through the complex nature of the themes of the large compositions. The first solo (beginning with the upbeat in measure 9 to measure 12) brings a harmonized soloistic version of the first violin theme, which is played here by all three groups, broken down into the smallest parts; the second to fifth eighths of the tenth measure are a tutti insertion to which the violins react soloistically, with a new scale theme (the middle of measure 10 to measure 12), while the cellos and violas accompany with a harmonized variation on the original bass theme (middle of measure 2 to measure 4). This solo episode is answered (measures 12–15) by the second half of the opening tutti (measures 4–8). Now the second solo follows (middle of measure 15 to measure 19); it is constructed rather like the first. Here, too, there is a tutti interruption in the second to fifth eighth in measure 17; however, here and in the following scale motive, the violas now play the violin part of the first solo, while the violins and cellos play the variant of the harmonized bass theme as accompaniment. In the following tutti (measures 19–20), the voices of the opening measures are exchanged; the violin theme is now played by the violas; the violins play the viola theme; for the time being, the cellos still play their own theme.

I hope these brief explanations serve to highlight an aspect of the design of this concerto that has received little attention. It seems to me to demonstrate quite clearly how the three different members of the violin family may be juxtaposed and compared with each other. Furthermore, we clearly see Bach's ability to distinguish "solo" and "tutti" in a work in which each part calls for only a single instrument, although all the instruments always play. It is accomplished with purely musical means of musicianship—a quite remarkable display.

In this concerto, Bach dispenses with a slow movement and uses two chords as a link between the two allegro movements, between which a small cadenza should probably be improvised. In this pure string concerto, this cadenza may be played only by one or several of the string soloists.

The second allegro contains almost no dialogue at all, which is very unusual in a Baroque concerto movement. Like a kaleidoscope the harmonies change, by half measures or by quarters (the 12/8 time is to be understood as triplet 4/4 time), while scurrying scales (in sixteenths), bell-like tone repetitions (in eighths) and complicated, interlocked spiccato triads (in sixteenths) jump back and forth between the single voices and voice groups. True concertante solos are found only in the second part (measures 15–17) for the first violin and (measures 35–37) the first viola.

In the *Fourth Brandenburg Concerto,* the designation "flauti d'echo" seems confusing at first. High piccolo flutes were occasionally used for this part, but they are much louder than the usual recorders, so that in such a case the orchestra really became an echo. It seems very likely, therefore, that normal recorders are meant. In the first movement, the roles of the concertino, the soloist group, are clearly distributed: the main soloist is the violin, seconded by the pair of recorders which later are further emphasized by a lyrical solo group (measures 157–185 and 285–311). The echo effect in the second movement may have been so important for Bach that he referred to it in the title of the concerto. The idea of the echo here is a repeated interruption of the melody, which would progress continuously without these echo insertions. The echoes are placed in those places in which one would in a sentence have to insert a comma; they force the listener to sit up and take notice. The effect apparently intended by Bach can be achieved only if the flutes are actually played at a distance or from a side room. In passages where they are treated independently (as in measure 4), the orchestra must compensate for this by playing more softly.

The andante designation of the second movement evidently applies here to the tempo and not to an "andante" character. The slow movement thus should be given a certain acceleration, with the pairs of eighth notes played unevenly (inégale). In this movement, the perfectly symmetrical arrangement is critically important; it corresponds roughly to the architecture of a Baroque palace and is frequently used by Bach in his large works as well. Four outer parts are grouped like a frame around a central piece (here measures 28–45), of which the first and the last differ only in an exchange of the outer voices. The second and fourth parts also correspond to each other, except that the echo passages in the fourth part seem compressed. The middle part contains new material and a new dialogue, because the recorders here are given solo statements. In the fifth part, the theme lies in the bass, the echoes of the first part (which corresponds symmetrically to it) are omitted; in the repetition they would have no meaning because the effect would no longer be fresh. It is very important for the interpretation to recognize this symmetry; the piece is played differently than if the parts were simply lined up behind each other.

Although the third movement must be attached directly to the preceding one, the recorder players have time to return to their places, because they do not begin to play again until measure 23. In this movement, all the thematic material is drawn from the first four measures.

The *Fifth Brandenburg Concerto* is the most modern of the six concertos, in terms of both its instrumentation and form. It is the first "clavier" concerto in music history (if we understand clavier correctly as the general term for a keyboard instrument). The two other solo instruments, subordinated in rank to the harpsichord, are the violin—an exemplary solo instrument throughout its development—and the transverse flute, which at that time had begun to replace the brilliant recorder. This tendency probably reflects the emergence of the "galant" and "empfindsam" or sensitive styles. As a solo instrument, the transverse flute was thus quite modern; its somewhat veiled tone, with rich tonal and dynamic nuances, was ideally suited for the new trend. Up to this time, its possibilities had never been completely recognized or exploited, but over the course of the 18th century the flute became the most popular of all solo instruments.

We must consider the role assigned to the harpsichord at the beginning of the 18th century in order to understand how striking its use in the *Fifth Brandenburg Concerto* must have been for listeners at the time, as well as to grasp the creative boldness underlying Bach's use of this idea. At that time the harpsichord was used only for solo music, rather like the organ, with which it was largely interchangeable. (The main focus was on the presentation of music composed in several voices, in the strict style; a keyboard instrument was not yet regarded as a "melody instrument.") Moreover, in chamber music and orchestral music, as well as in opera, the harpsichord was used for the basso continuo, i.e. it had to play all lowest voices and fill in and clarify the harmony. Because of the metallic plucked sound, an additional desired effect resulted: a rhythmical, structural quality which was necessary for much of the music of the 17th and 18th centuries. Because of this sound, which was very pronounced in the ensemble, rules developed for continuo playing which called above all for circumspection. The accompaniment was supposed to fill in, but never draw attention to itself, neither through artistic skill nor prolific passage work; imagination was to be shown in the style of playing legato passages and arpeggios. To this instrument, and naturally thereby also to himself as its player, Bach thus dedicated his first "Versuch" or attempt to juxtapose the concertizing *and* accompanying harpsichord to a small orchestra and two additional soloists. He found a thoroughly idiomatic tonal language especially for this instrument, and by assigning to the violin and the flute the same thematic material and the same musical figures, he moved the *tonal* differences of these instruments into the foreground. Different thematic material is consistently assigned to the ripieno, the orchestra, and the solos. The first eight-measure tutti is constructed like a complex rhetorical statement:

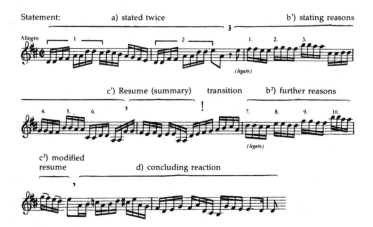

We might use a linguistic comparison to clarify just how this works:

a) the garden is beautiful 1) and large 2);
b1) (because) trees and flowers grow in it ... (1, 2 etc.),
c1) so it is a success!
b2) It also shelters deer and birds, etc. (7, 8)
c2) That is good
d) we are happy that we have such a garden.

The short tutti insertions also refer back to the parts of the first tutti:

a) measures 10, 13, 19, 35–37, 44, 49, 101–102, 109–110, 112–115;
b1, 2) measures 29–30, 40–41, 58, 59;
c) measures 31, 41 and 60;

the first part of the tutti theme is interrupted twice by a solo interjection (measures 12 and 113). The solo instruments react with new, very song-like themes which, however, are broken down by the harpsichord idiomatically into small note values. Only from measure 21 on do the violin and flute play a simplified sigh motive from the opening tutti; after measure 61, d) the tutti is taken (somewhat modified) into the solo vocabulary. From measure 71 on, the dialogue changes into a tone game.

For this Bach demands the bow vibrato of the ripieno violins and the viola, which he used so frequently, while the flute and the solo violin, over walking basses of the cello and chord arpeggios of the harpsichord, pass back and forth a very short, static theme. The wavy line notated in the flute and violin parts towards the end of this kaleidoscopic tonal game seems to call for a vibrating glissando—perhaps executed as a two-finger vibrato, which corresponds approximately to a quarter tone trill, rather than a regular trill. (To the best of my knowledge, Bach writes the sign only above chromatic progressions, probably indicating glissando. French contemporaries used it for a very wide vibrato.) In any case, this chromatic step is stressed here in an exciting manner, in pianissimo!

The slow movement is also composed in strict accordance with the concerto scheme, and the unchanged trio scoring is the special attraction. Solo and tutti are set off from each other only by differing themes, dynamics and different manners of playing. In the tutti sections, the harpsichord plays a continuo in the traditional sense, indicated by Bach by "accomp." and figuration. Five tutti sections are juxtaposed—seen superficially—to four solo sections. In truth, however, there are also five solo sections, because the fourth solo consists of two solo sections which are played without a pause. After the fourth solo section ending in measure 39, we wait in vain for the entry of the tutti. The listener is thus shaken out of his expectation and prepared for the imminent concluding finale.

The concluding allegro is imbued with the rhythm of the gigue and with hunting themes. In the course of the 18th century this basic rhythm became very fashionable for final movements of symphonies. Bach writes this 6/8 rhythm in 2/4 time with triplets

$$\text{♫♫ ♫♫} \text{, whereby (♫)}$$

dotted eighth and sixteenths should be adapted to the triplets. This notation is based on the rules for accentuation generally accepted at the time.

$$^{6}/_{8} \text{ ♫♫ ♫♫}$$

would have to be played with two accents that differ in strength;

$$^{2}/_{4} \text{ ♩ ♩}$$

has an accented and unaccented part of the measure. Naturally, this also affects the tempo. In this movement, the thematic material is the same for tutti and soli. One passage (after measure 79) is especially interesting: first, one of the solo instruments (at first the flute, after measure 89 the solo violin, after measure 99 the harpsichord) play, and later (after measure 148) the ripieno violins and the viola play a cantabile melody formed from the beginning of the theme and accompanied by two or three instruments soloistically in broken triads. Thus the ripieno players also participate in the solo material. This movement is constructed like a da capo aria: the repeat begins in measure 233, the fermata indicating the end is in measure 78.

The *Sixth Brandenburg Concerto* is basically similar to the *Third* in its scoring and style. Departing from the Baroque tradition, it is written exclusively for low instruments; the solo instruments are two violas. Providing contrast to them, predominantly in the tutti, are two gambas. Violas and gambas have more or less the same tonal range. Thus Bach juxtaposed them here as exponents of the two competing families of instruments, the violin family and gamba family. Moreover, since the mid-17th century the gamba had been the most distinguished solo instrument, together with the violin; the sound of the former had been compared to the "nasal voice of a diplomat." The gamba was never used in the orchestra, and Bach himself, with the exception of the *Sixth Brandenburg Concerto,* wrote only solos for it. This aristocratic solo gamba is here demoted to a lowly tutti instrument by the viola, of all instruments, a genuine and purely orchestral instrument, for which no solos had ever been written, and which to this time had not been thought of as a virtuoso instrument, as in the first and third movements, or as an expressive melodic instrument, as in the second movement. In the first half of the 18th century, an intense rivalry developed between the noble gamba—which was played delicately and nasally in salons for a refined circle of listeners—and the violin or the violoncello—which, with their loud, extroverted sound, could be played in large halls or even outdoors. It was often noted (Le Blanc *Defense of the Viola da Gamba*) that the brutal, vulgar violins with their thick strings were displacing the gambas. In this concerto, Bach confirms the victory of the violin family by allowing the gamba to be dethroned, not by the violin, but by the viola, the lowliest of all of the instruments of the family.

In this concerto as well, the solo-tutti division is again achieved primarily through musical and dynamic means, not through true soloistic playing. Tutti and solo themes are strictly differentiated. The first tutti consists of an inexorable, almost brutal competition between the two violas for the correct meter: the two voices chase after each other at the distance of only an eighth note, and we get the impression that each of the two instruments stubbornly wants to establish the downbeat. The other instruments play a hard, completely neutral accompaniment in evenly stamping eighth notes (only Bach could permit himself such a scorned way of writing), allowing neither of the violas to win. All six tutti sections in this movement are designed in strict accordance with this principle. In the first solo, which begins at measure 17 with the violoncello, elegance and volume are determined by the imitating gambas where they are included in the solo work, which is otherwise given to the violas and the violoncello. The second solo ends (measures 40–46) with a new interpretation of the first solo theme:

1st solo motif, m.17

new version, m.40

Through the seventh upbeat (instead of the leap of a fourth) the avoidance of through-imitation in the other voices and through the soft, chordal accompaniment by means of bow vibrato, piano, this theme now becomes a genuine solo with a highly expressive cantabile character which contrasts sharply with the following tutti. The means Bach uses to extract the greatest possible contrasts from this ensemble, which actually greatly lacks significant contrast, are noteworthy. The last tutti repeats the first, like a da capo, only shifted by a half measure. This shift, which occurs quite frequently in the works of Bach, as well as in the symphonic movements of Viennese classicism, shows that a measure is not necessarily defined by the bar line. The accents must here be the same in the first and last tuttis. Bach refrained, probably for notational reasons, from inserting a 2/4 measure before the last tutti (middle of measure 114).

The second movement is a duet of the two violas competing above an interesting split basso continuo: violone (contrabass) and harpsichord—the latter probably also an octave lower—play a bass conceived as a countermelody, which is broken up by the cello in quarter notes, andante. Very intense passing dissonances arise from this, but also impart to the movement a clear rhythmical gait. Then, in measure 40, the basses take up the theme, with the violas reacting in seemingly astonished confusion. Finally, the cello plays, we might even say usurps, the cadence (actually amounting to a cadenza) by means of a deceptive cadence (measures 54–55), and the conclusion of the movement, fading away, leads directly into the allegro finale.

Here, already in the first tutti, as in the first movement, the rhythm and meter are very clearly defined and at the same time called into question. Even though the movement begins with an upbeat involving a skip, it is already attached through syncopation to the third measure, so the violas seem to begin the measure on the last eighth. The chords played decisively against this, on the beat, by all others result, as in the first movement, in a struggle for the "right" measure. In this movement the gambas are completely excluded from the solo realm, which the violas especially, but also the cello, claim for themselves.

A few words in conclusion about the violone: in the 18th century the designation contrabass was quite rare; the large instrument of the violin and gamba family was usually called "violone." The cello also was often called by this name. In order to make things even more confusing, some German sources from the early 17th century designate only the six-string contrabass *gamba* as violone—and this very specialized nomenclature was unfortunately adopted by many present-day authors. In using sources from the time of Bach, clarity can be achieved, if at all, only from the notes, i.e. musically, not from names. The principle question is, of course, whether the violone part is to be played "loco," like a cello part or transposed down an octave, as a contrabass. In the Brandenburg Concertos, this question constantly comes up since Bach treated the "violone" part by no means in a uniform fashion. Thus in the *First Brandenburg Concerto* the part is called "violono grosso" and is always notated in the same register as the cello and bassoon. For this purpose Bach uses the lowest line of the score and also has the continuo— probably the harpsichord—play the same part *loco*. In the *Second Brandenburg Concerto* it is called "violone ripieno," i.e. orchestral bass. This part is notated in the next to the lowest line, because the bottom line is reserved for harpsichord and cello. Here there are in any case several solo accompaniments, for which Bach evidently did not intend the "violone."

I believe that Bach wanted true "contrabasses" for all six concertos, which originally must have been different instruments, or at least differently tuned. The violone parts are notated in various ways; thus we can recognize that Bach had a contrabass with low $\overline{C}$ for the first, second and third concertos; in the fourth and fifth concertos, the lowest tone of the instrument was evidently $\overline{D}$, which can be recognized by the fact that some passages are transposed upwards. In the sixth concerto, Bach even calls for a low $\overline{B}$-flat (last movement, measure 45); here the $\overline{C}$ string was probably tuned down for the movement or even for the entire concerto.

Since the contrabass part was normally derived in an undifferentiated way from the general bass part (cello, bassoon, harpsichord), the consistently written-out part in the Brandenburg Concertos is particularly informative; thus there are passages (e.g. measures 25, 26 and elsewhere in the second concerto), where Bach writes cello and bass in octaves, which, with the contrabass, become double octaves, a usage normally unnoticed today, probably because most contrabasses only go down to $\overline{E}$ and and musicians automatically transpose up the tones that lie below. This very important and pronounced effect also occurs in the fourth concerto (measures 29–30; 154–156), in the fifth (in many places) and sixth Brandenburg Concertos. In the latter two there are even triple octaves (fifth concerto, measure 134; sixth concerto, measure 65 ff.) Occasionally the continuo bass part is notated in the upper octave, which results in unisons, sometimes even two octaves higher, so that the contrabass sounds an octave higher than the cello.

We can therefore see, particularly in this score, the instruments Bach had at his disposal or wished to have (apparently different ones) and what variety he used in his registration (whether 8' loco, 4' upper octave, 16' lower octave or 32' two octaves lower than the cello part).

The *St. John Passion*

In the early years of the Christian church, from about the 4th century on, it was customary to read or sing, on the reciting tones, the story of the Passion of Christ as part of the Palm Sunday and Holy Week liturgies. Four clergymen usually participated: one sang the part of the narrator; the second sang the words of Christ; the third the utterances made by various persons such as Pontius Pilate, Peter, the High Priest, the woman, and so on; with the fourth singing the exclamations of the people. Sometime in the 9th century, a type of performance instruction based on letters of the alphabet was invented: for the evangelist, c=celeriter, or accelerated; for the words of Christ, t=tenere, held or sustained; for the other persons, s=sursum, or upwards (meaning these passages were to be sung higher). Other differentiating marks were added during the course of time. Even after the Reformation, the Passion continued to be sung in Lutheran churches in a similar way. Very soon thereafter, German Passion compositions were introduced which contained alternating monophonic and polyphonic parts, sung by the pastor and the choir. The forms became ever more varied, and free adaptations of the Passion were composed in the polyphonic style. Occasionally, the texts of the four gospels were combined.

German Passion compositions were written by almost all of the important composers of the late 16th and 17th centuries. An increasing number of songs (chorales) were inserted into the story of the Passion, which were often sung by the congregation. In the second half of the 17th century, the new Baroque forms of music drama arriving from Italy began to be utilized for Passion settings as well. Lyrical poetry and contemplative songs were frequently added to the biblical passages, and at times, sections of the biblical texts were even adapted, freely and poetically. Finally, after about 1700, the entire story of the Passion was adapted in the manner of a libretto (Menantes' "Der blutende und sterbende Jesus," B. H. Brockes "Der für die Sünde der Welt gemarterte und sterbende Jesus"); the emotionally charged language and dramatic form offered the most far-reaching possibilities for musical interpretation. Alongside these, the purely biblical Passion composition, which alone could be used in the liturgy, continued to be written and sung.

At the forefront of this development was the city of Hamburg, where Georg Philipp Telemann, Johann Mattheson, Reinhard Keiser, and George Frideric Handel (before he emigrated to England) were active. These men provided vigorous impulses to the city's musical life in every conceivable way, including concerts, operas and festival music. In Leipzig, where the cantor of the St. Thomas School was also the music director of the city, the situation was quite different. In cooperation with the city council, the music director was in charge of the music at four churches and also had to compose representative music for the city's official celebrations, although he had no responsibility for operas as Leipzig had no opera. The structure of the city's musical life was conservative—and so it was not until 1721, under Bach's predecessor Johann Kuhnau, that for the first time a modern form of Passion with polyphonic music was performed. Until that time, only the traditional chanted Passion performances were employed.

The *St. John Passion* was the first large-scale work that Bach wrote for Leipzig, the new locus of his professional life. Whether he had already composed it in Köthen and performed it on Good Friday 1723, prior to his officially assuming office in Leipzig, or a year later, has not been established with complete certainty. We know, however, that this work is the fruit of his activities in Köthen in both an intellectual and formal sense. Here, for the first time, Bach uses in a sacred work all the special refinements of the concertized style and of the instrumentation he had developed and tested in his many concertos, suites and sonatas.

Since the work was intended to be used in the Good Friday liturgy, the vesper service with sermon, the biblical text of the Passion—the 18th and 19th chapters of the Gospel of St. John which had to be used in its entirety—formed the textual basis. Bach supplemented this text with two passages from the Gospel according to Matthew: 26:75 "Da gedachte Petrus an die Worte Jesu..." and 27:51 "Und siehe da, der Vorhang im Tempel zerriss..." By including contemplative texts and song stanzas, Bach was able to redistribute the formal musical accents, which were largely predetermined by the various roles in the biblical text. Since he was not then collaborating with a writer, he took these texts from various poetical settings of the Passion and rewrote them himself. The contemplative character of these pieces was especially important to him, and for this reason he reshaped expressions that were overly personal so that they took on a more generalized quality. He tried to soften expressions that were especially crude or graphic. Bach's primary sources were the poetical works of Barthold Heinrich Brockes, a Hamburg city councilman ("Der für die Sünde der Welt gemarterte und sterbende Jesus, aus den vier Evangelien in gebundener Rede vorgestellet") and a St. John Passion by Christian Heinrich Postel. Brockes' work was widely known through musical compositions by Keiser, Telemann, Handel and Mattheson, while Postel's St. John Passion was put to music by Handel in 1704. We know that Bach was involved with this work in Köthen. The text of the arias "Von den Stricken meiner Sünden," "Eilt ihr angefochtnen Seelen," "Mein theurer Heiland," "Mein Herz, in dem die ganze Welt," "Zerfliesse, mein Herze in Fluten der Zähren" and the final chorus "Ruht wohl, ihr heiligen Gebeine" resulted from arrangements of texts by Brockes. The following juxtaposition of the text of an aria will indicate the way in which Bach approached this type of adaptation:

Brockes: Have the deep wounds of my soul been bound up by your wounds? Can I enter into Paradise because of your suffering and death? Is salvation near for the whole world? These are the questions of the Daughter of Zion. Jesus, in great agony, cannot answer; but he nods his head: "Yes."

Bach: My dearest Savior, let me ask you, as you are nailed to the cross and have said "It is finished:" have I been freed from death? Because of your pain and dying, may I inherit the kingdom of heaven? Has salvation come to the whole world?—Because of your great agony you cannot answer; but you nod your head and silently reply: "Yes."

The text of the chorale "Durch dein Gefängnis, Gottes Sohn" is taken from Postel's Passion, where it is the text of an aria. Bach changed only one word in the second verse, thereby altering the meaning of the text: instead of "muss" (must) he uses "ist" (is) so that the phrase reads "ist uns die Freiheit kommen."

Friedrich Smend was the first to convincingly describe the way in which the musical construction of the *St. John Passion* follows an ingenious formal design. The chorale "Durch dein Gefängis, Gottes Sohn, ist uns die Freiheit kommen" is the center, the core of the entire work. Grouped around this chorale, which explains the meaning of the events of Christ's passion like a brief sermon, are choruses of identical or very similar musical design, like the wings of a Baroque palace. Each of the two lyrical parts "Betrachte"-"Erwäge" and "Eilt, ihr angefochtnen Seelen" forms a group with two flanking choruses. These groupings correspond precisely to each other. This core begins and ends with chorales:

Chorale "Ach grosser König"
Chorus "Nicht diesen sondern Barrabam"
    "Betrachte"—"Erwäge"
Chorus "Sei gegrüsset, lieber Jüdenkönig"
Chorus "Kreuzige, kreuzige!"
Chorus "Wir haben ein Gesetz"

Chorale "Durch dein Gefängnis, Gottes Sohn"

Chorus "Lässest du diesen los"
Chorus "Weg, weg mit dem, kreuzige!"
Chorus "Wir haben keinen König"
    "Eilt, ihr angefochtnen Seelen"
Chorus "Schreibe nicht: der Jüden König"
Chorale "In meines Herzens Grunde"

The sections before and after this middle part of course are not as completely consistent in terms of symmetry, but correspondences can be clearly recognized which underscore the character of a grandiose framework. The opening chorus and final chorus (the last chorale does not belong here; for it represents the thoughts of Christians after the reading of the Passion); the pair of choruses, "Wäre dieser nicht ein Übeltäter" and "Wir dürfen niemand töten," is at the end of the front part of the frame, to which the chorus "Lasset uns den nicht zerteilen" at the beginning of the back part of the frame corresponds. The accumulation of arias in the beginning and final sections is thus explained in a meaningful way. This powerful structure with its wonderful architectural quality clearly raises Bach's first Passion well above those of his predecessors and contemporaries, who contented themselves with a simple stringing together of the individual numbers. The biblical Passion text does not lend itself to a meaningful musical formation, since the people's choruses, especially important for an audible division, are by no means arranged according to formal musical considerations. Despite these very difficult problems, Bach created a work not only possessing the deepest musical expression in detail, but also revealing a convincing and monumental overall structure.

Bach performed his *St. John Passion* about four times during the course of his career in Leipzig. He changed certain details for each performance. Sometimes these changes represented improvements, but at other times they were simply adjustments in keeping with new situations. These changes have come down to us in various parts used in Bach's performances. They give us a fairly clear idea of how he modified his wishes to reflect practical possibilities. He recorded the final version of the work in a score written during the last years of his life. Bach wrote the first 20 pages himself, leaving the rest to be completed by one of his students. However, this latter part contains numerous corrections in Bach's own handwriting.

Since the orchestra available to Bach consisted in part of students, with a constant turnover of players, the master had to adapt his instrumentation to new sets of performing conditions: once he used oboes d'amore instead of oboes da caccia, muted violins instead of violas d'amore. Instead of the lute he once used a harpsichord, at another time the organ. Of course, these were emergency solutions resorted to so the work could be performed at all; they were dropped when no longer needed. But Bach also introduced a few genuine improvements; he had a bassoon play with the cellos in all of the choruses and a few of the arias; he wrote "Tutti li strumenti," meaning that all instruments should play along in the tenor aria "Ach mein Sinn," which was originally accompanied only by string instruments (as is usually the case today, oddly enough), but, judging from a preserved bassoon part, probably only the introduction, the interludes and the postlude. The very precise forte and piano markings in this aria can only be meant as tutti (with winds) and solos (only strings), as was common at the time. In the choruses "Sei gegrüsset, lieber Jüdenkönig" and "Schreibe nicht: der Jüden König" he had the flutes and oboes represent the howling of the mob. But playing in a key which then was difficult for wind instruments, they were not loud enough. Bach therefore added several but "not all" the violins.

There has been much debate over the last 100 years concerning the extent to which the organ or the harpsichord was and should be used for the continuo. Although the discussion is very likely to continue, at present it is assumed with a fair amount of certainty that in his sacred works, Bach basically preferred the organ, even for the recitatives. But when necessary, when an organ could not be used (as in a repetition of the *St. Matthew Passion*) or when he had no lute (as in the second or third performance of the *St. John Passion*), he turned to the harpsichord, which was viewed as a "worldly" instrument, used primarily in opera and for chamber music, but which was available in the Leipzig churches.

Musicologists have also hotly debated the question of whether the chorales were also sung by the congregation or were performed solely by the choir and the orchestra. This question has been difficult to resolve because we know today that in some places, including Hamburg, chorales, which were set to music in a rather simple fashion, at that time were also sung by the people. However, it is unthinkable that Bach's congregation joined in the singing of the chorales. They were not even included in the printed texts of the Passions. Nor could the congregation have sung along; the chorales vary so greatly in their range, and some are much too high to be sung by an untrained group. Moreover, Bach's subtle ornamentations, which differ in each chorale, could not be sung by ordinary folk. It is completely unthinkable to the musically trained person that Bach's incredibly fine and often extremely complicated harmonic and rhythmical structures would have been condemned to be drowned and destroyed in the singing of the congregation. One might also reflect on the faulty harmonies which would result in these wonderful compositions through octave doubling (when a congregation sings, the men usually sing the melody one octave lower, thus at times singing even lower than the bass!). These chorales were never intended to be sung by the congregation; rather, they symbolize the congregation in the overall context of the Passion composition. The description published in the Saxon pastor Christian Gerber's *Historie der Kirchen Zäremonien in Sachsen* has often been applied, certainly with little justification, to Bach's Passions. Gerber wrote: "The story of the Passion, which was heretofore sung so de simplici et plano, simply and piously, is now played with many instruments in a most artful way, and at times mixing in a setting of a Passion hymn, which the entire congregation sings, and with many instruments playing along. When this Passion music was played for the first time in a distinguished city [probably

Dresden] with twelve violins, many oboes, bassoons and other instruments, many people were astounded and did not know what to make of it. Many high ministers and noblewomen were present at a chapel for nobility and sang the first Passion hymn from their books with great devotion: when this theatrical music began, all these people were extremely amazed . . ." During Bach's lifetime, it is unlikely that his music was perceived as theatrical or operatic, although it was regarded as very demanding. Bach himself would never have tolerated "theatrical" music in church. Moreover, under the terms of his contract he was explicitly obliged "to arrange the music so that it does not appear operatic, but rather induces contemplation in the listeners." The "noblewomen" in Dresden were thus probably shocked by a completely different piece of music.

Bach had to rely in Leipzig on an ensemble that was almost scraped together. He had a chorus of no more than 24 singers, boys and young men, including the soloists for the Passion performances. Like all boys' choirs, the composition of this group changed constantly. A boy alto or soprano can sing for three to four years at best before his voice changes, since a thorough training is required beforehand.

It must be assumed that Bach had molded the group of St. Thomas pupils, whom he used for large and difficult tasks, into a first class ensemble that was largely able to realize his intentions. Since choruses at the time sang only the music of the period, stylistic problems hardly existed. The constant singing of complicated double-choir motets, which formed the chief responsibility of the St. Thomas pupils, provided marvelous training in virtuoso polyphonic choral singing. It is likely that coloraturas which are regarded today as especially difficult were at that time familiar to any well-trained choirboy.

The instrumental ensemble consisted of town pipers (the official musicians of the Leipzig city council), older St. Thomas pupils, and university students. Since Bach conducted the student Collegium Musicum, a group that had been founded by Telemann, for many years, he was able to draw upon the best musicians of this ensemble to strengthen his own group. But there were also times when, due to lack of funds, he did not have an adequate number of good musicians available. Bach's feelings about this matter are recorded in his "Kurtzer, jedoch höchst nöthiger Entwurf einer wohlbestallten Kirchenmusik" (Short, but very necessary proposal for a well-appointed church music). His preferences for the composition of his musical ensembles are described in detail here. His ideal orchestration included three first and three second violins (Bach's predecessor Kuhnau at times used four), two violas, two cellos, a contrabass, three oboes, bassoon and, as needed, flutes, trumpets and kettledrum which, incidentally, exactly corresponds in its proportions to the arrangement called for by Quantz in 1752: ". . . with eight violins one must have: two violas, two violoncellos, a contraviolone, two oboes, two flutes . . .″). This seems a small group to us, but we should remember that the chorus, measured against today's oratorio choruses, was also small; that there was very little room in the choir lofts; and above all that the musical unity of choruses, arias and recitatives, which was very important to Bach, would have been distorted with a larger ensemble.

The acoustics of the church also enhanced and blended the sound of these limited groups. We have many accounts of how important it was to composers of the period that their works and their ensembles were appropriate to the halls where they were to be played. Bach's fine sense for hall acoustics has been explicitly documented: Forkel, his first biographer, who had this information from Philipp Emanuel Bach, wrote: "Nothing escaped his sharp eye that was related in any way to his art and could be used to discover new artistic advantages. His attention to adapting great pieces of music to places of different [acoustic] qualities, his very experienced, keen ear with which he noticed the smallest mistakes in the most heavily scored and complex music . . ."

Bach's fine musical sensibility also lies behind his subtle and varied instrumentation. In each aria of the *St. John Passion*, different instruments are employed. Subtle sound combinations such as lute and violas d'amour, or transverse flutes and oboe da caccia, underscore the affect of these arias. The affect, the musical speaking expression, was, after all, an essential compositional principle in Baroque music and the subject of complicated theory. Bach's musical interpretation of the text extends from emphatic rhetorical sermons comprising entire movements, such as the tenor aria "Ach mein Sinn," to the isolated painting of individual words. It also includes, however, the entire symbol-language of the time: graphic musical symbols, if a graphic image was to be evoked through a musical phrase—the movement of rising or falling, waves of water, lashes of a whip, etc. Such symbols are evident in the notational picture, such as the rainbow, represented by notes in Aria 23,

as well as numerical symbols with a wide range of meaning. Thus Bach's works reveal an almost incomprehensible complexity of rhetorical, symbolic and musical elements.

A lively eye-witness account of the rehearsal of a major work has been left to us by Johann Matthias Gesner, rector of the Thomas School in Leipzig from 1730 to 1734:

> You would call all this . . . completely insignificant if you . . . could see Bach, to take an example, for not long ago he was my colleague at the Thomas School in Leipzig. How he plays our harpsichord, for example, with both hands and all fingers . . . or that basic instrument, the countless pipes of which must be blown with bellows, how he races over the

keys, here with both hands, there with fast feet! Yet he pays attention to everyone and everything at the same time and leads 30 or even 40 musicians, this one with a nod of the head, another by stamping his foot, including a third with a cautioning finger to observe rhythm and beat . . . how amidst the loudest playing of the musicians, although he himself has the most difficult part, he notices immediately if something is wrong somewhere, how he holds the whole thing together . . . ; how he feels the beat in all parts of his body, tests the harmonies with his keen ear, sings all the voice parts with his own limited throat . . . I believe that friend Bach by himself surpasses Orpheus.

Bach's son Philipp Emanuel and his student Johann Friedrich Agricola write: "He was very accurate in directing and very sure of the right tempo, which he usually took very fast." In 1758 Jakob Adlung wrote: "Those people seem to be correct who have heard many artists, but all agree that the world has known only one Bach."

The *St. Matthew Passion*

Immediately after Bach completed the *St. John Passion,* his first great oratorio on the last days in the life of Christ, he began to work on the *St. Matthew Passion.* Work on this Passion extended over several years and was by no means finished even when it was first performed on Good Friday 1729. Although neither score nor parts for this performance have been preserved, substantial evidence supports the view that the work as we know it—as it has come down to us in a magnificent hand-written score and a complete set of parts, most of which are in Bach's own handwriting—only received its final form after an extended series of revisions and rearrangements. Since a knowledge of the architecture of the work helps one understand it, I will briefly recount the evolution of its structure through these different stages. I basically follow the convincing analysis of Friedrich Smend.

Like many of Bach's instrumental works from his years in Köthen, the *St. John Passion* is built symmetrically around a mid-point. Initially it seemed obvious that this successful principle, which had imparted a convincing unity and a clear architectural structure to the *St. John Passion,* should also be used for the new work. Bach actually arranged the movements that he first composed along these lines. As a textual basis for the madrigalesque parts he used Picander's "Erbauliche Gedancken auf den Grünen Donnerstag und Carfreitag . . . 1725" (Edifying thoughts on Holy Thursday and Good Friday . . . 1725), although he changed the text in many places.

For an axis of symmetry, a focal point of the work, the passage that suggested itself is the only one in the *St. Matthew Passion* that is literally repeated: the cry of the people, "Lass ihn kreuzigen" (crucify him). The architectural mid-point in this first draft of the work is indeed located there.

Chorale: "Wie wunderbarlich ist doch diese Strafe"
Evangelist: "Der Landpfleger sagte"
Pilate: "Was hat er denn Übels getan?"
Soprano: "Er hat uns allen wohlgetan"
        "Aus Liebe will mein Heiland sterben."

These pieces are in every respect lifted from the total work, both textually (the meaning of the innocent suffering of Jesus is portrayed) and musically (through an instrumentation depending upon wind instruments in alto and soprano registers, which create a mood of detachment). Moreover, it is noteworthy that this central point in both Passions occurs at what is, in terms of content, precisely the same place;

that is when Pontius Pilate undergoes a change of heart. In a manner very similar to the *St. John Passion,* choruses and arias are built around this central point and are coordinated musically with each other, so that a clearly discernible framework results.

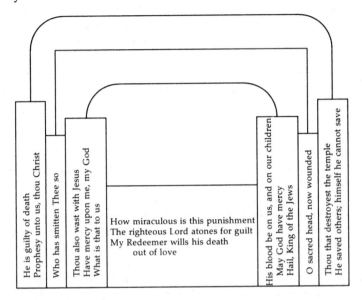

The other intervening movements ("Gebt mir meinen Jesum wieder," "Befiehl du deine Wege," "Können Tränen meiner Wangen," "Ja, freilich will in uns das Fleisch und Blut," "Komm, süsses Kreuz") were not included in this first version. The framework of the entire piece, the parts before and after this symmetrical middle block, was designed very like the *St. John Passion.*

It is probable that at this point Bach stopped working on the *St. Matthew Passion* for several years. When he returned to it, he had a completely new concept in mind. Picander had expanded his poetry, probably in collaboration with Bach, adding many arias, several of which were now interposed by the composer between the existing parts. Bach thereby destroyed the original symmetry, which evidently had become unimportant. Four additional chorale stanzas, based on the melody "Herzlich tut mich erfreuen" ("O Haupt voll Blut und Wunden" had been the only one previously set) were added, each one step lower, up to the death of Christ, which now became the central point toward which the entire work moved—"Erkenne mich, mein Hüter" in E major, "Ich will hier bei dir stehen" in E-flat major, "Befiehl du deine Wege" in D major and "Wenn ich einmal soll scheiden" in C major. Bach imparts to this last chorale the deepest, most personal and grief-filled feelings upon the death of Christ. Never before had a chorale text been interpreted musically in such emotionally charged harmonies. This chorale and the words of the people around the centurion, "Wahrlich, dieser ist Gottes Sohn gewesen"—intended to make comprehensible the basis of Christian faith arising out of the events of the Passion—now comprise the "heart piece" of the work.

Bach had originally composed the final chorus of the first part, the chorale fantasy "O Mensch bewein dein Sünde gross," as the opening chorus for the *St. John Passion*. After the final revision of the earlier version, it was replaced by the chorus "Herr unser Herrscher." It is probable that Bach finally included it in the *St. Matthew Passion* because this magnificent movement would otherwise have been lost as a torso; but it fits here perfectly.

The Double Choirs
The most obvious feature of the *St. Matthew Passion* is the use of two choirs. If we consider the enormous financial and personal difficulties with which Bach had to cope in order to perform his great works, we can understand how important the effect of the double choir must have been to him. It was difficult enough in Leipzig to put together a simple orchestra with three first and three second violins and the necessary wind instruments, but with two choirs, the instrumentation had to be doubled. His problems with the chorus and the soloists were no less serious. Bach worked tirelessly to improve the abilities of his chorus so that he could have at least two or three good singers on each part. Why did he make it especially difficult for himself by demanding a double chorus?

A few words about the use of two choirs might help to clarify this point. Even the early antiphonal liturgical singing—between lead singers and choral schola, or between several groups, or between clerics and the people—is based on two choirs: choruses or soloists positioned at various places in the church alternate in singing. The vivid impression created by this type of singing is enhanced when, for example, the words of the cantor are repeated by a large group, or when several groups sing to each other in one great dialogue. This way of singing made the congregation a part of the ceremony in a very intimate way. It is no wonder that this very festive and impressive manner of singing was also taken up in art music.

Around 1550, the Dutchman Adrian Willaert wrote his famous "Salmi spezzati," psalm compositions distributed between two choruses, for the San Marco Cathedral in Venice. This work is regarded as the first systematic, large-scale experiment with the use of two choirs. It ushered in the flowering of this way of composing in Venice over the following 100 years. The shape of San Marco Cathedral, with its cruciform ground plan and choir lofts situated opposite each other, probably also played a role in the genesis of this style. The main purpose of using two choirs— or better, several choirs, for soon more and more music-making groups were set up throughout the church—was probably to create a marvelously festive feeling, with the whole building resounding from all directions in a gigantic dialogue: a truly Baroque idea. This compositional technique spread very quickly and resulted in a unique style of composition written for several choruses, not only for vocal but also for instrumental music. Smaller groups, even individual soloists, were contrasted with large orchestras or choruses of singers. The Baroque concerto, in which soloist and tutti groups make music with and against each other, has here one of its important roots. One of the most sweeping works of this genre was the famous Salzburg festival Mass, which had long been attributed to Orazio Benevoli (for the dedication of the cathedral in Salzburg in 1628), although it was probably written around 1670 by a Salzburg composer. Its 53 parts were divided among 12 different choirs. In the 17th century, polychoral works were composed in many countries outside of Italy, including England, France, Austria and Germany. Their major purpose was to represent the dialogue aspect of music in a fantastically many-layered way complete with Baroque magnificence and theatricality, usually at particularly festive occasions. When Bach composed his *St. Matthew Passion,* the vogue of polychoral effects had already receded, being replaced by other musical qualities. Bach had written several motets for double choir, mostly for solemn funeral sermons upon the deaths of high personages in Leipzig. Here the use of two choirs served only for enrichment and to achieve a broader tonal spread, and was thus intended to underscore the solemnity of the occasion.

From its very beginnings another factor is the critical element in the *St. Matthew Passion:* the character of the dialogue. Picander's poetry was certainly based on this principle. Of all Bach works this one has the largest dimensions, and the display of the richest conceivable musical resources is certainly a major reason for this manner of writing. The use of two choruses here is, however, more than a magnificent play of sounds; it is intended to present the passion text and the contemplative poetic dialogue as a grand musical dialogue of two sound groups. Picander's text, based on the story of the Passion according to St. Matthew, is a contemplative dialogue between the Daughter of Zion and the faithful. The Daughter of Zion, the Old Testament personification of Jerusalem in the Book of Isaiah, is thought of by Christians as a symbol of the Church as bride of Christ. Originally, Bach had probably had all the text passages of the Daughter of Zion sung soloistically, above Chorus I of the opening chorus. Later he emphasized the universal nature of this figure; she is now no longer a tangible personality. Thus he could have her words sung by each of the soloists, even by the chorus.

If we study the various stages of the work, we can see that the use of two choirs, initially not of great importance, gradually moved into the foreground and became increasingly significant. At the first performance at St. Thomas Church in 1729, the two choirs probably stood on the right and left-hand sides of the choir loft, so that they could be accompanied by a single organ. In the violin solos in "Erbarme dich" and "Gebt mir meinen Jesum wieder," the soloist of one orchestra was accompanied by the ripieno players of the other orchestra, which is only possible if they are not positioned at a great distance from each other. The vocal soloists also were in all probability common to both choirs, so that there were only four soloists. As the work evolved, the division of the choirs became more radical. At the second performance in 1736, according to the report of the sacristan Rost, "both organs in St. Thomas" were heard, which means that the two choirs with their orchestras were positioned opposite each other at the east and west ends of the church. This positioning required that each orchestra was to be assigned its own continuo instrument. Now the violin solos were also added, one to each orchestra, and, as a final and most important step, each choir was given its own complete solo quartet.

In assigning parts to the two choirs, Bach basically gave the words of the Daughter of Zion to the first choir, those of the faithful to the second, while the evangelist and Christ belong to the first choir. This principle is also maintained for the one-choir arias and choruses. The arias and recitatives of the first choir are sung, so to speak, by the Daughter of Zion ("Du lieber Heiland du—Buss und Reu," "Wiewohl mein Herz in Tränen schwimmt—Ich will dir mein Herze schenken," "Erbarme dich," "Er hat uns allen wohlgetan—Aus Liebe will mein Heiland sterben," "Ja freilich will in uns das Fleisch und Blut—Komm, süsses Kreuz," "Mache dich mein Herze rein"). The arias of the second choir are sung by various personifications of the faithful ("Blute nur, du liebes Herz," "Der Heiland fällt vor seinem Vater nieder—Gerne will ich mich bequemen," "Mein Jesus schweigt zu falschen Lügen stille—Geduld," "Gebt mir meinen Jesum wieder," Erbarm es Gott—Können Tränen meiner Wangen"). Bach never designed arias to specific, concrete persons, e.g. Peter "Erbarme dich" or Judas "Gebt mir meinen Jesum wieder." Such an approach would have rendered the work much too theatrical. The action is carried exclusively by the gospel texts; the texts of all polyphonic sections are observations based on the spirit of the situation. They were written to convey more general reflections. Thus he deleted or rewrote passages where aria texts in the poetry are spoken by biblical characters.

The double choir is therefore an essential component of the musical and poetic concept in the polyphonic part of the *St. Matthew Passion*. How do the biblical texts relate to this plan? This question has to do primarily with the choirs of the apostles, Jews and high priests, since the speaking persons were automatically assigned to the first choir; only the two false witnesses are sung by the second choir. The excited and at times frenzied choruses of the high priests, elders and the people are written for two choirs, without dialogue. Here, by means of the calls and cries resounding from all sides, the impression of an excited crowd of people is created ("Ja nicht auf das Fest / Er ist des Todes schuldig / Weissage / Was gehet uns das an / Lass ihn kreuzigen / Sein Blut komme über uns und unsre Kinder / Gegrüsset seist du / Der du den Tempel Gottes zerbrichst / Andern hat er geholfen / Herr wir haben gedacht"). When smaller groups speak, only one chorus sings; the apostles are represented consistently by the first chorus ("Wozu dienet dieser Unrat / Wo willst du / Herr, bin ichs"). The small group that challenges Peter in the palace of the high priest is sung by the second choir ("Wahrlich, du bist auch einer von denen"). Two short choruses are dramatically distributed, "Etliche" (some) sing (first choir): "Der rufet dem Elias," the "Andern" (others) thereupon (second choir): "Halt, lass sehen." The movements expressing the commonality of all Christians are sung by both choirs together. These movements therefore are actually monochoral. Bach stresses this through the notation in his score: while all double choirs, including those in which the two choirs are practically identical, were written out by Bach in two separate sets of parts, all of the chorales, the chorale adaptation "O Mensch, bewein dein Sünde gross" and "Wahrlich, dieser ist Gottes Sohn gewesen" are notated as one.

The two choirs were clearly so important to the composer that he undertook the solution of considerable technical difficulties in order to be able to implement their use in a consistent way. The performance material written by Bach himself clearly reveals what the master wanted to have played and sung by whom. It would have been quite impossible to have the vocal solos of the first and second choirs sung by the same singers, because they are contained only in the choral parts of each respective choir. It would also have been impossible to play instrumental solos—for example the two gamba solos—from one location, or to have one continuo player accompany both choirs. In the respective, very carefully written and figured parts, only rests are indicated in the pieces for the other choir.

The double choir feature also poses an acoustical problem. We know that Bach was well versed in practical acoustics; at his time it was still a professional matter of course that the speed of harmony changes and modulations had to be adapted to the resonance time of a given hall. This adaptation to a performance space is particularly important in a work employing two choirs positioned at some distance from each other, so that the acoustics of the place have a great effect on the performance. A Gothic church with reverberant acoustics would destroy the effect of such a tightly harmonized work. The Church of St. Thomas in Leipzig today has rather echoing acoustical qualities, a fact occasionally taken by musicologists as an indication that very slow tempos were used. At the time of Bach, however, the church had wooden paneling, so that, as calculations have shown, when several hundred people were in attendance, it had approximately the same resonance as a very good concert hall. Thus it was ideally suited for the harmonically complicated works of Bach, especially for the great demands in terms of clarity that are posed by the *St. Matthew Passion*.

The musical separation of the choirs is only meaningful if the two choirs are also separated spatially. When, as in the usual Passion performances, they are positioned close together or even joined in the concert hall, Bach's allocation of the soloists becomes meaningless. Even today, one solo quartet almost always sings the solos of the first and second choirs. To be sure, the division into two orchestras and choirs is not perceived by today's listeners, since the listeners, unless they are seated in the first row, can perceive no difference in the direction from which the sound emanates.

The Text

If one revises and corrects not only the musical, but also the literary text of the work on the basis of the autograph score and the parts, many differences appear from the text usually sung today. In my opinion, the original text should be sung, even when it employs unfamiliar, archaic forms of words. After all, quite a number of such words have been sung in the *St. Matthew Passion* all along, e.g. "Ihr *wisset*, dass nach *zween* Tagen Ostern wird." The retention of certain forms and the modernization of others, a compromise generally practiced today, seems inconsistent to me. The *St. Matthew Passion* is based on this text with its diction, pronunciation and with the punctuation of Picander's personal feeling for language and therefore should also be performed in this way. The most important difference is found in the second stanza of the chorale "O Haupt voll Blut und Wunden," where the text should read, and does read in Bach: "das grosse Weltgewichte wie bist du so bespeit." This text is correct; "das grosse Weltgerichte" (as is still sung frequently today) is a falsification and distortion of the meaning of the original text. Nor are the punctuation marks used in accordance with modern rules of grammar, but rather in accordance with the less strictly defined usage of the 18th century. This is important for the performance because they are very often included in the composition.

Remarks on Individual Movements

The work begins in E minor, a key which Mattheson—a musician and musical author of the age of Bach—calls "very pensive, profound, making one feel sorrowful and sad, but in such a way that one still hopes to find consolation . . ." This characterization corresponds, as do many in Mattheson's tabulation, precisely to Bach's intent. It is interesting that the theme of the opening chorus was evidently inspired by a tombeau (dirge) by Marin Marais, the gambist at the court of Louis XIV; the correspondence is undeniable. We know that Bach had a high regard for

French composers and that he kept himself abreast of their work. Thus it is very probable that he obtained copies of the printed gamba works of Marais. A second indication also points to an acquaintance with the works of Marais: none of Bach's compositions for the gamba is actually written in a gamba-like fashion, in terms of playing technique. In many of Bach's works, the gamba provides a special, tender or mournful tonal color, which provides wonderful contrasts with the other string instruments and the winds, above all the recorders. The instrument is used in a truly French soloist manner in the two gamba arias of the *St. Matthew Passion,* especially in that of the first choir "Komm, süsses Herz." The dotted rhythm, the broad leaps, the ingenious runs and, above all, the rich chords are, in gamba terms, truly French. Forqueray and Marais wrote their gamba solos in this manner. Bach must have known their works in order to suddenly write in a style so completely new to him.

The chorale of the first choir, "O Lamm Gottes unschuldig," was originally not sung, but rather played only on the organ, or on both organs, with registration that stood out clearly ("Rückpositiv Sesquialtera"), in an early version even with doubling by wind instruments. This is by no means unusual, for the melody was commonly known and every listener must have understood it to symbolize a textual reference. In the last version of the *St. Matthew Passion,* Bach evidently had this chorale sung, probably by a group of boys who were not yet ready for polyphonic singing. He wrote a separate part, "soprano in ripieno," which contains this as well as the chorale "O Mensch bewein dein Sünde gross," indicating that this choral fantasy was originally planned to be sung with a greatly augmented soprano group.

In the words of the liturgy of the Last Supper "Trinket alle daraus," ". . . des Neuen Testaments" and "zur Vergebung der Sünden," the violin plays a characteristic theme probably intended to represent the gesture of holding up the chalice.

In the following contemplative aria this theme is taken up by the oboes d'amore also lifting up the cup, as it were, in order to show it to the faithful.

The old theory of tonality is revealed in a particularly beautiful way in the dialogue "Ich will bei meinem Jesu wachen—so schlafen unsre Sünden ein" (I shall watch [be awake] near my Jesus). "C minor is a very sweet but also sad key . . . it should be a piece which induces sleep . . ." Also in the final chorus (response of the second choir) "Ruhe sanfte, sanfte ruh," the same feeling is expressed in C minor.

As is always the case in the works of Bach, the chorales are harmonized in very individual ways; often, each word is interpreted harmonically. Bach had used this principle since his youth in the chorale accompaniment in church. A critique of his organ playing in Arnstadt in 1706 has come down to us: ". . . that he made in the chorale many unusual variations, mixing in many strange tones, so that the congregation became quite confused." This criticism also demonstrates, however, how attentive listeners of the time were and how anything that deviated from the familiar was immediately noticed.

In the chorale fantasy "O Mensch, bewein dein Sünde gross," the "cross" theme

is taken up repeatedly by the violin and oboe: an imaginary cross hangs over the entire chorus. Since it had been composed as an opening chorus for the *St. John Passion,* one might say that this work opens with a grand image of the cross. In the *St. Matthew Passion,* the movement serves as a monumental conclusion to the first part preceding the sermon, but yet the cross symbolism is not so compelling at this place. Bach now transposed the chorus to E major, as ". . . E major expresses a desperate or quite deathly sadness incomparably well . . ."

The aria "Ach, nun ist mein Jesus hin" was originally designed for the bass soloist; it was assigned to the altist only after the last revision after 1741. The correction is clearly evident in the score. Picander took the text of the faithful (second choir) in this dialogue from *Solomon's Song of Songs* (5:17): "Wo ist denn dein Freund hingegangen?"

The two false witnesses are portrayed in a very graphic way. The second sings mechanically after the first, as if he had to be careful to parrot a text that had been drummed into him. The text distribution in the Judas scene is curious. The answer of the high priest and the elders is sung by the double chorus, "Was gehet uns das an," but the words of the high priests are sung by only two soloists, "Es taugt nicht, dass wir sie in den Gotteskasten legen." According to the *Gospel of St. Luke,* there were two high priests, Anas and Caiphas, a fact which may explain the two-voice effect. Their words are written in red in Bach's score, as are those of all individual speaking parts.

The bass recitative "Am Abend, da es kühle war" is in G minor, a key that held particular meaning for Bach. "G minor is almost the most beautiful of all keys, because it not only mixes seriousness with a cheerful sweetness, but also conveys unusual grace and charm."

Symbolism

Like all of Bach's great works, the *St. Matthew Passion* is replete with symbols, tone painting and numerical riddles. If these elements mean little to us today—an age in which all types of symbolic languages have become alien—it is nonetheless important to know that this encoding is characteristic not only of Bach, but is consistent with the prevailing ideas of the period. In those days, music was perceived as language in a much more direct way than is the case today; it was thought to have countless possibilities of expression. This vocabulary is hardly significant to us now, since we are no longer familiar with it and it therefore no longer comes naturally to us. At best, we can reconstruct it in individual cases. But it is perhaps useful to know that we perceive only isolated aspects of the statement made by Bach's music, that much immediately grasped by the listener of his time passes us by completely unnoted.

The tone painting found in his musical language is perhaps most readily understood by us. The string orchestration of Christ's recitatives is undoubtedly intended to represent a halo illuminated briefly before the words of Christ.

The figure, for instance, represents sobbing ("von meiner Augen Tränenflüssen); weeping is also very realistically portrayed in the aria "Erbarme dich." The violin solo in "Gebt mir meinen Jesum wieder" represents the glistening money that has been tossed onto the ground. Many examples of more or less obvious tone painting can be found in each individual piece.

In addition to tone painting and key characteristics, the late Baroque musical doctrine of the affections offered an extensive vocabulary which Bach mastered in a sovereign fashion. Every sentence, in addition to its obvious textual meaning, also amounts, on a more profound level, to a "musical sermon." The listener of today who is accustomed to enjoying the aesthetic qualities of music, who has no practice in understanding Baroque "tonal discourse," must have virtually every musical expression explained. Each age has its own way of listening to music, which means that we can constantly discover new facets in works that operate on as many levels of meaning as the oratorios of Bach. It is almost as if listeners in different decades and centuries wandered through these colossal works, constantly discovering new sides, new, unsuspected beauty, but they can never encompass the work in its totality and in all its details.

The number symbolism that appears throughout the work is even more difficult to recognize than the rhetorical-musical intentions of the composer. One must not ascribe to Bach any kind of special role as an initiator of cryptic numerical art. He often said that he wanted nothing to do with mathematics. Thus Philipp Emanuel wrote to Forkel: ". . . the deceased was, like myself and all true musicians, no friend of dry mathematical matters." These number games never were thought of as mathematics, but rather as a part of the musical language of symbols. Recently, musical researchers, including F. Smend, Jansen and S. Helms, have uncovered many coded numbers . Some can easily be detected by a skilled listener, while many are so interwoven in the music that they can only be detected through an examination of the score. The Jews call upon the law in 10 double choruses (the four choruses of the Roman soldiers naturally are not counted), which represent the 10 commandments. In the chorus of the apostles who ask "Herr, bin ichs," the word "Herr" (Lord) is sung 11 times, once for each apostle with the exception of Judas. Instead of Judas' "Herr," we hear immediately "Ich bins, ich sollte büssen . . ." In the duet of the high priests, the bass plays to the end of the melisma "legen" (= put down) 30 notes: the pieces of silver are counted out; only then do the high priests continue to sing.

But there are much more complicated and hidden numbers, e.g. when a quoted biblical passage is to be indicated by the number of tones or pitches. In the recitative "Und siehe da, der Vorhang im Tempel zerriss . . ." the 32nd notes in the continuo below the three text passages: 1. "Und die Erde erbebete," 2. "und die Gräber täten sich auf," and 3. "und stunden auf viel Leiber der Heiligen, die da schliefen," result in 18, 68 and 104 notes, respectively: the earthquake is described in Psalms 18, 68 and 104.

Similar numerical references are found in almost each part of the *St. Matthew Passion*. Bach used the most varied methods to this end. He encoded words according to the numerical alphabet, and the resulting numbers were also concealed, like numbers in the text or references to biblical passages, in some form in the music. This side of Bach's work deserves attention primarily for the fact that at no time does the music suffer as the result of being placed on this Procrustean bed. Bach's mastery of the technique of composition was so nearly perfect that he gleefully sought such additional challenges to test his own prowess.

The History of Interpreting Bach's
Mass in B Minor

Though we know very little about Bach's own performances of his *B Minor Mass*, it is unlikely that he ever performed the work in its entirety. Friedrich Smend recently postulated that the work is not a coherent whole, but rather a fortuitous compilation of four distinct works for the Lutheran service, which were written down by Bach in one collected volume. This supposition seems somewhat far-fetched to me. The fourth section—consisting of the "Osanna," "Benedictus," "Agnus Dei" and "Dona nobis pacem"—has no plausible place in the Lutheran service, and it is completely unsuited as music to be played during the distribution of the Eucharist, because of its elaborate and festive instrumentation, employing a double choir, kettle drums and trumpets. Nonetheless, it is certain that the work, the individual parts of which were written over the course of many years, was assembled at a late date, probably in the last years of Bach's life. It does not seem possible to me that this could be due to chance, since that which is "collected" in this score represents a complete Latin mass, in proper sequence and with a unified setting and key. The reuse of the "Gratias" from the "Gloria" in the "Dona nobis pacem" stands out, and probably can be interpreted as an attempt to give cohesion to the entire work.

Bach completed the score of the *B Minor Mass* ca. 1746–1748, at a time when he was writing his great cyclical works, *Die Kunst der Fuge* and *Ein Musikalisches Opfer*. The inclusion of previously composed works (the "Sanctus") in this score and the enlarging of it into a complete mass by the adaptation of other suitable compositions can be viewed as evidence that, in addition to his Passions and other major cycles, Bach wanted to leave behind a great Latin mass.

Does this imply that Bach, who was an orthodox Lutheran, created an ecumenical or even a "Catholic" mass composition? Such a plan would not have been so unthinkable as it was seen in later times. After all, in his dedicatory preface to the *Missa* he had written to the Catholic King August III: ". . . I offer myself in humblest obedience at any time to the most gracious requests of your royal majesty for the composition of sacred music . . . to demonstrate my indefatigable diligence . . ."—thus offering to compose Catholic church music.

Smend's views relating to the performances of the parts of the *Mass* and their origin seem convincing to me. Accordingly, the *Mass*, i.e. the "Kyrie" and "Gloria," was probably first played on April 21, 1733, on the occasion of the homage paid to the heir to the hereditary title of Elector of Saxony, after the death of August the Strong, having been composed for this occasion. The "Credo," the Nicene Creed, was probably composed on the occasion of the festive rededication of the renovated St. Thomas School on June 5, 1732. The "Sanctus" was, according to Georg von Dadelsen, given for the first time at Christmas 1724. The following movements, "Osanna," "Benedictus," "Agnus Dei" and "Dona nobis pacem" are all reworkings of older compositions. Upon completion of the entire manuscript in the last years of Bach's life, they were included along with the "Sanctus" in the complete volume.

After Bach's death, the score came into the hands of his son, Philipp Emanuel. In 1786, about 40 years after the work had been created, Philipp Emanuel performed the "Credo" of the *Mass in B Minor,* although he evidently felt that he had to make several important changes. It is interesting to observe how even the generation after Bach, including his own sons, had moved away from tradition in the direction of a modern symphonic sound. The general musical taste of the time had distanced itself so far from the tonal ideas of the late Baroque that some things no longer seemed acceptable. In Bach's autograph score of the *B Minor Mass,* we find traces of bold interventions by Philipp Emanuel Bach. He added countless legato slurs in his father's original score, added dynamic marks and even changed the instrumentation. Most importantly, he seems to have disliked the violin-oboe mix which was a key component of Baroque orchestral sound. In the duet "Et in unum Dominum," he nonchalantly scratched out the instruction "et hautbois" beside the first and second violins. This deletion is particularly drastic because the important concertante division into solo and tutti is based precisely on the sounding or silence of the oboes d'amore. He also composed introductions for a few movements. As a result of these alterations, the work was so changed that it must have seemed quite modern to the listener of 1786. But what makes the "arrangement" of Philipp Emanuel so interesting for us is the fact that, despite all the changes made in response to the new musical preferences of the time, the balance between chorus and orchestra and those of the individual choral and orchestral parts was preserved. It never occurred to Philipp Emanuel to strengthen the orchestra or the chorus in terms of numbers.

In the year 1800, Karl Friedrich Zelter became director of the Berlin Singakademie. As a student of Fasch and an admirer of Philipp Emanuel Bach, he was particularly interested in cultivating the "old masters." By 1811, the Singakademie had begun to study the *B Minor Mass.* There were no public performances for some years since the difficulties posed by the work were too great. Finally, in 1827, Zelter performed the "Et incarnatus est" in a choral concert; in 1828, Spontini, the head of the Berlin Opera, performed parts of the "Credo." By the time of Zelter's death in 1832, the chorus had become so familiar with the work that his successor, Rungenhagen, was able to perform large sections of the *Mass* in 1834. All these performances presented the work in a heavily edited form, with the addition of composed introductions and completely different instrumentation. Unlike Philipp Emanuel Bach, these arrangers no longer had the kind of intimate relationship to this music which would have made it impossible for them to intervene in its musical substance; they ignored the demands for balance that are based on the score.

The choruses consisted of at least 100 singers. Spontini used an orchestra of 12 first and 12 second violins, 12 violas, 12 cellos and 8 contrabasses; the winds included clarinets, horns, bassoons, but no oboes or trumpets! Similar changes both as to the numbers of performers (170–200 people) and instrumentation are found in all performances of this period: Bach dressed in the musical garb of Carl Maria von Weber! We can well imagine how this meticulous score must have sounded in such a thick instrumentation with so many participants. Many obbligato parts were either not played at all or were inaudible. What remained was a magnificently harmonized monumental sound. Perhaps the listeners of the time, who were no longer accustomed to sophisticated polyphony, were satisfied with this chordal Bach sound. Perhaps the arrangers felt that the music was all too overcharged and regarded the remaining torso of powerful harmonic development, free from complicated embellishment, as the true musical manifestation of Bach's genius.

In any case, we should not find fault with those who rediscovered Bach, since no direct tradition existed that looked back to his own performances. Except for the Hamburg performances of Philipp Emanuel of 1786, which were developed out of a completely different spirit, those Berlin attempts 70–90 years after the work was completed were undertaken under totally new musical conditions. No one had ever heard a work of Bach as the composer had intended it. People were completely at home in the musical world of Beethoven, Weber, and Mendelssohn. The context in which Bach's choral works had been composed—the school and church of St. Thomas, the small boys' choir, the small orchestra—was unknown and would have been incomprehensible at this time. The intoxicating sound of mixed mass choirs had just been discovered and the overpowering, large Romantic symphony orchestra had just been created. The traditional was no longer valued on its own merits, but had to be adapted to this "much more beautiful" new world of sound! We must keep in mind that this period was alive with musical vitality.

Our present-day musical life is based on the middle-class concert life that evolved during this period. This is natural and acceptable as far as the music of Romanticism or post-Romanticism is concerned. After all, there is a performance tradition linking the music of that time to the present, and this uninterrupted tradition guarantees a minimum of basic, instinctive knowledge needed to understand such music. Baroque music suffered a completely different fate, as it was gradually integrated into the musical life of Romanticism (which still prevails today). It was romanticized musically as well as formally. Bach sounded somewhat like Brahms or Bruckner; his music was performed on the same instrument, the Brahms-Bruckner orchestra. Later, the most serious interventions in Bach's scores were reversed, but there remained, as in the *B Minor Mass*, the overall impression of a colossal choral work full of the greatest difficulties. Since then, the best performances have always had an element of giantism.

There hardly is a choral work of any place or period so closely related to the development of choral unions, singing societies and academies which were founded at the beginning of the 19th century, as Bach's *Mass in B Minor*. This work, which was never performed in its entirety during his lifetime, understandably appeared to all choruses as the greatest and most difficult work of all, and so at one time or another, each had to take up the challenge that it represented. As heirs of the twofold performance traditions of the 19th century and of the time of Bach, great difficulties confront us in present-day performances. A flawless balance can be achieved only using this historical apparatus. Certainly, these magnificent works should not be eliminated from the modern repertoire simply because it is almost impossible to perform them flawlessly. But the self-assured conductor of a present-day performance should be aware that all of his choices represent compromises. A reduction of the size of the chorus and orchestra is not enough to bring about a better balance, since the individual instruments have been so modified over the past 200 years that completely new conditions exist today.

In the typical modern performance, no attention is paid to such considerations: entire portions of the score seem to be erased, we do not hear certain passages, and if we did not see the musicians playing or the vocalists singing, we would think that they are pausing. The same is also true of many recordings. For example, when a choral part is played in thirds or sixths with *one* wind instrument, it makes musical sense only if the number of singers is very small, or if multiple wind instruments are used. There are many such passages in the *B Minor Mass*: for example, in the "Kyrie," measures 35–36, "Et expecto," measures 27, 29, 31, 69, 71, 73. Similar problems of balance arise also in the "Et resurrexit," where the two flutes are played for stretches quite independently and must remain audible against both the chorus and the orchestra. Also the reenforcement of the trumpets by the flutes in measures 101–105 is only plausible if the flutes are not completely drowned out by the trumpets. From these few randomly chosen examples it is evident that the distribution of the voices and instruments, weighed most subtly by Bach, loses its meaning completely if even one link is changed in this complicated chain. The resulting chaos can be avoided only by radical interventions in the instrumentation. This area represents an important task confronting modern Bach interpreters.

In preparing to record Bach's *B Minor Mass*, we cast about for a new solution to the practical problems associated with the performance of this work: we aimed at nothing less than to recreate the original sound. Even though it was clear to everyone involved that we could work only with approximations, and that in many areas we would be forced to rely on experimentation and guesswork, nonetheless our success, our actual experience of playing the music, demonstrated the basic validity of such an undertaking. It surprised us all when we encountered very few balance problems in this very complicated work. The recording engineers only had to record; they served no kind of corrective function. The chorus and orchestra were each recorded with one stereo microphone, and everything was audible. The natural trumpets did not drown out the transverse flutes, the orchestra did not overpower the chorus, or vice versa. Every participant had repeatedly performed the work in other interpretations in concert halls and had concluded that it was impossible to achieve a meaningful balance. The small number of boys' voices, and the orchestra, which used original instruments exclusively and duplicated precisely the number of players used at the time of Bach, automatically supplied the solution to all problems of transparency.

In the famous petition Bach submitted to the Leipzig city council on August 23, 1730, he called for a minimum of three or four singers for each part; for an orchestra without doubled wind instruments, he requested two or three first and second violins, two violas, two cellos and one violone. If we compare these figures with those cited by Quantz (1752): "For six violins one takes one viola, one violoncello, and a contraviolone and one bassoon," "with eight violins belong two violas, two cellos" etc., or with the orchestra of the Hamburg Opera in 1738: eight violins, three violas, two cellos, two contrabasses and winds, the instrumentation that we had selected (eight violins, two violas, two cellos, a contrabass and single winds) in relation to the corresponding room acoustics would have been regarded as a rather festive orchestration at the time of Bach.

Orchestras that would be considered large today were used in those days only for open-air performances. The composers employed completely different styles for large and small ensembles, for performances in church and chamber. Quantz described the "open-air style" of the festive opera by Fux, *Costanza e Fortezza*, performed in Prague in 1723: "An opera was performed out-of-doors with 100 persons singing and 200 playing . . . Although it consisted largely of movements which looked stiff and dry enough on paper, nonetheless in the open air and with such large forces it had a much greater effect than a song with many embellishments and fast notes." Composers were also expected to take into consideration the technical (stage) resources, the performers available, and acoustical conditions.

From those who heard Bach's own performances we learn that "when he wanted to express strong emotions, he did not do this, like others, through exaggerated forcefulness, but through harmonic and melodic figures, i.e. through inner artistry." It will certainly be still some time before Bach's major works are widely accepted as compositions conceived more or less as chamber music. The 150-year-old Romantic Bach tradition with its massed choirs and orchestras is still all too dominant. In the colla parte playing of the orchestra with the chorus the large choral sound to which we are accustomed today blurs the tonal colors carefully chosen by the composer. Similarly, the symphonic sound of the Brahms orchestra normally used today destroys the balance between the orchestral parts, as well as between the individual groups of instruments. Moreover, a meaningful dynamic balance must prevail in the alternation of solo arias and choral passages; the overall effect must develop on *one* tonal level. Delicate vocal and instrumental solos must not be allowed to disappear between powerful choral blocks; the music must move forward without a break. In the 18th century, these relations were still common knowledge, when, for example in England in the colossal Handel festivals, the solos were often doubled or tripled.

The dynamic relationship between choruses and solos also applies within the choruses. In a work like the *B Minor Mass*, in which the choruses are so dominant, the individual solos otherwise would not be understandable in a formal sense. As W. Ehmann has convincingly demonstrated, Bach's choral practice is based on the old division into "Concertisten" and "Ripienisten." These expressions were still used by Bach in his petition to the Leipzig city council mentioned earlier.

After about 1600, it was customary to enliven sacred vocal music by means of rich, almost organ-like registrations. This was achieved by setting up several separate choirs, and by using choral groups of different sizes, from the solo quartet to the full choir. These differences in ensembles were sometimes explicitly called for, but normally they were the responsibility of the performers, as was true of so much performance practice in Baroque music. As an example we might cite the autograph of the "Sanctus." Here the word "tutti" is found on the lower margin of the score (measure 88). This implies, at any rate, that the number of performers in this piece varied, which was so self-evident that it did not need to be specifically indicated. Over the course of time, certain types of musical notation developed for these choral and solo groups of different sizes. This meant that most of the choral "registrations" were implied by the way a passage was written and are immediately recognizable in the appearance of the score. These choral registrations can be compared to the freedom of the organist to interpret a work through appropriate registration—which is almost never prescribed. It is a similar case with the orchestra. Here, too, one resorted to all possibilities, from enlisting large groups of various sizes to purely soloistic playing. While explicit instructions are often found in the scores, much is left to the judgment of the conductor. Markings such as piano and forte are often references to solo and tutti scoring.

The *Mass in B Minor* basically enlists a five-part choir, with two sopranos, alto, tenor and bass. In the few four-part choruses, unison singing of the two soprano sections (in the "Kyrie" II, "Gratias," "Patrem," "Dona nobis pacem") or only one of the two (in the "Crucifixus") is called for. The six-part "Sanctus" and the double-choir "Osanna" are exceptions, in which the chorus was evidently intended to be split even further. Because of this five-part writing, Bach called for five soloists: two sopranos, alto, tenor and bass. Even though a division of the two bass arias among two basses could be defended because of their different tessitura, nonetheless the combining of the two soprano parts and of the alto part for one soprano and one alto, as it is usually practiced today, does not correspond to Bach's intention. He clearly prescribed what was to be sung by the first soprano, the second soprano and the alto. Despite the low tessitura of the second voice, the "Christe eleison" is evidently meant to be performed by two sopranos with similar timbre. A distinction between the sound of the two voices through different voice types, as is called for in "Et in unum Dominum," is not desired here. Because of the tessitura, the solo aria "Laudamus te" is assigned to the second soprano.

Remarks on Individual Sections
The "Kyrie" I, "Christe" and "Kyrie" II were probably composed for the previously mentioned celebration of homage to the new ruler in St. Thomas Church. The rhythm ♪ | ♩ ⁊ ♪ ♩ ⁊ ♪ | ♩ which pulsates through the entire "Kyrie" I can probably be understood as a very intensive musical and rhetorical gesture of supplication: "Herr, erbarme dich unser" (Lord, have mercy on us). It is also used in this sense by other 18th century composers. The duet "Christe eleison" radiates peace and unity; the mood of pleading supplication in the first "Kyrie" seems resolved. This impression is conveyed above all by the simplicity of the movement; the two soprano parts are largely homophonic, which is quite unusual for Bach; they amount to *one* doubled voice, as it were, which is further underscored by their similarity. The instrumental setting is also extremely simple: the violins play in unison richly articulated figures which are spun out into infinity above an ostinato bass that hardly participates in the thematic action.

The "Kyrie" II is a four-part fugal choral movement in the "old style" of Netherland polyphony. This type of writing was described (notably in Italy, after the appearance of the concertizing style around 1600) as "prima prattica" and was preserved above all in Catholic sacred music as the official church (Palestrina) style until well into the 18th century. The instruments which play colla parte exclusively objectify the living statement of the choir, but also provide contour and articulation for the strict form and thereby facilitate our understanding of the complicated patterns of polyphony.

The "Gloria" probably was intended as the festive music for the ruler. Based on a lost instrumental concerto, the complete instrumental parts were first written in score form with the choral parts added later. This was done so organically and so convincingly that a new and fitting piece resulted. Arnold Schering writes of Bach's method: "Bach's easy mastery of all technical aspects made it possible for him to solve with ease tasks that appeared almost to defy solution, such as the addition of a choral movement to an existing instrumental movement."

The "Et in terra pax" is, to be sure, a new composition, added without a break to the "Gloria." The undulating pairs of eighth notes—played and sung slightly unequally—are intended to represent peace and tranquility. In a grand climax, the different instrumental groups, at times individually and at times jointly, take up choral phrases in such a "speaking" way that they fairly call out to each other the message of peace, until peace is at last represented as a final victory in the brilliant sound of the clarino trumpets. The "Laudamus te" is probably to be understood as the song of angels on high. The solo violin, playing in a register that was very high for the time, rejoices above a transparent string texture without the low fundament of the contrabass; the mood is one of pure rapture and joy, free of loud exuberance. The almost instrumental coloraturas of the soprano compete with the violin: a contest of heavenly songs of praise.

For the "Gratias," Bach used the opening chorus of his church cantata 29. Musically and in terms of its message this chorus fits ideally into the new framework. The German text of the cantata chorus is practically a translation of the Latin: "gratias agimus tibi—propter magnam gloriam tuam" (In the cantata: "We give thanks to you, God, we proclaim your wondrous deeds.") By minor melismatic changes, Bach altered the accentation: "und verkündigen deine Wunder" becomes "propter magnam gloriam tuam."

Even though the choral movement remained basically the same, through many small changes it was so thoroughly adapted to the new text that it seems to be an original composition. All parodies—

adaptations of other works—in the *B Minor Mass*, particularly those found in the "Gloria" and the "Credo," are selected and handled with such care that the original is surpassed in most cases by the new version. One has the impression that only now has the movement found its ultimately correct place.

The performance material for the "Domine Deus" provides an interesting insight into performance practice. Although in all modern scores all sixteenth notes of the solo flute are notated evenly, many of them slurred in pairs, the flute part written by Bach himself deviates through the use of other types of rhythm. This rhythm is found only in the first measure and is an important indication that in the case of Bach also, equal note values must often be played unevenly (*inégale*). Descending tied groups of two notes were often performed in "Lombard" rhythm (this is the term used for this reverse type of dotting), without having to be explicitly indicated. This type of rhythm appears not only in the solo part, but is also found in the original second violin and viola parts, though only where the figure in question appears for the first time. To the best of my knowledge, there is no score in which these very important and interesting types of rhythm are printed or described. The "Lombard" rhythm probably should be played only in this descending sixteenth-note theme and not, by analogy, distributed across the entire movement, because the "analogous" treatment of similar passages, which is today often called for in principle, does not at all correspond to Baroque practice.

The "Qui tollis" proceeds directly from this movement. Although "Lente" or "Adagio" is written above it in the parts, nonetheless the *tempo* remains approximately the same as in the preceding movement. The *movement* slows down, however, since the eighth-note motion in the bass now changes to a constant beat in quarter notes. The harmonic points of rest are now spaced more widely: in the "Domine Deus" they occurred at the distance of quarter notes—now in the "Qui tollis," of a whole measure. The Italian tempo marking therefore expresses here no absolute retardation, but rather one that is written out. This movement is taken from Church Cantata 46. In the latter, too, we find thorough agreement between the old and the new texts: "Schauet doch und sehet, ob irgend ein Schmerz sei wie mein Schmerz, der mich troffen hat" (*Lamentations of Jeremiah,* Chapter 1:12). The Protestant theologian Friedrich Smend says: "The text from the Lamentations cannot be interpreted more profoundly by Lutheran theology than as a prophecy of the Savior to whom all Christianity is praying: 'Qui tollis—You who take away the sins of the world, have mercy on us . . .' " Here we find more far-reaching changes from the original composition; the instrumental prelude and the middle part were omitted, the quarter note motion of the cello was added, the entire piece was transposed down a third. The new musical version is so successful and perfect that I am convinced that basing it on an existing composition cannot have been a question of economy, but rather of Bach's belief that he could conceive of no better musical form to match this content.

The two following arias—"Qui sedes" and "Quoniam"—belong together, since the text of the second represents a response to the first. The instrumentation and the style of composition can hardly be more different: in the "Qui sedes," the alto voice concertizes with the instrumental alto, the oboe d'amore, featuring similar thematic and general musical style. The strings simply form an articulated and full-voiced obbligato continuo. In contrast, the "Quoniam" is carried by four equal but completely different partners: the bass voice, the natural horn, the two bassoons which are always used together, and the basso continuo. Each of these groups has its own completely distinct thematic material. The horn is probably intended to express the majesty of Christ, especially in its striking opening theme. In this aria, the articulation is indicated with particular care, not only here, but in other passages of the work as well; many are written-out rhythmic vibratos. This homage to Christ leads directly into the jubilant final chorus "Cum Sancto Spiritu in gloria Dei patris, Amen." The instruments indicating the glory of the ruler, the clarino trumpets and kettle drums, illuminate the rich pattern of movements: the musical parallel to the "Gloria" is very evident. Like two powerful Baroque pillars, these two choruses frame the entire "Gloria."

Like the "Gloria," the "Credo" of the *Symbolum Nicenum* represents a rounded architectural design, symmetrical as in all of Bach's longer works.

```
┌────────Credo – Patrem
│
│   ┌────Et in unum
│   │
│   │   ┌─Et incarnatus est
│   │   │ Crucifixus
│   │   └─Et resurrexit
│   │
│   └────Et in spiritum sanctum
│
└────────Confiteor – Et expecto
```

The movements which correspond to each other are coordinated in form and weight. The block "Incarnatus-Crucifixus-Resurrexit" should be seen as a whole, as the heart of the "Credo." In the "Credo," the Gregorian melody is carried by seven voices (five-part chorus and two violins) above an andante bass which expresses the steadfastness of faith. The "Patrem" is an adaptation of a chorus from Church Cantata

171, "Gott wie dein Name, so ist auch dein Ruhm bis an der Welt Ende." Smend demonstrates that from the theological viewpoint as well, "the choice of the original image has not been made by chance, but with great care."

The duet "Et in unum Dominum" requires particular attention, since in the original autograph score there are two versions of this piece. For our interpretation, we selected the first version, in which the text is set up to and including "Et incarnatus est de Spiritu sancto ex Maria virgine et homo factus est." The "Crucifixus" originally followed. Bach later inserted the chorus "Et incarnatus est" and wrote, probably to avoid text repetition, a new version of the two singing voices of the "Et in unum Dominum," whereby the text was so drawn out that it now ended at "descendit de coelis." We cannot help but notice a loss in unity of text and music. In the original version the text is commented on, in the accompanying solo instruments, by musically "speaking" turns of phrase. For example, at about measures 59–60 the descending thirds of the strings at "descendit de coelis"; or the descending scale, already heard in the first part at "natus" which now at "et incarnatus est" is fully carried out; or the unexpected change of key at "et homo factus est," which is intended to symbolize the transformation from a divine to a human nature. To accommodate the new text some of the voice-leading had to be changed, but the instrumental part remained unchanged. By this shift in text, words of the "heavenly sphere" move over into the "earthly" sphere. As a result of this inconsistency, the symbolism of the accompanying instrumental music loses its original meaning. There are some indications that Bach later reversed this change. The repetition of the words "et incarnatus est" in the following chorus seems to me particularly beautiful and compelling. This is probably meant to represent man's acceptance of this article of faith. This chorus brings the musical gesture of the descent from heaven (measures 59–60 of the preceding duet) as a distinctive theme. Throughout this movement the unisono violins repeat a version of this descent that is ornamented by suspensions, thus putting the rest of the text under the motto of the first three words.

The following "Crucifixus," in the same tempo as the "Et incarnatus est," only the note values are doubled, is a passacaglia. It may seem strange to us today that Bach selected a dance form for this, of all passages, since we usually associate joy and merriment with the dance. Originally, however, dancing was a basic means of human expression that could encompass man's varied emotions. (For the final chorus of the *St. Matthew Passion*, Bach even selected the form of the minuet!) This passacaglia, which is derived from the cantata chorus "Weinen, Klagen, Sorgen, Zagen ist der Christen Tränenbrot," presents itself as a sorrowful lament for the dead. The unexpected harmonic turn of the E minor piece, six measures before the end, and the concluding cadence to

G major, allow this music of mourning to end on a note of hope and consolation.

Like the "Gloria," the "Et resurrexit" chorus is based on a lost instrumental concerto, although more sweeping changes were necessary here. In the place of the bass solo "Et iterum venturus est" there was originally probably an instrumental solo. The strong predominance of the instrumental in this movement reminds us that at the time of Bach, the playing of an instrument was regarded as a kind of speaking in tones, so that it was fully equal in value to singing. The instruments join in the jubilation of the singers, shaping the text in their own way. The bass aria "Et in Spiritum sanctum Dominum" takes up the sound and form of the duet "Et in unum Dominum." This time the two oboes d'amore, which there had been used only to add color to the tutti sound, are, as solo instruments, equal partners with the singing voice. The relation of the two pieces was also emphasized by Bach's son, Philipp Emanuel, when he scratched out the designation "hautbois" in the first piece, and in the second wrote "*also* without oboes with 2 violins."

As in the introductory "Credo," the five-part choral writing of the "Confiteor" is supported by an andante bass that moves in steady, relentless quarter notes, until this bass changes, at "peccatorum," to full measures of accented bow vibrato. This passage is also marked adagio in order to underscore the change of expression. The following text "expecto resurrectionen mortuorum" (I look for the resurrection of the dead) concludes this movement, with the musical accent on "mortuorum." The same text is repeated once more at the beginning of the next movement, marked Vivace e Allegro: suddenly, as if only now the full meaning of the text had become clear—that the talk is not of the *dead,* but of the *resurrection* of the dead—jubilation breaks out with all available power. This final chorus of the "Credo" is one of the most magnificent examples of how Bach bestowed a new and final shape on earlier works. The original version of this chorus is "Jauchzet ihr erfreuten Stimmen, steiget bis zum Himmel nauf" from Cantata 120. Only the main part of this chorus was used, with many details omitted while others were added. The most important change is probably the addition of a fifth voice to the four-part choral movement. The fugato insertions—five now, instead of four in the same space—clearly reveal Bach's awesome technical mastery. In this movement there are three musical themes:

"Expecto"
expressing expectation

"Jauchzet"
a primarily instrumental theme, later
taken up by the choir, and

"Steiget"

which symbolically represents the awaited resurrection of man

The "Sanctus" had been composed long before the parts of the *Mass* were finally assembled. It is the only piece we know with certainty that Bach performed several times. The ♪♪ groups of course are to be played as triplets, so that the whole first part is in continuous triplet rhythm. The only alternative would be over-dotting ♪·♪ but this was ruled out according to the practice of the time by the slurs. The musical form of the "Sanctus" is related to the "Adagio/Fugato Allegro" coupling of the church sonata, and therefore derives from instrumental music.

The only movement for double chorus is the "Osanna." This is an adaptation of the opening chorus of the homage cantata "Preise dein Glücke gesegnetes Sachsen" (215); Bach used only the main part, but without a prelude. In this chorus he dispensed with changes not necessitated by the new Latin text. In keeping with the very "worldly" Baroque concept of God, it did not seem strange for grand homage music for a local ruler to be pressed into service as homage music for Christ.

In the "Benedictus," the solo instrument is not indicated. For this register, only the violin and transverse flute are possible, since the piece is too high for the oboe of the age of Bach. Along with Smend, we decided in favor of the flute, because the piece is very unviolinistic, but well-suited for the transverse flute. The lowest tone (d') of the transverse is never surpassed: this would hardly happen in a Bach violin solo.

Although the "Agnus Dei" was not composed originally for the *Mass*, its model "Ach bleibe doch, mein liebstes Leben" from the *Ascension Oratorio* (BWV 11) deviates quite radically from this movement. Such far-reaching changes go beyond the parameters of a simple retexting.

Bach took the music of the "Gratias" from the "Gloria" note for note for the "Dona nobis pacem." This transcription has often been considered unsuccessful and carelessly executed, as concerns the text, but also because this movement—a middle movement in the "Gloria"—was judged inappropriate for the conclusion of the work as a whole. The rousing conclusions of individual parts, of the "Gloria" and the "Credo," it has been said, surpass that of the *Mass* as a whole. I submit that Bach, a brilliant musical architect, was better acquainted with all of the pros and cons, particularly with regard to reusing already composed pieces, than were any of his critics, and that he selected this movement after careful consideration. The wonderfully compelling prayer of thanks in the

"Gloria" had to touch the heart of each listener; why should the words "Give us peace" not sound with the same music expressing heartfelt thanks. Can there be a more meaningful conclusion to the last great choral work of Bach than this linking of gratitude for peace with a prayer for peace?

Wolfgang Amadeus Mozart:
Discussions of His Works

Mozart's Dramatic Technique as Reflected in his *Idomeneo* Correspondence

It rarely happens in the process of creating a new work that a composer provides a written commentary on his endeavors. A rare opportunity to catch this kind of glimpse into an artist's workshop is provided by Mozart's correspondence with his father from the winter of 1780/81. At this time he was composing *Idomeneo* in Munich, while his father at home in Salzburg maintained contact with the librettist. For the first time in his life, Mozart was left completely to his own devices, having traveled alone from Salzburg to Munich, his first venture quite independent of his father. Unlike many modern psychologists, I do not view such a bond as somehow negative. Mozart's father devoted himself to the education of his son, whose genius precluded conventional schooling, with the greatest sensitivity and a profound sense of responsibility. Inevitably, the moment had to come when the son would become independent; musically, he had been independent for a long time. Certainly, his father made suggestions. Mozart used his father's ideas when they agreed with his own vision; where this was not the case, he rejected them freely and confidently. However, he was dependent in matters of daily life, and his father feared with some justification that, left to himself, he would have difficulties with the mundane demands of simply staying alive.

The young Mozart remained in Munich for months while composing the opera, writing a letter to his father almost every other day. The entire process of composition—which could not have been done in Salzburg because at the time, operas were practically "custom-designed" for the singers—is documented in this correspondence between father and son. It is the most interesting and most complete correspondence about a musical work that I know. (Fortunately, the letters of Mozart's father have also been preserved.) It ends—naturally enough—on the day on which his father came to Munich for the first performance. This is unfortunate, because the last changes in the work are therefore not documented.

Idomeneo remained one of the works that Mozart most loved and which touched him deeply and intimately. In the loving tension between Idomeneo and Idamante, he may have felt a parallel to his relationship with his father. He obviously identified with Idamante, even while composing the work, and he regarded the so-called death quartet as special and personal to the end of his life. In a reliable report about a performance of this quartet that took place in a private home much later, during his years in Vienna, it is said that Mozart himself sang the part of Idamante—probably in falsetto—and was so overcome by emotion that he was unable to continue. This opera is more closely connected with Mozart's life story than any of his other works.

In his letters from Munich,* Mozart often refers to problems that he encountered with the singers; he also recounted his views on vocal style and technique. Among the questions which most concerned him were those touching on the borderline between speaking and singing, between speech and music, a matter which from the time of Caccini and Monteverdi has been the central problem in music drama. Mozart discussed this question extensively in a letter about the death quartet "Andrò ramingo e solo . . ."

> I have just had a bad time with him [Raaff, the singer of Idomeneo] over the quartet. The more I think of this quartet, as it will be performed on the stage, the more effective I consider it; and it has pleased all those who have heard it played on the clavier. Raaff alone thinks it will produce no effect whatever. He said it to me when we were by ourselves. (December 27, 1780)

Raaff objected to this piece because it does not contain a cantabile melody. His criticism is very interesting, for it indicates that even at that time the legato was a major concern of singers. While the composer wanted more emphasis on a spoken text, the singer wanted a great melodic line with which to show off his voice!

> "Non c'è da spianar la voce. It gives me no scope." As if in a quartet the words should not be spoken much more than sung. That kind of thing he does not understand at all. All I said was: "My very dear friend, if I knew of one single note which ought to be altered in this quartet, I would alter it at once. But so far there is nothing in my opera with which I am so pleased as with this quartet; and when you have once heard it sung in concert, you will talk very differently." (December 27, 1780)

Mozart expressly calls for a speaking type of singing here. This "speaking-singing," cantar recitando in the style of Caccini, or better "singing-speaking," recitar cantando, was the central point in the shaping of a recitative for Mozart and his contemporaries. When he heard a "duodrama" (melodrama) in 1778 in Mannheim, he was thrilled:

> You know, of course, that there is no singing in it, only recitation, to which the music is like a sort of obbligato accompaniment to a recitative. . . . Do you know what I think? I think that the most operatic recitatives should be treated in this way—and only sung occasionally, when

* All translations of the correspondence are taken from *The Letters of Mozart and His Family,* Translated by Emily Anderson, Volumes II, III, Macmillan & Co., Ltd., London and Basingstoke, 1938.

the words can be perfectly expressed by the music. (November 12, 1778)

These passages from his letters also provide information on the relationship between singer and composer. Raaff insists on his inherent right to have his part modified to reflect his taste and his wishes. But Mozart says clearly:

"I have taken pains to serve you well in your two arias, I shall do the same with your third one—and shall hope to succeed. But as far as trios and quartets are concerned, the composer must have a free hand." Whereupon he said that he was satisfied. (December 27, 1780)

This clearly shows that in ensemble, the drama is what is important; beautiful singing is secondary. Mozart was absolutely intransigent on this point. We should reflect on the situation in which the two men found themselves: Raaff was 60 years old, a world-famous singer with immense authority; Mozart was still almost a child, his authority stemming solely from his ability. But he knew exactly how the music drama taking shape in his mind had to be formed. According to his letters, Mozart had the most trouble with Raaff, who as a younger man had been one of the luminaries of the florid Italian vocal style. Lionized by the public, these artists had an overblown self-image and frequently tyrannized composers. In those days, singers simply assumed they could dictate to the composer how they wanted their arias to be composed! If the composer did not comply with the wishes of his singers, he was criticized, indeed, he would have been thought unsuitable as a composer. In the relationship between singer and composer, the singer was the star for whom the composer had to work.

The modifications that Raaff wanted were many; he rejected Idomeneo's final aria, for example, because five "i's" appear in the last verses, which, as is known, do not sound good and are difficult to sing.

The other day he was very much annoyed about some words in his last aria—rinvigorir—and ringiovenir—and especially vienmi à rinvigorir—five i's!—It is true that at the end of an aria this is very awkward. (December 27, 1780)

His father is less circumspect in this matter, since he answers:

In regard to "vienmi a rinvigorir" it is true that there are five i's, but it is also true that I can pronounce the phrase twenty times without any inconvenience, in fact with the greatest rapidity and ease. . . . Basta! to please everyone the devil himself may go on altering and altering. Signor Raaff is far too pernickety. (December 29, 1780)

Raaff further demanded that the final aria correspond precisely to his notion of lyrical singing. Because he was not satisfied with Varesco's writing, he suggested that Mozart use a peace aria from a Metastasio opera, with which he had enjoyed great success. Mozart should simply include this text in his composition—which would have been a serious insult for the librettist Varesco. The only solution Mozart could find for this calamity was that a new, improved text had to be written. Finally, after an unsuccessful attempt ("The aria for Raaff which you have sent me pleases neither him nor myself. . . . Besides, the aria is not at all what we wished it to be.") [November 29, 1780], he received a text from Varesco which also met with Raaff's approval. Mozart composed the wonderful aria "Torna la pace," and Raaff loved it! Then, at the end of the rehearsal period, this aria, which had been created with so many struggles, was cut for dramatic reasons! When Mozart had the course of the dramatic action of the completed work in front of him, he eliminated a few arias, accompagnatos and recitatives. It is remarkable: The composer expends effort, time and imagination on these magnificent arias, but sacrifices them ruthlessly when he recognizes that these radical cuts are necessary for the good of the work as a whole. The aspect of dramatic correctness was more important to Mozart in making his decisions than purely musical considerations. Dramatic expression, what Monteverdi called truthfulness, was also more important to him than purely musical beauty.

Things went back and forth for six weeks. The son writes that this or that point has to be changed, the father then must go to the librettist—a court chaplain in Salzburg—to have the changes implemented. About the quartet, as in most questions of interpretation, the father and the son are in complete agreement:

> I need not say anything about the quartet, for which declamation and action are far more essential than great singing ability or his everlasting "spianar la voce." In this case, action and diction are the necessary qualities. (December 29, 1780)

This correspondence indicates how precise Mozart's ideas were, how he distinguished between what belonged to the realm of the singer and that of the composer, where he could yield to the wishes of the vocalist, and where—in the interest of the dramatic structure—he had to stubbornly assert his authority as composer.

These letters reveal illuminating details concerning the relationship between composer and singers as well as between composer and librettist. In Mozart scholarship of the 19th and early 20th centuries, we read again and again that, although Mozart was certainly a great composer, he was so wrapped up in his musical phantasies that he indiscriminately put inferior texts to music. How could such frivolous pieces as *Lucio Silla* still be performed today, or *Così fan tutte*—the silliest of all! These texts, it is claimed, have to be rewritten, if the music is to be "saved." Poor Mozart, some feel, knew nothing about texts. But today we are gradually coming to realize that such criticism was both wrong and premature; that these operas have been misunderstood because they involve depth and sharpness of diction, far surpassing anything that was expected from an opera in the 19th century. And we are also discovering that composers like Mozart, Schubert and even Verdi, who has been the target of the same reproach, were extremely concerned with each individual word.

A brief digression back to Monteverdi may be appropriate at this point. Monteverdi worked out each of his operas together with his librettist. In some cases the librettist actually lived near the composer, so that the two could constantly collaborate, revise, tinker with the smallest details. A similar working method linked Mozart and his librettists, particularly Da Ponte, but also Stephanie (*Die Entführung aus dem Serail*) and Schikaneder (*Die Zauberflöte*). In Mozart's collaboration with all three, a significant amount of his own input can be discerned in the shaping of the text.

The early Italian opera seria differed formally from the new music drama. In his youth in Milan, Mozart had to write such works, using finished librettos which occasionally had also served other composers. The technique of opera seria called for the solution of certain standard problems: the love duet, the revenge aria, the cemetery scene, etc. The texts were expected to observe certain general rules and were largely interchangeable. Raaff's desire that Mozart use a peace aria by Metastasio illustrates this idea in the case of the completely unsuitable example of *Idomeneo*. The ideas Mozart had in mind for his kind of music drama could not be realized within the seria conventions.

It is revealing and significant that Mozart describes *Idomeneo*, his first work in the new manner, not as opera seria, but rather as dramma per musica. Here, for the first time, he feels responsible for the entire work, for the text as well as for the music, and writes not a note of music for words that he did not fully accept. It can therefore be said that each of the operas that followed *Idomeneo* is entirely Mozart's text as well as music. For if Mozart did not approve of the text, he insisted on its being changed. He worked with the librettist and, when necessary, even by himself, until he came up with the results that he was looking for. We can follow this approach quite closely from the correspondence about *Idomeneo*.

So if today we claim that the music is good but the text weak, we criticize Mozart himself—and we should tread cautiously on such ground. Mozart accepted the text, as it appears in the definitive version. If an opera text composed by Mozart seems silly to us, this implies a criticism of the composer. After all, if something was not to his liking, he could have asked for changes at any time, and he did so again and again. His instinct for drama relates by no means only to the music, but also to the opera as a whole. When the librettist Varesco called for extra pay for the many changes required by the artistic director of the Munich performance, Mozart wrote:

> Meanwhile tell Varesco from me that he will not get a farthing more out of Count Seeau than was agreed upon—for all the alterations were made, not for the Count, but for me . . . (January 18, 1781)

In the age of Mozart, a meaningful music drama could result only from close collaboration between composer and librettist. Today, in a similar fashion, such a composition can performed in a meaningful way only if the conductor and stage director work together closely and harmoniously. Unfortunately, what is actually a joint endeavor often receives separate reviews: the stage direction was intelligent and good, but the musical performance left something to be desired, or the other way around. The conductor shares responsibility if the stage director's approach is not musically well-founded; during rehearsals, he must represent the intentions of the composer. A stage director who is musical will gladly heed his advice. But when the conductor arrives shortly before the opening performance and encounters an almost completely rehearsed performance—which is what usually happens—he can only resign himself to his fate. Then he thinks: no matter what happens on the stage, we will just play our beautiful music. This very common attitude is disastrous for opera. No operatic performance should ever take place if the stage director and conductor have not worked closely together, or if each does not support the entire performance, including the aspect that is the domain of the other! This symbiosis of stage director and conductor is very like the relationship that exists between the actual authors of an opera: its composer and librettist.

One more example of Mozart's involvement in the writing of the libretto:

> In the last scene of Act II Idomeneo has an aria or rather a sort of cavatina between the choruses. Here it will be better to have a mere recitative, well supported by the instruments. For in this scene, which will be the finest in the whole opera (on account of the action and grouping which were settled recently with Le Grand), there will be so much noise and confusion on the stage that an aria at this particular point would cut a poor figure—and moreover there is the thunderstorm, which is not likely to subside during Herr Raaff's aria, is it? The effect, therefore, of a recitative between the choruses will be infinitely better. (November 15, 1780)

This observation refers to the final accompagnato of Idomeneo in Act Two, "Eccoti in me barbaro Nume," between the choruses "Qual nuovo terrore" and "Corriamo fuggiamo." Mozart describes this scene as the "most beautiful in the whole opera"—in reality it is the most terrible, but it expresses exactly what he wants to say, and therefore it is beautiful. To Mozart, the concept of beauty does not necessarily imply something pleasant. In this scene, an apparent monologue, Idomeneo admits that he alone is responsible for all the misfortune. He had promised a sacrifice to Nettuno, but now, since it involves his son Idamante, he cannot keep his vow. This monologue is in truth a great dialogue between Idomeneo and Nettuno. The awesome god of the sea speaks not a word in the whole opera, but he is nonetheless omnipresent in the orchestra, from the overture on. In this accompagnato, we hear his terrible "No" to the timid plea of Idomeneo that he might forego the sacrifice of the innocent victim. It is a powerful example of non-verbal tonal discourse. In the language of Mozart, as in that of Monteverdi, "beautiful" thus means something like *right* or *true*.

This same striving for "compression" is also found in his correspondence about Act Three:

> It was considered much superior to the first two acts. But the libretto is too long and consequently the music also (an opinion which I have always held). Therefore Idamante's aria, "No, la morte io non pavento," is to be omitted; in any case it is out of place there. (January 18, 1781)

Of course, this means "out of place" in a dramatic sense, because if Idamante sang the aria, the other singers would have to "stand around" in a meaningless way on stage. Mozart is well aware that such cuts, as necessary as they might be, mean a loss in musical terms:

> But those who have heard it with the music deplore this. The omission of Raaff's last aria too is even more regretted; but we must make a virtue of necessity.

"Raaff's last aria" is, of all things, "Torna al pace," the aria that Mozart had created at the cost of so much effort and conflict in order to pacify his singer. It comes after the long accompagnato of Idomeneo, which ends with the words "Oh Creta fortunato, Oh me felice." After an orchestral recitative (accompagnato), the listener of the time expected an aria; the few exceptions to this formal convention rule were regarded as sensational. After Mozart had eliminated the aria, this last recitative, the painful resignation of Idomeneo, became the end of the opera! The absence of the aria which resolved everything in happiness and release of tension is even more noticeable because of the jubilation chorus which now directly follows. In a formal sense, after all, this chorus does not belong to the main action, but is the beginning of the great concluding divertissement: choral march "Scenda Amor"/Ballett-chaconne. This concluding jubilation now seems superimposed, painful. It abruptly interrupts Idomeneo's unfinished monologue and thereby implies "Enough, your time is up." The premature rejoicing shocks us. The guilt of Idomeneo deprives him of every initiative; he may not even sing his final, "happy end" aria.

Here, too, we realize that the cut, which is regrettable only in musical terms, results in great dramatic compression; the effect derives from the music itself, from the shocking collision of the accompagnato with the final apotheosis. Idomeneo's last accompagnato is isolated in the finale and in terms of its key, as well. After Elettra's raging, which ends in D minor, there comes a strangely disturbing yet soothing E-flat major chord, to which the conspicuous clarinets and horns lend a mysterious and romantic sound. The accompagnato of Idomeneo ends in B-flat major, the key of the aria which had been eliminated. Without this, the conclusion of the recitative seems like taking a breath for something that never happens, something that is brutally shunted aside by the jubilant D major chorus.

It is remarkable and highly consistent that Mozart finally removed the only aria of this opera which displays a perfectly relaxed, happy emotion. The entire work is characterized by threats (Nettuno), conflict (Greeks/Cretans), tension (father/son, the two rivals Ilia and Elettra) and fear. Happiness and peace of mind are constantly sought, but hardly ever within reach; they are constantly threatened on all sides. The same lack of fulfillment is also reflected in the few happy moments of Idamante, as in those of Ilia and Elettra. For Idomeneo himself there are no such moments, because the ominous vow always hovers in the background. The piece contains not a single quiet andante or adagio aria where everything is peaceful and beautiful. The music of Idomeneo's final aria was probably originally intended to be the great resting point of the opera. And this of all the arias was finally torn out by Mozart, because the work could not be allowed to move towards a peaceful conclusion. Until the end, the tragic mood prevails—a sequel probably would have been a similar tragedy. In this struggle for a fitting conclusion to the opera, we truly have a glimpse into Mozart's workshop; we can sense what he was striving for in all the discussions with the librettist, in the grappling with various musical versions.

Mozart's search for an adequate form for the oracle scene gives us a deep insight into his concept of drama.

> Tell me, don't you think that the speech of the subterranean voice is too long? Consider it carefully. Picture to yourself the theatre and remember that the voice must be terrifying—must penetrate—that the audience must believe that it really exists. Well, how can this effect be

produced if the speech is too long, for in this case the listeners will become more and more convinced that it means nothing.

This scene is structured with great dramatic effectiveness. If something is terrifying, unnerving, its dramatic impact is gradually lost if it is presented in a long-winded speech. At the first chord, the audience perks up their ears, but the longer this subterranean voice speaks, the more the initial interest flags, and the effect will be lost. I find it almost incredible that such a young composer could so precisely assess such an impact which, after all, presupposes some experience of life.

He continues:

> If the speech of the Ghost in Hamlet were not so long, it would be far more effective. It is quite easy to shorten the speech of the subterranean voice and it will gain thereby more than it will lose. (November 29, 1780)

Mozart obviously not only knows his Shakespeare, he even competently criticizes him. When Varesco's proposals for cuts did not go far enough, he writes:

> The speech of the oracle is still too long and I have therefore shortened it; but Varesco need not know anything of this, because it will all be printed just as he wrote it. (January 18, 1781)

At this point, although he had already shortened the oracle scene twice, he found it still too long. The additional cuts were carried out by the composer himself, without involving the librettist. Mozart felt that, out of consideration for Varesco, the libretto should be printed in an uncut version. This never occurred because the artistic director insisted that, due to the extensive discrepancies, only the version that was actually played should be printed in the definitive libretto. It was customary at the time for the public to be able to purchase the text of a new opera prior to attending a performance—an opportunity for the audience to familiarize themselves ahead of time with the content of the work. Thus the listener would not have to devote all of his attention simply to following the story line of the action on stage.

There were ultimately four versions of the subterranean voice, each shorter than its predecessor. Mozart wanted this speech to have a ghostly, unreal character. He therefore had it accompanied by two horn players and three trombonists who, like the singer, are to stand behind the stage. He intended that the three trombones play only these few chords in the whole opera. The artistic director of the Munich theater rejected Mozart's request for trombones on the grounds that they were too costly. After a fierce argument, the composer had to relent.

In addition to many other minor rows with Count Seeau, I have had a desperate fight with him about the trombones. I call it a desperate fight, because I had to be rude to him, or I should never have got my way. (January 11, 1781)

Mozart unfortunately did not "get his own way," for in the first performance "La Voce" was accompanied by woodwinds. This was a serious loss—even aside from tonal considerations—because the woodwinds had to play from the orchestra pit and could not be placed behind the stage. I find fault with the version used for the first performance with the woodwinds for this reason. From his letters, we know that this represented only an compromise solution as far as Mozart was concerned.

After a few performances in Munich, Mozart never again performed his *Idomeneo* on the stage. Although he always had it in the back of his mind, it never worked out. A stage performance in Vienna in 1781 was thwarted by Gluck, since that year his *Iphigenie* was performed in German and his *Alceste* in Italian, so that all of the leading singers were already under contract. Furthermore, the "excellent poet" Alxinger, who was supposed to translate *Idomeneo* into German, was occupied with work for Gluck. Mozart wanted to perform his opera not only in German, but in a completely new version with the bass Fischer as Idomeneo and the tenor Adamberger as Idamante.

Finally, in 1786, Mozart was able to put on a concert performance at the Palais Auersperg; however, certain social considerations made some changes necessary. On this occasion, Idamante was sung by a tenor, and a long violin solo had to be added for Count Hatzfeld, a prominent violinist in the concert and social life of Vienna, whose wife sang the role of Elettra. The pieces added for this performance are beautiful; the so-called "Viennese version" is a true concert version, even though many opera houses use it for the stage.

We see that this invaluable correspondence clearly explains the motivation underlying many of Mozart's decisions. This insight into his working approach to music drama is extremely important for interpreting these operas today. We will also judge the various versions of the later operas differently if we hold the key to understanding the changes made by Mozart. We will also be on guard against hasty judgments because we have seen that Mozart approached his work self-critically and conscientiously.

Mozart's *Requiem:* His Only Work with an Autobiographical Element

Thoughts and Impressions

In discussing this work, I do not want to present a scholarly musical analysis, but rather to share some impressions formed by a musician in the process of coming to terms with Mozart's *Requiem.*

First of all, I felt the cohesion, the overall design of the piece and its architecture in a much more convincing way than ever before—despite the fragmentary score and the additions made by Mozart's student Süssmayr, which have been so harshly criticized. It does not seem to me that these additions are an alien body musically, since their essence is Mozart-like. I cannot believe that an inferior composer like Süssmayr, whose compositions never go beyond banal mediocrity, could have of his own accord completed the "Lacrimosa" and composed the "Sanctus," "Benedictus" and "Agnus Dei." Even the possibility that the rest of the composition may have served to inspire Süssmayr cannot convince me that this music stems from him. As far as I am concerned, these movements also originate with Mozart, be it that some material was available to Süssmayr in sketched form, or that, in the course of their collaboration, Mozart might have played these compositions for him so that they somehow took hold in his mind. The clear qualitative discrepancy between the composition as such and Süssmayr's instrumentation of these movements further strengthens my conviction.

From Mozart's letters we know that thoughts on death and religious ways of dealing with death were familiar to him and accepted as a part of life. In 1787, at the age of 31, he writes to his sick father:

> As death, when we come to consider it closely, is the true goal of our existence, I have formed during the last few years such a close relationship with this best and truest friend of mankind, that his image is not only no longer terrifying to me, but is indeed very soothing and consoling. And I thank my God for graciously granting me the opportunity . . . of learning that death is the key which unlocks the door to our true happiness. I never lie down at night without reflecting that—young as I am—I may not live to see another day . . . (April 4, 1787)

The death quartet from *Idomeneo,* which he had written 10 years before the *Requiem,* already impresses me as being his first, very personal confrontation with his own death. Throughout his life, Mozart, who identified with Idamante, had an unusually strong emotional attachment to this opera, and particularly to this quartet. It is said to have moved him to tears, so that he could not continue singing when he once performed it in Vienna, himself singing the role of Idamante. There is also a report about a rehearsal of the *Requiem,* at which shortly before his death the completed passages were tried out. At the "Lacrimosa" Mozart burst into tears and was unable to go on.

The entire work seems to me to be a deeply personal confrontation; terrifying and upsetting, since the composer normally made a clearcut distinction between his personal life and his art. The instrumental prelude is a dirge using bassett horns and bassoons, with the low and high strings alternately playing sobbing figures, which represent weeping in the music of Mozart. This quiet mourning is harshly interrupted by the forte beats of the trombones, trumpets and kettle drums in the seventh measure. Death is not only a gentle friend, but the doorway to the feared judgment. Here I find for the first time, perhaps like Mozart himself, that the official liturgical text becomes a personal, stirring confrontation. Death comes at some time to everyone—but what will happen to *me*! After "luceat eis" (may light illuminate their pathway forever) in measures 17–20, the imploring general plea ends on a hopeful note of consolation: all will be well, because there is mercy.

The "Kyrie," the prayer for divine mercy, intensifies from the impersonal fugue into ever more personal, imploring homophonic calls: Lord, You *must* have mercy on me! The juxtaposition of the general with the personal is particularly stark in the Sequence: the Dies Irae paints an uncompromising picture of the terrors of the Last Judgment, the sternness of the Judge ("cuncta stricte discussurus!"), the Tuba mirum describes the awakening of the dead to be judged: nothing will go unavenged ("nil inultum remanebit")—the movingly personal and anxious question then comes: "What will I, poor man, then say?" . . . Or the crass juxtaposition of the powerful king in Rex tremendae with the self, with me: "Save me, Source of Grace," which in the Recordare leads into a moving and deeply trusting prayer. "You have redeemed me by Your suffering, Your efforts must not have been in vain." This movement was particularly important to Mozart, according to the testimony of Constanze. I understand Mozart's special religious and musical attachment to this movement because he has the personal element of the relationship to God emerge so strongly. The possibility of loving mildness of the Judge who was previously described as implacably severe is now represented with great feeling. We hear this particularly in two passages: "You who pardoned Mary Magdalene, *let me also hope*" (measures 83–93), and "Let me be among the sheep at Your right hand" (measures 116–end).

In the "Confutatis," which contains from the outset the juxtaposition of "everyone-myself," the intimate personal relationship to God is underscored in the last sentence, "Be with me when I die," both harmonically and in the confident, trusting musical interpretation of the text. Here I hear the voice of Mozart himself, pleading on his own behalf with all the urgency at his command, like a sickly child who looks trustingly at his mother, and all fear disappears.

Discography (Selection)

Nikolaus Harnoncourt

JOHANN SEBASTIAN BACH

Johannes-Passion, BWV 245
Equiluz, van t'Hoff, van Egmond,
Wiener Sängerknaben,
Chorus Viennensis,
Concentus musicus Wien
LP 6.35018 (3 LPs) EK
DMM
MC 4.35018 (2 MCs) MH TIS
Grand Prix du Disque

Johannes-Passion—Excerpts
Equiluz, van t'Hoff, van Egmond,
Wiener Sängerknaben,
Chorus Viennensis,
Concentus musicus Wien
LP 6.41069 AH

Matthäus-Passion, BWV 244
Soloists: Wiener Sängerknaben,
Esswood, van Egmond,
Schopper, King's College Choir,
Cambridge
Concentus musicus Wien
LP 6.35047 (4 LPs) FK
DMM
MC 4.35047 (3 MCs) MR TIS
Premio Della Critica Discografica
Italiana, Edison-Preis

Mattäus-Passion, BWV 244,
Arias and Choruses
Concentus musicus Wien
LP 6.42536 AH

Matthäus-Passion, BWV 244,
Arias
Concentus musicus Wien
LP 6.41136 AQ
MC 4.41136 CQ

Mass in B Minor, BWV 232
Hansmann, Iiyama, Watts,
Equiluz, van Egmond
Concentus musicus Wien
LP 6.35019 (3 LPs) FK
DMM
CD 8.35019 (2 CDs) 2A
Deutscher Schallplattenpreis,
Grand Prix du Disque

Missa 1733, Kyrie—Gloria
Hansmann, Iiyama, Watts,
Equiluz, van Egmond, Wiener
 Sängerknaben,
Chorus Viennensis,
Concentus musicus Wien
LP 6.41135 AQ

Christmas Oratorio, BWV 248
Esswood, Equiluz, Nimsgern,
Wiener Sängerknaben,
Chorus Viennensis,
Concentus musicus Wien
LP 6.35022 (3 LPs) FK
DMM
CD 8.35022 (3 CDs) 2B

**Die Weihnachtsgeschichte aus
dem Weihnachtsoratorium,**
BWV 248
Soloist: Wiener Sängerknaben,
Esswood, Equiluz, Nimsgern,
Wiener Sängerknaben,
Chorus Viennensis,
Concentus musicus Wien
LP 6.42102 AQ

THE CANTATAS
First complete recording with
authentic instruments. Complete
texts and scores included.
40 albums.
Erasmus-Preis.

Motets
Singet dem Herrn ein neues Lied,
BWV 225; Der Geist hilft unserer
Schwachheit auf, BWV 226; Jesu,
meine Freude, BWV 227; Fürchte
dich nicht, BWV 228; Komm,
Jesu, komm, BWV 229; Lobet
den Herrn, BWV 230
Bachchor Stockholm
Concentus musicus Wien
LP 6.42663 AZ
DMM DIGITAL
MC 4.42663 CY CrO$_2$
CD 8.42663 ZK
Deutscher Schallplattenpreis
Caecilia-Preis

Der zufriedengestellte Äolus
Zerreisset, zersprenget,
zertrümmert die Gruft, BWV 205
Kenny, Lipovśek, Equiluz, Holl,
Arnold-Schönberg-Chor,
Concentus musicus Wien
LP 6.42915 AZ
DMM DIGITAL
CD 8.42915 ZK

ORCHESTRAL WORKS
**Brandenburg Concertos
Nr. 1–6**
Concentus musicus Wien
LP 6.35620 (2 LPs) FD
DMM DIGITAL
MC 4.35620 (2 MCs) MH

**Brandenburg Concertos
Nr. 1, 2, 4**
Concentus musicus Wien
LP 6.42823 AZ
DMM DIGITAL
MC 4.42823 CX
CD 8.42823 ZK

**Brandenburg Concertos
Nr. 3, 5, 6**
Concentus musicus Wien
LP 6.42840 AZ
DMM DIGITAL
MC 4.42840 CX
CD 8.42840 ZK

**Suites Nr. 1, BWV 1066;
Nr. 2, BWV 1067**
Concentus musicus Wien
LP 6.43051 AZ
DMM DIGITAL
MC 4.43051 CY CrO$_2$
CD 8.43051 ZK

**Suites Nr. 3, BWV 1068;
Nr. 4, BWV 1069**
Concentus musicus Wien
LP 6.43052 AZ
DMM DIGITAL
MC 4.43052 CY CrO$_2$
CD 8.43052 ZK

Suites Nr. 1–4
Concentus musicus Wien
LP 6.35046 (2 LPs) DX
MC 4.35046 (2 MCs) ME TIS
Deutscher Schallplattenpreis
Grammy

Harpsichord Concerto Nr. 1,
BWV 1052; Sinfonia from the
Concerto, BWV 1045
(Fragment); Double Concerto, BWV 1060
Herbert Tachezi, Harpsichord,
Alice Harnoncourt, Violin,
Jürg Schaeftlein, Oboe,
Concentus musicus Wien
LP 6.41121 AS TIS

Harpsichord Concerto Nr. 1,
BWV 1052; **Nr. 10,** BWV 1061
Gustav Leonhardt, Anneke
Uittenbosch, Herbert Tachezi,
Harpsichord,
Concentus musicus Wien
Leonhardt-Consort/Leonhardt
LP 6.42488 AQ
MC 4.42488 CQ

Musical Offering, BWV 1079
Concentus musicus Wien
LP 6.41124 AZ
DMM
MC 4.41124 CY CrO$_2$
Edison-Preis

Sinfonia, Movements from the
Cantatas, BWV 18, 21, 29, 31, 35,
42, 49, 244
Concentus musicus Wien
LP 6.41970 AQ

Chamber Music—Vol. 1
Violin Sonatas, BWV 1014–1019
Alice Harnoncourt, Violin,
Nikolaus Harnoncourt, Gamba,
Herbert Tachezi, Harpsichord
LP 6.35310 (2 LPs) FX

Chamber Music—Vol. 2
Flute Sonatas
Leopold Stastny, Frans Brüggen,
Flute, Herbert Tachezi,
Harpsichord, Alice Harnoncourt,
Violin, Nikolaus Harnoncourt, Cello
LP 6.35339 (2 LPs) FX

Chamber Music—Vol. 3
3 Gamba Sonatas
Concentus musicus Wien
LP 6.35350 (2 LPs) FX

Violin Concertos—Vol. 1
Concerto for Two Violins,
BWV 1043; Violin Concertos,
BWV 1042, BWV 1041
Alice Harnoncourt and Walter
Pfeiffer, Violin,
Concentus musicus Wien
LP 6.41227 AZ
DMM
MC 4.41227 CY CrO$_2$
CD 8.41227 ZK

Violin Concertos—Vol. 2
Concerto for Violin, BWV
1056; Concerto for Oboe
d'amore, BWV 1055; Concerto
for Violin, BWV 1052
Concentus musicus Wien
LP 6.42032 AW TIS

Violin Concertos
BWV 1041, 1042,
1043, 1052, 1056, 1060
Alice Harnoncourt, Walter Pfeiffer,
Violin, Jürg Schaeftlein, Oboe,
Concentus musicus Wien
LP 6.35610 (2 LPs) DX

Magnificat, BWV 243

Georg Friedrich Händel:
Utrecht Te Deum
Palmer—Lipovšek—Langridge
Wiener Sängerknaben,
Arnold-Schönberg-Chor,
Concentus musicus Wien
LP 6.42955 AZ
DMM DIGITAL
MC 4.42955 CY CrO_2
CD 8.42955 ZK

HEINRICH IGNAZ FRANZ BIBER

**Schlachtmusik, Pauernkirchfahrt
Ballettae, Sonate**
Concentus musicus Wien
LP 6.41134 AS TIS

**Requiem, Sonata St. Polycarpi à 9,
Laetatus sum à 7, Dreikönigskantate**
Wiener Sängerknaben, Soloists:
Equiluz, van Egmond,
Concentus musicus Wien
LP 6.41245 AQ

JOHANN JOSEPH FUX

Concentus musico instrumentalis . . . 1701
Sernade à 8, Rondeau à 7, Sonata
à Quattro
Concentus musicus Wien
LP 6.41271 AQ

GEORGE FRIDERIC HANDEL

Alexander's Feast
(Cäcilien-Ode, 1736)
Palmer, Rolfe-Johnson, Roberts,
Bachchor Stockholm,
Concentus musicus Wien
LP 6.35440 (2 LPs) EK
DMM
CD 8.35440 (2 CDs) ZA

Belshazzar, Oratorio
Tear, Palmer, Lehane, Esswood,
Concentus musicus Wien
LP 6.35326 (4 LPs) GK
Edison-Preis

Giulio Cesare Highlights
Esswood, Alexander, Murray,
Concentus musicus Wien
CD 8.43927 ZK

Jephtha
Hollweg, Linos, Galle, Esswood,
Tomaschke, Sima,
Concentus musicus Wien
LP 6.35499 (4 LPs) GK
DMM
MC 4.35499 (3 MCs) MR
CD 8.35499 (3 CDs) ZB
Deutscher Schallplattenpreis

Ode for St. Cecilia's Day
Palmer, Rolfe-Johnson,
Bachchor Stockholm,
Concentus musicus Wien
LP 6.42349 AZ
MC 4.42349 CY CrO_2
CD 8.42349 ZK

Messiah
Gale, Lipovšek, Hollweg,
Kennedy, Stockholmer Kammerchor,
Concentus musicus Wien
LP 6.35617 (3 LPs) FR
DMM DIGITAL
MC 4.35617 (3 MCs) MU
CD 8.35617 (3 CDs) ZB

Concertos
Concerto F Major, Concerto
D Minor, Concerto G Minor,
Sonata à 3 F Major, Concerto D Major
Concentus musicus Wien
LP 6.41270 AW TIS

**Alexander's Feast-Concerto—
Concertos for Organ, Oboe, Violin**
Alice Harnoncourt, Jürg Schaeftlein,
Herbert Tachezi
Concentus musicus Wien
LP 6.43050 AZ
DMM DIGITAL
MC 4.43050 CY CrO_2
CD 8.43050 DIG ZK TELDEC

Concerti grossi, op. 3
Nr. 1, 2, 3, 4a, 4b, 5, 6; Oboe
Concerto Nr. 3
Concentus musicus Wien
LP 6.35545 (2 LPs) EX
DMM
CD 8.35545 (2 CDs) ZA

Concerti grossi, op. 6,
Nr. 1–12
Concentus musicus Wien
LP 6.35603 (3 LPs) FR
DMM DIGITAL
CD 8.35603 (3 CDs) ZB

Organ Concertos, op. 4 & op. 7
Herbert Tachezi, Organ
Concentus musicus Wien
LP 6.35282 (3 LPs) FK
CD 8.35282 (3 CDs) ZB

Water Music—Complete
Concentus musicus Wien
LP 6.42368 AZ
DMM DIGITAL
MC 4.42368 CY CrO$_2$
CD 8.42368 ZK

Trio Sonatas
Sonata B Minor for Traverso,
Violin and B.c., op. 2, lb;
Sonata D Minor for 2 Violins and
B.c., op. 2, 3; Sonata D Minor,
Oboe, Violin and B.c.; Sonata
F Major for Recorder, Violin, and
B.c., op. 2,5
Frans Brüggen, Recorder, Alice
Harnoncourt, Walter Pfeiffer,
Violin, Herbert Tachezi, Harpsichord
LP 6.41254 AQ

Utrecht Te Deum
J. S. Bach: Magnificat,
BWV 243
Palmer, Lipovšek, Langridge,
Wiener Sängerknaben,
Arnold-Schönberg-Chor,
Concentus musicus Wien
LP 6.42955 AZ
DMM DIGITAL
MC 4.42955 CY CrO$_2$
CD 8.42955 ZK

JOSEPH HAYDN

The Creation
Gruberova, Protschka, Holl,
Arnold-Schönberg-Chorus
Wiener Symphoniker

The Seasons
Blais, Protschka, Holl,
Arnold-Schönberg-Chorus
Wiener Symphoniker

CLAUDIO MONTEVERDI

L'Orfeo, complete recording
Berberian, Kozma, Hansmann,
Katanosaka, Rogers, Equiluz,
Egmond, Villisech,
capella antiqua, München,
Concentus musicus Wien
LP 6.35020 (3 LPs) FK
CD 8.35020 (2 CDs) ZA
Deutscher Schallplattenpreis,
Edison-Preis

L'Orfeo, excerpts
Berberian, Kozma, Hansmann,
Katanosaka, Rogers, Equiluz,
Egmond, Villisech,
capella antiqua, München,
Concentus musicus Wien
LP 6.41175 AN

L'Orfeo
Il Ritorno d'Ulisse in Patria
L'Incoronazione di Poppea
Complete recordings with
original instruments
Concentus musicus Wien
LP 6.35376 (12 LPs) JY

L'Incoronazione di Poppea,
Complete recording
Donath, Söderström, Berberian,
Esswood, Langridge, Equiluz
Concentus musicus Wien
LP 6.35247 (5 LPs) HD
Deutscher Schallplattenpreis
Grand Prix du Disque, Premio
Della Critica Discografica
Italiana
Art Festival Prize, Japan
Grand Prix du Disque, Canada

Lettera amorosa—Lamento
d'Arianna—Disprezzata
Regina—A Dio, Roma from
''L'Incoronazione di Poppea''
Cathy Berberian, Mezzosopran,
Concentus musicus Wien
LP 6.41930 AW TIS

Cathy Berberian sings
Monteverdi
Arias from L'Orfeo,
L'Incoronazione di Poppea, Madrigals
and Songs
Concentus musicus Wien
LP 6.41956 AQ

Vespro della Beata Vergine
Marian Vespers, 1610
Hansmann, Jacobeit, Rogers,
van't Hoff, van Egmond,
Villisech, solos by Wiener
Sängerknaben, Monteverdi Chor,
Hamburg,
Concentus musicus Wien
LP 6.35045 (2 LPs) DX
Grand Prix du Disque

**Combattimento di Tancredi e
Clorinda—Lamento dell ninfa**
Schmidt, Palmer, Hollweg
Concentus musicus Wien
LP 6.43054 AZ
DMM DIGITAL
MC 4.43054 CY CrO$_2$
CD 8.43054 ZK

WOLFGANG AMADEUS MOZART

Idomeneo, Complete recording
Hollweg, Schmidt, Yakar, Palmer,
Equiluz, Tear, Estes, Mozart-
orchester & Chor des
Opernhauses Zürich
LP 6.35547 (4 LPs) GX
DMM DIGITAL
CD 8.35547 (3 CDs) ZB
Prix Mondial du Disque
Caecilia-Preis
Preis der Deutschen Schallplattenkritik

Mass in C Minor, KV 427
Laki, Equiluz, Holl,
Wiener Staatsopernchor,
Concentus musicus Wien
LP 6.43120 AZ
DMM
MC 4.43120 CY
CD 8.43120 ZK

Thamos, König von Ägypten,
KV 345
Thomaschke, Perry, Mühle,
van Altena, van der Kamp,
Niederländischer Kammerchor,
Collegium Vocale, Concertgebouw
Orchestra
LP 6.42702 AZ
DMM DIGITAL
MC 4.42702 CX
CD 8.42702 ZK
Preis der Deutschen Schallplattenkritik

Requiem, KV 626
Yakar, Wenkel, Equiluz, Holl,
Wiener Staatsopernchor,
Concentus musicus Wien
LP 6.42756 AZ
DMM DIGITAL
MC 4.42756 CX
CD 8.42756 ZK

Serenade Nr. 7 D Major, KV 250
"Haffner Serenade"
March D Major, KV 249
Staatskapelle Dresden
LP 6.43062 AZ
DMM DIGITAL
MC 4.43062 CY CrO$_2$
CD 8.43062 ZK DIG

Serenata Notturna, KV 239
Notturno, KV 286

Symphony Nr. 25 G Minor,
KV 183,**Symphony Nr. 40,**
G Minor, KV 550
Concertgebouw Orchestra,
Amsterdam
LP 6.42935 AZ
DMM DIGITAL
MC 4.42935 CX
CD 8.42935 ZK

Symphonies Nr. 29 A Major,
KV 201;**Nr. 39 E-flat Major,**
KV 543
Concertgebouw Orchestra,
Amsterdam
LP 6.43107 AZ
DMM DIGITAL
MC 4.43107 CY CrO$_2$
CD 8.43107 ZK

Symphony Nr. 33 B-flat Major,
KV 319, **Symphony Nr. 31 D Major,**
KV 297 ("Paris")
Concertgebouw Orchestra
LP 6.42817 AZ
DMM DIGITAL
MC 4.42817 CX
CD 8.42817 ZK

Symphony Nr. 34 C Major,
KV 338, **Symphony Nr. 35**
D Major, KV 385 ("Haffner")
Concertgebouw Orchestra
LP 6.42703 AZ
DMM DIGITAL
MC 4.42703 CX
CD 8.42703 ZK

Symphony Nr. 38 D Major,
KV 504 ("Prague"), **Symphony
Nr. 41 C Major, KV 551**
("Jupiter")
Concertgebouw Orchestra
LP 6.48219 (2 LPs) DX
DMM DIGITAL
MC 4.48219 CY CrO₂

**Symphony Nr. 40 G Minor, KV 550,
Symphony Nr. 25 G Minor, KV 183**
Concertgebouw Orchestra
LP 6.42935 AZ
DMM DIGITAL
MC 4.42935 CX
CD 8.42935 ZK

"Posthorn Serenade", KV 320,
Marches D Major, KV 335,
Nr. 1 and 2
Peter Damm, Posthorn,
Staatskapelle Dresden
LP 6.43063 AZ
DMM DIGITAL
MC 4.43063 CY CrO₂
CD 8.43063 ZK

Gran Partita, Serenade Nr. 10
B-flat Major, KV 361 (170a)
Wiener Mozart-Bläser
LP 6.42981 AZ
DMM DIGITAL
MC 4.42981 CX
CD 8.42981 ZK

**Concerto for 2 Pianos and Orchestra
Nr. 10 E-flat Major,**
KV 365 (316a); Chick Corea:
Fantasy for two pianos; Friedrich
Gulda: Ping-pong for two pianos
Friedrich Gulda, Chick Corea,
Clavier, Concertgebouw
Orchestra
LP 6.43961 AZ
DMM DIGITAL
MC 4.43961 CY CrO₂
CD 8.43961 ZK

Piano Concertos Nr. 23 A Major,
KV 488, **Nr. 26 D Major, KV 537**
("Krönungskonzert")
Friedrich Gulda, Piano,
Concertgebouw Orchestra
LP 6.42970 AZ
DMM DIGITAL
MC 4.42970 CY CrO₂
CD 8.42970 ZK

Horn Concertos Nr. 1–4
Hermann Baumann, Naturhorn,
Concentus musicus Wien
LP 6.41272 AZ
DMM
MC 4.41272 CX
CD 8.41272 ZK

Organ Works
Adagio and Allegro (Adagio)
F Minor for a mechanical organ
KV 594; Epistle Sonata F Major,
KV 244; Veroneser Allegro, KV 72a;
Leipzig Gigue in G, KV 574; Fantasia
F Minor, KV 608; Epistle Sonata C Major,
KV 328; Andante F Major, KV 616
Herbert Tachezi, Organ, Members of
Concentus musicus Wien
LP 6.41117 AH TIS

MOZART AND ANTONIO SALIERI

Der Schauspieldirektor
Prima la Musica, Poi le Parole
Alexander, Hampson, Holl
Concertgebouworkest Amsterdam
CD 8.43336 ZK

ANTONIO VIVALDI

**Il Cimento dell'Armonia e
dell'Inventione**
12 Concertos op. 8: The Seasons,
La Tempesta di Mare, Il Piacere,
La Caccia
Concentus musicus Wien
LP 6.35386 (2 LPs) EK
DMM
MC 4.35386 (2 MCs) MH
Grand Prix du Disque

**Concerti à cinque,
à quattro, à tre**
Frans Brüggen, Recorder,
Jürg Schaeftlein, Oboe,
Otto Fleischmann, Bassoon,
Alice Harnoncourt and
Walter Pfeiffer, Violin,
Nikolaus Harnoncourt, Cello,
Gustav Leonhardt, Harpsichord
LP 6.41239 AW TIS

**Concerto for Oboe A Minor;
Concerto for Traverso, Oboe,
Violin, Bassoon and B.c. G Minor;
Concerto for Bassoon E Minor;
Concerto for Strings G Minor**
Concentus musicus Wien
LP 6.41961 AW TIS

JOHANN DISMAS ZELENKA

**Hipocondrie—Sonata for
2 Oboes, Bassoon and B.c.;
Overture à 7 concertanti**
Concentus musicus Wien
LP 6.42415 AW